TRANSFORMING NURSERY
EDUCATION

Transforming Nursery Education

Peter Moss and Helen Penn

P·C·P
Paul Chapman
Publishing Ltd

Paul Chapman Publishing Ltd
144 Liverpool Road
London
N1 1LA

British Library Cataloguing in Publication Data

Moss, Peter , 1945–
Transforming nursery education
1. Nursery schools   2. Education, Preschool
I. Title   II. Penn, Helen
372.2′16

ISBN 1-85396-308-9

Typeset by Whitelaw & Palmer Ltd, Glasgow
Printed and bound by Athenaeum Press, Gateshead, Tyne & Wear

A B C D E F G H   9 8 7 6

Contents

Preface

At present, services for young children are both inadequate and irrationally organised . . . Both nationally and locally, the present division of responsibility between social services and education authorities makes little sense. Not only is the division difficult to justify, but it perpetuates anomalies of payment, availability and placement . . .

A more integrated service for children under five, under the auspices of a single authority, and a willingness to make education services accept responsibility for the day-care needs of older children would bring the question 'why five?' into even sharper focus . . .

All the issues raised here require study, experiment and discussion. But to undertake this implies a readiness to admit the need to review and change the well-established forms of provision on which future developments have been planned. Today's services are not simply inadequate in quantity; they are also fragmented and unresponsive to changing needs.

(Tizard, Moss and Perry, 1976)

WHY WE HAVE WRITTEN THIS BOOK?

Early childhood services in Britain have a lot going for them. A long and rich tradition of innovative work, by individuals and organisations. A resourceful and committed workforce. Membership of a European Union which provides many opportunities for cross-national exchange and collaboration.

Yet despite these considerable advantages, early childhood services are in a critical state and at a critical stage. The services are fragmented, inflexible, incoherent and full of inequalities, unable to meet the changing and varied needs of families. They rely on a workforce most of whom are poorly paid and poorly trained. Like many other parts of the national infrastructure, early childhood services suffer the consequences of chronic under-resourcing.

In a centralised state such as Britain has increasingly become, much of the responsibility for the critical situation we are now in must be assigned to the action, or inaction, of successive governments. There has been a history of missed opportunities to develop a national policy on early childhood services.

Instead, obstacles have actually been placed in the way of the future development of such a policy, as a result of policy measures introduced elsewhere without consideration given to their consequences for early childhood services – for example, education legislation over the last 15 years which has virtually ignored early childhood services while having major implications for them. Developments have been allowed to go forward unhindered without considering their longer-term implications or the relative merits of different development options – for example, the growth of a large unsubsidised private market in 'day care' services or the expansion of part-time nursery classes. Growing numbers of public and private agencies (e.g. TECs, the Home Office, employers) have identified an 'interest in early childhood services, but this proliferation has increased fragmentation and lack of coherence as different agencies focus narrowly on one particular service role or one particular group of service users. Questionable concepts and structures have gone unquestioned – for example, starting compulsory and primary schooling at 5 (or, for most children in Northern Ireland, 4) and the validity of dividing early childhood services into two separate systems labelled 'day care' and 'education'. Legislation has been introduced requiring local authorities to review their early childhood services – but no parallel duty has been placed on central government to do the same nationally.

Instead of the development of a national policy on early childhood services based on continuous debate and regular review, there has been a history of occasional, narrowly focused government initiatives: for example, the 1972 Education White Paper, the Government's conference on 'Low-Cost Day Provision for the Under Fives' in 1976, the 'day care' parts of the Children Act 1989, the childcare disregard introduced in the 1993 budget. Most recently, there has been the decision to provide vouchers for pre-school education for all 4 year olds.

There are some positive features to emerge from this latest proposal, in particular the recognition that education can and should take place across the whole range of services for 4 year olds, not just in nursery schools and classes. But these cannot disguise the fact that, once again, an opportunity for a more fundamental rethink of early childhood services has been missed. The voucher scheme does not come out of a wider review and analysis of current early childhood services and future options. There has been no questioning of ends, no discussion of the various values that might underpin services, no review of means, no assessment of different options for service development. Consequently, the voucher scheme is irrelevant to the main issues confronting early childhood services.

Because none of the succession of government initiatives has been grounded in any longer-term and developmental process of political and public debate about early childhood services, each has failed to identify, define and address the critical questions. What are the functions of early childhood services? What age range should these services cover? On what values and principles should services be based? In the light of these questions, what are the most appropriate types of service provision? Should there be an integrated or split system of services? Should there be coherence across services in certain areas? What training is needed for staff? What are the costs and what are the benefits of early childhood services? Who should contribute to these costs and on what basis should costs be allocated between responsible parties? How should early childhood services relate to education and other services for older children?

Without answering these questions, it is impossible to judge, for example, whether vouchers as a method of funding are in the best interests of children, families and early childhood services. Without answers to these questions, there is little chance of creating a national policy and a national framework for implementing that policy which will enable Britain to move beyond individual examples of good practice to an integrated and coherent system of early childhood services that will meet the needs of all our children and parents. Without answering these questions, there can be no vision, a critical ingredient of policy and practice.

We have observed this sad state of national affairs over the last 25 years, while at the same time being involved in initiatives and developments in this country and abroad which have shown what could be done, given sustained political commitment and understanding. We have been driven to write this book by a combination of frustration, concern and hope. Frustration, because of a failure of vision and action, brought home vividly by the quotation at the beginning of this preface – written 20 years ago but still applicable today. Concern, because we fear that the situation in Britain may soon reach a point of no return. Hope, because we know what is possible, from what we have seen in this country and abroad; and because we are aware that many of our ideas are also shared by others (for example, Pugh, 1994).

This book is a contribution to the development of debate about ends, means and values in early childhood services. We offer a vision of a comprehensive, integrated and coherent early childhood service for children from 0 to 6, which would be the first stage of the education system but equally committed to meeting other needs of children and parents including care, socialisation and support. We also offer specific proposals for making this vision a reality, in the course of which we have tried to grasp firmly some of the most painful nettles. We suggest that the debate about ends and means must be accompanied by a debate about values, not just what values we wish to adopt or reject but the priority we attach to different values.

WHY HAVE WE CALLED THE BOOK *TRANSFORMING NURSERY EDUCATION?*

Nursery education is one of the main services we have for young children and it has many good and enduring features; it is the most widespread, well-known and respected publicly funded early years service. But we think that nursery education as it is presently understood and delivered is inadequate. It is a limited service, part-time, short-term and for a narrow age range of children, predicated on a view of mothers at home and available to look after their children; and whose main task is to prepare and funnel children into primary school. To state this is not to denigrate what currently exists, but to begin the process of examining how nursery education might develop.

We suggest that given the fundamental changes in social context and the direction of recent theoretical perspectives, which we explore in later chapters, it would be sensible to rethink nursery education – in terms of who it is for, how long it is available, and the prominence of curricular initiatives and children's learning as its central goal.

But the need for development and transformation goes beyond nursery education. It is not only nursery education which is inappropriate. We think most forms of services have major shortcomings. It is one of our central contentions that the legacy of years of neglect is a large amount of service provision that is ill-suited to provide the type of comprehensive, multi-functional and responsive early childhood service we envision. Yet when public, political and media attention pays one of its fleeting visits to early childhood services, the discussion assumes more of the same. As well as nursery education there are hundreds of private nurseries geared to the need of employed parents for care, but which often ignore children's need for education or the need to provide a community resource. Children with high levels of social need are segregated into yet another system of services – 'day care' organised by social services departments – and are also often excluded from education. Other places are provided by playgroups which offer a meagrely resourced part-time service dependent on cheap female labour; or by childminders who are also poorly resourced and often ill-trained and ill-paid.

But things do not have to be like this. The services we have in Britain today are not inevitable. They are not the consequence of regular and reflective review. There is no intrinsic reason why 'nursery education' should be equated with classes tacked on to primary schools in which, if lucky, children will spend a few hours a week during less than a year of early childhood. The best features of today's 'nursery education' – and some of the practice is undoubtedly good – could be applied in a new context. A transformed nursery education could be at the centre of a new comprehensive, integrated and coherent early years service.

There is a role for privately managed services, parent and community-run services and school-based services in the system of early childhood services that we propose. But the system requires transformation of what we have, not more of the same; it requires clear direction to be given to service development, not leaving development to the free play of market forces. It requires recognition that services are social and cultural institutions, not mere purveyors of services to private consumers. It requires a new, broader view of 'nursery education', which might become the generic name for the 0 to 6 early childhood service we propose, an umbrella title spanning a range of community-based services, all capable of meeting a variety of needs including care, socialisation, support and learning.

THE PLAN OF THE BOOK

Transforming Nursery Education begins and ends with our vision of a comprehensive, integrated and coherent early childhood service. We start with a chapter setting out this vision, exploring the principles that would be necessary to provide a service system capable of delivering high quality, flexible and multi-functional services to children from 0 to 6 years and their parents. We end it with a chapter on how this vision might be fulfilled, letting our imagination run riot and offering three examples of services in the year 2000 – fictitious examples, but based on projects that we have come across or which have been sent to us.

In between we offer a critique of what is already available, from a number of different perspectives. We look at evidence of what parents want which, we argue, is well in tune with our vision. We show what the current plethora of services means in terms of what is actually on offer to children and parents in one local community. We look at the staff who work in the current services, and at the poor deal most get in terms of training, pay and conditions. We look at the history of nursery education, a perspective which helps explain how we have got to be where we are today, as well as at contemporary practices in nursery education. We emphasise that from both these perspectives, historical and contemporary, there is more than one way to conceptualise and deliver nursery education.

We explore initiatives in Britain, and services in two European countries, where our vision of a comprehensive, integrated and coherent early childhood service has already partly or wholly been translated into practice. We consider the costs, benefits and funding of such a comprehensive, integrated and coherent early childhood service and make some specific policy suggestions about the steps which should be taken at national level in the UK to achieve this service. It is here in particular that we have had to grasp nettles by putting forward our conclusions about some long-running and contentious issues such as staffing and financing.

We have tried to make the book lively and down to earth, using examples to illustrate our points. Where positive examples are given, and we have had permission, we have used real and identifiable cases. Where the examples are more negative, we have been careful to disguise them. Some of the examples are real cases. In other instances we have composited cases drawing from several examples known to us. We hope that in doing so we have been able to mirror the 'real world' in representing the dilemmas that parents, workers, politicians and other stakeholders commonly face in addressing and trying to resolve the complex issues of early childhood services.

Acknowledgements

We would like to thank Mary Hart, Maureen Leck, Margaret Orchard and Robin Duckett for their help with preparing Chapters 8 and 12. We are also very grateful to a number of colleagues for their comments on earlier drafts, including Angela Hobsbaum, Sally Holtermann, Gill Haynes, Susan McQuail, Sue Owen, Richard Stainton and Margy Whalley. They did not agree with all of our views and conclusions, and as authors we take complete responsibility for the contents of the book, including any mistakes it contains. Finally, our thanks are due to Loveday Penn and Clemency Penn for their help in preparing the text.

1

An Early Childhood Service for the Twenty-First Century

Basic to a good society is that children are welcome, are given a good environment during childhood and are the concern of the whole society. Children have a right to secure living conditions that enhance their development. Preschool has an important function in children's lives. It offers a comprehensive programme and is a source of stimulation in the children's development. It gives them a chance to meet other children and adults and to be part of an experience of fellowship and friendship. It is a complement to the upbringing a child gets at home.

(Family Aid Commission, Sweden, 1981)

Social change and most notably the high levels of women in the workforce means that parents are increasingly looking for help with childrearing and seeking solutions outside of the family. In the effort to respond to the needs of parents the local authority has made a considerable effort to increase the number of crèches . . . there are now twice as many as in 1977. But in this field it is not enough to provide a lot of facilities; you have to make sure they are good. Above all we have tried to make sure that your child is as happy as possible. This booklet [about the 225 nurseries for children under 3 funded by the municipality of Paris] *gives you a glimpse of the life of children in the crèche, and helps to inform you about what is going on and is a basis to satisfy yourself that the crèche is not only offering care, but is a place which truly contributes to the development of your child.*

(Jacques Chirac (as Mayor of Paris), France, 1986)

This Government sees early childhood care and education as having priority among its social policies. To assist in establishing a more equitable system of early childhood care and education the Government formed a working group . . . 'Education to be More' is the report of that working group. It is a timely document. The Government has already made public its proposals for the reform of education administration. 'Education to be More' fits into that framework. It is a responsible document. Too frequently reports to Government stress the need but do not document the means. 'Education to be More' outlines steps to provide the required services. It is an important document. The care and education received by and given to a young child is

*crucial to her or his development. Crucial, not just to the individual but to
the society in which they will grow up and become adults.*

(David Lange, then Prime Minister of New Zealand and
Minister of Education, 1988)

VISION IS ESSENTIAL

We start this book by offering our vision of a comprehensive, integrated and
coherent early childhood service, concerned to meet a wide range of needs
among children and their parents, but in particular needs for learning,
socialisation, care and support. We adopt this visionary approach deliberately
and unashamedly. For vision is neither an optional extra nor a self-indulgent
distraction.

Vision provides answers to essential questions. Where do we want to get to
and why? For what purposes and for whom do we think services should be
provided? The expression of vision makes beliefs and values, means and ends
transparent and open to debate.

Vision inspires and motivates. It expresses belief in the long-term value of an
enterprise and commitment to progress. It offers the prospect of a better
tomorrow, which today's hard work and effort will contribute to achieving.
The development of good early childhood services depends on the
development of long-term, co-operative and committed relationships between
all the parties involved: shared and sustained vision is at the heart of such a
partnership.

Lack of vision is harmful. Britain has never had a national policy on early
childhood services based on a considered, informed, sustained and broad
public vision. There have been long periods of public neglect, when options
have been regularly closed off in a thoughtless manner because early childhood
has not had a regular and valued place on the public agenda. These periods
have been interspersed by spasms of political activity which fail to identify or
address critical questions about direction, purpose and concept because they
draw on no shared and sustained vision. As a consequence of this singularly
visionless past and present, services and their staff, children and their parents
suffer.

As well as a manifesto for the future, our vision implies a critique of the past
and present. It is a rejection of the status quo. In outlining our vision, we are
also explaining why we wish to move away from the present situation and
what we think is wrong with it.

A COMPREHENSIVE, INTEGRATED AND COHERENT
EARLY CHILDHOOD SERVICE

At the end of the twentieth century, Britain needs an early childhood service
that is comprehensive, integrated and coherent, offering equal access to
flexible, multi-functional and high quality services for all young children from

0 to 6 and their parents. These are fine words. But what do they mean? Are they purely rhetoric, or do they have substance? And if they have substance, what are their implications?

A comprehensive service

The early childhood service would be comprehensive in several ways. It would be equally accessible to all children and all parents. It would pay equal attention to children under and over 3 years and to parents whether or not they are employed. All services would be open to children with disabilities and other special needs; there would not be a separate system of welfare services for a minority of families considered at risk or inadequate. Nor would there be one system of services for employed parents and their young children and another system for non-employed parents and their children. Central to our vision is the concept of a single, encompassing system, replacing the present fragmented and compartmentalised systems – an 'early childhood service' to replace 'child care for working parents', 'day care for children in need', 'nursery education for 3 and 4 year olds' and so on.

The early childhood service would be comprehensive because it would address a wide range of needs. There are five 'core' needs that an early childhood service must ensure all individual services provide for, although individual services would be encouraged to meet other personal, family or community needs, over and above these core needs. These core needs are of critical social and economic importance. The case for an early childhood service stands or falls by its ability to meet these needs.

1. Learning

Early childhood is an important time for learning. Not just from 3 years or 5 years, but from the earliest age, children have the ability to learn and, we would argue, the right to the widest range of opportunities to enable them to do so. The family, of course, plays a vital and major role, providing many unique opportunities for learning. But an early childhood service can complement the home, providing other unique learning opportunities.

An early childhood service must ensure individual services provide learning opportunities for the full age range of children, not just over 3s but also under 3s. In our vision, services would offer a range of experiences to enhance all aspects of children's development, cognitive, linguistic, social, emotional, aesthetic, sensory, physical and moral. As well as the stimulus of other children and adults and varied materials and equipment, there would be exciting buildings, extensive space indoors and out imaginatively used, an emphasis on visual art, music and dance, good food well cooked, gardens to tend, plants to grow and animals to care for, maximum involvement for children in the making of decisions and respect for children's autonomy.

These opportunities for learning would stand children in good stead for compulsory school and the National Curriculum. Recent authoritative reports have made a clear case for the longer-term educational benefits of early learning, although such evidence is frequently cited outside its specific context and used cavalierly (Woodhead, 1988). But in our view the case for providing young children with opportunities for learning is more fundamental than preparation for schooling and later life. Early years, the period up to 6 years, is a stage of life that is important in its own right, and not just for its contribution to later development and achievement. Learning at this stage may improve later performance: but, first and foremost, learning enables children to achieve their *present* potential, and enriches and fulfils their *present* life. Each stage of education should be valued in its own right, and not simply viewed as a springboard for reaching future goals.

2. *Care*

An early childhood service must provide safe and reliable care. As we discuss in detail in the next chapter, parental employment is increasing rapidly, and a modern society must be organised to ensure that the subsequent care needs of children are well met – although, as we also argue, the challenge of increasing parental employment requires far more than just the provision of safe and secure non-parental care. Care needs to be not only safe and reliable, but available at the times when parents need it for their work.

But safe and reliable care is needed for more than just children with employed parents. It is needed for children whose parents are seeking employment or are training or studying. It can also be needed for children whose parents are not employed or training or studying, to help these parents with their other family responsibilities or simply to give them some time to themselves, a break from the otherwise continuous round of caring.

3. *Socialisation*

Conviviality is important to all of us; friendship and ease and pleasure in communication with others is in one sense what life is about. An early childhood service should, we believe, be convivial. It should offer opportunities for young children to socialise with other children and adults, a place to complement the intense, vital but often limited range of child and adult relationships within the nuclear and extended family.

4. *Health*

An early childhood service should actively promote good health. Good health means an absence of illness but, more fundamentally, an ambition to secure for each child a positive feeling of physical and mental well-being. This ambition should influence every aspect of the service, including the preparation and eating of meals, the physical environment, opportunities for exercise and other daily activities.

5. *Support*

Finally, an early childhood service can contribute in a variety of ways to support for children and parents. In recent years, there has been increasing recognition of the part early childhood services can play in helping families that are facing extreme difficulties and stresses; this is one reason why the Children Act 1989 placed a duty on local authorities to provide 'day care' services for children 'in need'. In practice, this duty is mainly confined to a small minority of highly distressed or dysfunctional families who come to the notice of social workers and meet often stringent criteria for getting assistance.

A comprehensive system of early childhood services would provide a more widespread and general source of support, helping the generality of young families in the business of getting by in everyday life, while at the same time able to meet more acute and complex needs. There are few families which do not need some support at some stage of early parenthood. Parenthood is a watershed. It profoundly affects how you manage your time and how you relate to others. The transition to parenthood is a critical period. Many parents need opportunities to reassess their circumstances, develop new friendships and mutually supportive social networks. Support for those that need it can take many forms: informal opportunities to meet and be convivial; group work on a wide range of issues; individual counselling and advice; the organisation of adult learning and recreational activities; arranging services that are not readily available elsewhere in the local community. The provision of safe, secure and reliable care not only frees parents to work or study, which may itself be the best way of supporting many parents, but supports family functioning. The potential contribution of early childhood services to the development of friendships and social networks has already been mentioned. Underlying these specific examples is the support that stable and reliable services offer families in a society that is increasingly insecure and unpredictable.

Interdependence of core needs

Although spelt out separately, these core needs are in practice interdependent. Socialisation and conviviality create important opportunities for learning, and vice versa. Children's learning would be inhibited without safe and secure care, which in turn provides many opportunities for learning. Healthy children will be better able to learn and socialise, while the excitement of learning and the pleasures of conviviality will enhance children's health and feeling of well-being. Opportunities for learning, care and socialisation may be denied unless services can also accommodate and work with stressed and distressed children and parents, but access to services offering learning, care and socialisation opportunities may have an important part to play in supporting and helping such children and parents, as well as families with less demanding needs.

So, central to the concept of the 'early childhood service' would be a commitment to meeting a variety of needs and a recognition that these needs are in practice closely linked, indeed, in many cases, inseparable. The basis of the service would be an holistic approach to young children and their families. This means that individual services must be multi-functional and flexible, adapting themselves to the needs of families rather than expecting families to fit themselves, as best they can, to what services choose to offer.

The wider benefits of early childhood services

There is another sense in which an 'early childhood service' would be comprehensive. Children and parents would naturally be a central concern. But a truly effective and comprehensive early childhood service would have wider objectives and would benefit others.

An early childhood service is one of the conditions needed to ensure an effective and sufficient labour supply; it is essential therefore for employers. An early childhood service, primarily offering community-based provision, can support the cohesion of local communities, not only bringing together children and their parents and forging links and networks between them, but also involving young children with older children and adults in the neighbourhood. Like the local school, the local surgery and local shops, local services for young children are a necessity for any successful local community, contributing to its identity and functioning and making it a more desirable place to live and work.

Last, but not least, an early childhood service contributes in many ways to meeting the objectives of a healthy and prosperous society, through its contribution to children, parents, employers and local communities. This is why we emphasise that the early childhood service we envision is an essential part of the social and economic infrastructure, a socially cohesive force in society.

An integrated and coherent framework for services

When we talk about an 'early childhood service' we refer, like the 'health service', to a total system of provision which includes a wide range of individual services operating within a single and common framework to ensure a consistent and equitable approach across individual services. We describe this framework in detail in Chapter 11, but outline the main elements here. There would be an encompassing early childhood *policy* and *legislation*. *Administrative responsibility* for the service would reside with one department at national and local levels. There would be a common system of *funding* for all services involving a mix of public funding, to cover the greater part of the cost, and parental contributions. There would be a common system of *staff training*, *pay* and *conditions*, again across all services, ensuring coherent standards and possibilities for workers to move between services; the level of basic training and pay for most staff would be comparable to that of teachers. Last but not least there would be an integrated approach to *standards* and *quality*.

Within this common framework, there would be scope for diversity in type and management of services and choice for parents. The early childhood service would consist of a network of publicly supported individual services in each neighbourhood, offered by a range of providers, including local authorities, voluntary organisations, community and parent groups and worker co-operatives. Private services might also be part of the network if they can meet funding conditions.

Diversity and parental choice, however, would need to be balanced against other considerations. They would not be the only or the dominant value of the early childhood service, but one of several values to be taken into account in determining how to develop the service. Other important values include equality of access, social cohesion of local communities, responsiveness to the needs of families and local communities and co-operative, long-term relationships – between parents and individual services, between different individual services and between these services and the local authority.

Parents would be offered some choice between services and a real choice, not the false impression of choice that arises today when so many functions depend on parents' ability to pay and offer a very limited range of services. For importance would be attached not only to offering some diversity of provision, but to services being affordable and responsive to the varied and changing needs of local families and communities. Rather than parents shopping around until they found a service that nearest met their needs, we envisage an emphasis on services that would be sufficiently flexible and multi-functional to meet those needs locally. Put another way, in our vision parents would be offered a large measure of diversity and choice within individual services rather than just 'take it or leave it' choices between different services.

We see public funding being deliberately used to promote and ensure certain common conditions across all services – for example, appropriate staff training, pay and conditions, stimulating physical environments and parent involvement in management. But it would also be used to encourage the development of multi-functional individual services capable of providing for the core needs of learning, care, socialisation, health and support, and of responding flexibly to the varied needs of their local communities. For example, the conditions attached to public funding would challenge nursery education and playgroups to transform themselves – away from providing a narrowly defined and inflexible part-time and short-term service for 3 and 4 year old children, towards the development of broader models of school-based and parent-run early childhood services.

Funding conditions would be used to encourage the development of services that were not only multi-functional and flexible, but also 'age-integrated', that is, able to take children across the full 0–6 age range and including, in some cases, out-of-school provision for older children. Age integration offers a number of advantages, including continuity for children, the opportunity for children, parents and staff to develop and sustain relationships and more possibilities for siblings to attend the same service. While we envisage a range of centre-based services – some attached to schools, others free-standing – there would be an important place too for organised family day care schemes, with appropriately trained and paid family day carers (childminders) and access for them and their children to a range of support services and centre-based services.

Equal access

To be equally accessible to all children and parents, and therefore comprehensive, the early childhood service must meet various conditions, over and above being open to all children whether or not they have special needs. The service has to be responsive to particular local needs and demands; for example, in rural areas families must be able to reach the services they use.

But above all unless there are enough places at free or affordable prices for all children whose parents want to use the service there is no possibility of equal access. We stress the principle of affordability. Ensuring access to good quality services cannot be left to the private market and parents' ability to pay, any more than access to schools or health services – not least in a society where nearly two-thirds of people live in households where income is less than the average, where one in three children now live in poverty (defined as living in families with incomes below half the national average) and where inequalities in income have been growing in recent years rather than diminishing (Department of Social Security, 1993; Commission on Social Justice, 1994; Jenkins, 1994; Goodman & Webb, 1994; Central Statistical Office, 1995a).

We think it would be reasonable for parents to make some kind of financial contribution to the cost of the early childhood service, as they currently do in other countries; but most of the costs would come from public funds. More specifically, a portion of attendance time, equivalent to full-time school hours, would be free of charge to parents and therefore entirely publicly funded. For children attending for longer hours, funding for the additional hours would come from a mixture of public funding and parent contributions adjusted to take account of family income, family size and other relevant circumstances. No family would pay more than a specified proportion of total household income. Such an arrangement ensures affordability, while avoiding the charge that a totally free service disproportionately benefits employed parents. These proposals are explored further in Chapter 10.

Good quality

We want to see good quality services. What does good quality mean in this context? In the first place, a service that can achieve its objectives. But that begs the question, what objectives? For defining quality means defining what objectives are sought for which groups.

Our vision does not require one absolute definition of quality, handed down and prescribed for all services. Rather it treats quality as an essentially relative and dynamic concept, rooted in values and beliefs that would vary in a plural society and change over time. Quality therefore is subject to different perspectives, understandings and meanings. We elaborate on our perspective in the last chapter when we envision our ideal services, but we recognise that others may well have different visions of quality based on valuing different ideals.

On the other hand no society can permit an entirely relative approach to quality in services; 'anything goes' is unlikely ever to be acceptable. There must therefore be a common core of objectives, based on a common core of values that all services must conform to and build into their definition of quality; for example, equality between children. But beyond that core, there can be scope for considerable diversity in how quality is interpreted. The process of definition becomes critical in this context: how are definitions arrived at? and by whom?

While we value professional skill and integrity highly, an important requirement in our vision is an inclusive process whereby parents, workers, children and other stakeholders in services work together in developing, implementing and reviewing definitions of quality, in a wider community context of debate and enquiry about values, objectives and policies. 'Quality' should be the product of thoughtful and self-reflective services and genuine partnership between 'stakeholders' that goes beyond parents and staff exchanging information and views about individual children to making decisions about the nature, ethos and running of services. This model once again leads us to value co-operative, long-term relationships – within individual services, between individual services and between services and the wider community – based on reflective and well-documented practice by staff and a caring, respectful and reflective dialogue between all stakeholders (see Moss and Pence, 1994, for development of this approach to quality).

0 to 6 – the first stage of the education system

Our vision has implied, but so far has not sufficiently stressed, the importance of regarding 0–6 as the first stage of the education system. We think it is iniquitous that children who are barely 4, (in some cases we have come across not even 4) should be starting primary school. It is putting the clock back to the beginning of the century and losing so many of the educational gains that we have painfully acquired. It brings us no advantages in national competitiveness – countries where children do not start school until 6 or 7 outperform us by the time those children are 16 (Dearing, 1995). Moving compulsory school age to 6 years would bring Britain into line with nearly every other European country (the only other EU countries where compulsory primary schooling starts before 6 are Luxembourg and the Netherlands).

The early childhood service we envision would cover the first third of childhood, and would be the first stage of the education system. Compulsory school age would begin at 6, but this change would be accompanied by a guaranteed place in the early childhood service for all 5 year olds, followed in succession by a guaranteed place for 3 and 4 year olds and then for all children under 3 years; a 'guaranteed place' might vary, according to need and parent wishes, between a full day place and a weekly 'drop in' of a few hours for a child and her parent. We recognise that at present early admission to school is a popular option in the absence of alternative services. It does after all offer a full-time school-based free service. We are proposing instead an educationally orientated service free in school hours, but with added advantages and without the disadvantages of the present system.

This change would ensure a period of continuity for children, parents and staff alike, of at least three years – from 3 (or earlier) to 6. During this time, relationships can be nurtured, age-appropriate work with young children can be developed and common standards, for example levels and training of staff, can be applied. This would replace the current turbulence experienced by many children today. In a matter of two years or less, these children find themselves passed from home to playgroup to nursery class, before being deposited at 4 years into crowded reception classes of primary school, during which process they experience three different staffing regimes.

The changes that we are proposing would fundamentally alter the relationship between early childhood services and the rest of the educational system. 'Early childhood' would no longer be an appendage of compulsory schooling, epitomised by the small nursery class tagged on to the primary school giving a year's half-day provision before children move on to reception class. Instead, 'early childhood' would become a separate, distinct and substantial stage in the education system, of equal standing to primary and secondary stages. Indeed, the multi-functional and flexible nature of the early childhood service might well pose a challenge to these later stages; instead of the first stage of education accommodating itself to the demands of primary and secondary education, these later stages might need to consider what lessons they could learn from the early childhood service.

A VISION OF CHILDHOOD

So far, we have offered a vision of an early childhood service, comprehensive, integrated and coherent and equally accessible to all children and parents. But our vision must go beyond an early childhood service. An early childhood service cannot be considered in isolation. An early childhood service assumes certain other conditions, concerning childhood, parenthood and society. Those conditions shape the service, but are also in turn shaped by the service. We recognise that children are primarily a private and parental responsibility, but they are also a social responsibility – all children are our common future. We should not limit our social concern to a small minority defined as 'in need' by social welfare legislation and agencies. This is not to deny that some children have special needs or more needs than others, but to recognise that all children have some important needs that early childhood services can help to meet.

Our vision of an early childhood service assumes a view about childhood. More broadly, it assumes a society developing a children's culture. What do we mean by children's culture? First, and foremost, a society that recognises children, including those under 6, as citizens, with rights and a call on a fair share of society's resources, not just dependent on their parents' ability and willingness to pay. A society with a children's culture is also concerned with integrating children into all aspects of life and with listening to what they have to say, for example about the services they use, because people want to listen and because they believe that what children say is important.

One consequence of developing an early childhood service within an emerging children's culture would be an emphasis, in discussing the objectives and evaluation of services, on what that service can do, here and now, to improve the quality of everyday life of young children, to provide them with opportunities for learning, to enhance their current well-being and development and to increase their integration into the wider society. Longer-term goals, for example enhancing school performance, would be considered important and valuable, but no more compelling as a reason for providing services than the immediate, 'here and now' benefits. In this way, the early childhood service we envision and the wider children's culture challenge the current trend of increasingly viewing and valuing young children for the school children, the adolescents and the adults they would become; instead, they point to a more balanced view in which young children would be valued and respected for what they are as well as for what they might become.

Our vision of an early childhood service assumes not only valuing young children but work undertaken with them. That work is as important, as demanding and as valuable as work with older children, which is why we emphasise a coherent staffing system based on parity of training levels and pay with teachers. Low levels of training, poor pay, third-rate conditions of employment are a statement about how society views both young children and working with them. It is also a recipe for a variety of ills, including high staff turnover and instability for children, poor quality provision and exploitation of a predominantly female workforce.

Our vision of an early childhood service does not, however, assume the continuance of a predominantly female workforce. In the interests both of children and parents, the workforce in a comprehensive early childhood service must reflect the make-up of the communities and society it serves. This means representation of the ethnic, linguistic and cultural diversity of communities and society. It also means substantial representation of men, working with the full age range of young children.

Increasing male involvement in early childhood services will not just happen by itself. It will need to be an explicit and accepted objective, implemented through a carefully considered strategy which would also ensure that employment opportunities for women are not diminished, compatible objectives when services are being expanded (for a discussion of such a strategy, see Jensen, forthcoming). But increasing men's involvement in paid work with young children needs to be part of a broader approach which encourages and supports men in general to assume a more equal share of the work and responsibilities involved in caring for children – an approach based on a public recognition that this is a movement to be nurtured, but not compelled, and which would benefit not only children, but also potentially women, the wider society and, of course, men themselves (EC Childcare Network, 1994a; Moss, 1995).

An early childhood service itself can play an important role in this process of supporting change in gender roles and relationships. Individual services can provide opportunities within a safe and secure environment for men and women to explore these issues and the possibilities for change; this is one example of the support role in practice (see Ghedini et al., 1995). In this context, a comprehensive early childhood service is one that enjoys the active participation of men as well as women, and where 'parent' involvement really means involvement by both fathers and mothers.

PARENTAL EMPLOYMENT

Finally, our vision of an early childhood service must be set in the context of developments in parental employment. Trends in parental employment determine some of the needs that the service must be able to meet, both for children and for parents. There is also a policy dimension. As the number of employed parents increases, there is an increasing need for a public policy to help parents reconcile employment and caring for children, in a way that ensures quality of life for children, parents and families and equality of opportunity for women and men. A comprehensive, integrated and coherent early childhood service would be an important part of that policy.

But though a necessary condition for reconciling employment and caring for children, an early childhood service is not sufficient. Other parts of the policy include the introduction and development of a statutory right to Parental Leave and other forms of leave for employed parents (discussed in more detail in Chapter 11) and active measures to support and encourage increased participation by fathers in the care and upbringing of children. Both measures might affect the demand from parents for the early childhood service, especially when children were very young.

As with early childhood services, the emphasis on a strong public policy in this area recognises the strong public interest in children and families (as well as, of course, the strong public interest in ensuring effective use of the labour force, which such a policy would encourage). It also recognises the fact that only government, representing society, can adequately comprehend and represent the many needs and interests involved – the well-being of children and families, equality for women, effective and efficient use of the labour force. But important as public policy is, it is not enough.

Equally important are major changes led by employers and trades unions, with government support, to make the workplace more responsive to the needs of workers with children. We do not of course mean this in the extremely narrow sense of workplace nurseries, which we see as an unsatisfactory and segregated service. We envision a wide tranche of measures and changes in workplace culture which would recognise and support the caring roles and responsibilities of employed women and men, including those arising from the care and upbringing of children.

SUPPORTING PARENTING

There is currently a considerable debate about parenting skills. There are obvious benefits to introducing all boys and girls (not just non-academic girls) to parenting skills. However, the debate is often without social context and with little reference to the negative and limiting employment and other conditions which constrain how men and women bring up children. At some point most parents experience stress – with sleepless or bedwetting children or with unforeseen family crises which undermine how families function. We envisage services which enable parents to reassess their position and to support the choices which parents make – to work or not to work, to seek advice or relief from stress, to lessen the isolation of non-stop caring, or as a base from which to seek further education and training, to be convivial or not.

Our view of parenting is that it is not only about mothers and fathers and their relationship with their children but is also about the possibility of empowering men and women to have more control over if and how much they work and when they work, and how much time they choose to spend with their children. Ideally they should be able to make these decisions without putting at risk their position in the labour market (if they have one) where to 'drop out', as opposed to taking leave, carries ever increasing risks for future employment prospects. The vision is about helping parents, mothers and fathers, to find a satisfactory and satisfying balance between employment and caring for children (using the term 'caring' in its broadest sense), as well as other important aspects of personal and social life. A comprehensive, integrated and coherent early childhood service has an important part in achieving that vision.

VALUES AND BELIEFS

Vision, like quality, is an expression of values and beliefs. Our vision for a comprehensive, integrated and coherent early childhood service is based on the importance we attach to a number of related values and concepts: citizenship; social cohesion; equality of opportunity; democracy and inclusion; the importance of co-operative, respectful and long-term relationships; responsiveness to diversity and change; the social significance of parenting; and the importance of caring for and bringing up children. Last but not least, our vision is based on the idea that early childhood is a period that is important in its own right as well as being vital for future development, and should be a time of discovery, excitement, fun, sociability, growing self-confidence and zest in learning.

This is a weighty list and an inversion of the usual justification for early childhood services. We do not expect early childhood services to change the world – as has not infrequently been claimed for nursery education. On the contrary, we want comprehensive, integrated and coherent early childhood services because the world is changing. Such services are an expression of our values; an essential part of a better and more just society.

2

The Parents' Perspective

SIX FAMILIES

Hazel *has two boys: Jo, aged 4 and Sam, aged 18 months. She works as a secretary and her husband is a lecturer. They would dearly like Jo to go to a nursery class, but the childminder, who is elderly, cannot manage to take him. Despite this, and the reservations they have about the childminder, Hazel and her husband continue to use her because they do not want to have different arrangements for the two children. The childminder's charge of over £120 a week takes up a large part of the family income, but Hazel and her husband consider it just about worthwhile to ensure Hazel keeps her job.*

Agnes *is Nigerian. She came to Britain as a young bride to an older husband, and saw it as her duty to bear his children. She now has three young children – a 4 year old, a 2 year old and a new baby – but has refused to have more children, defying both her husband and her church. As a recent immigrant, and a mother at home with small children, Agnes has been very isolated. She lives in a small flat, with a lodger, and space is very restricted. The children are bilingual (Agnes speaks to them in Ibo and English) and in common with many bilingual children are slow at speaking. Their frustration shows in frequent screaming.*

Despite these difficulties, Agnes, with great determination, has taken an access course to enter for a law degree, and would dearly like to go on with her studies. But she finds this impossible because she cannot afford to pay for the necessary care arrangements for her children. Her son and daughter would love the local nursery class, but it only takes 4 year olds for two-and-a-half hours a day. Because she did not understand the system properly, Agnes did not get her son's name down on the entry list in time, but in any case feels she cannot manage the journey of a mile each way twice a day with all three children in tow and for such a short period of time. So she uses the local playgroup, which is nearer but held in a draughty church hall with constantly changing volunteer staff. There is little understanding of the children's language difficulties or their need for consistency – and the few hours a week on offer costs Agnes £10 which she can barely afford.

Coral *had an abusive partner who is now in prison. She drinks and this sometimes makes her foul-mouthed and abusive. She is isolated and has no friends. She has a son, John, aged 5, who not surprisingly is often aggressive and uncooperative. He would have benefited from relaxed play in a group setting and some kind of structure in his life. But Coral was too depressed and disorganised to take him to the local nursery class, which in any case refused to have him when the health visitor asked because they felt he was too much of a problem and they have insufficient staff to cope. Coral has not yet registered John for school and is unlikely to do so until she is forced. She gives excuses for not having got round to it. She thinks vaguely that she would like to take up her former job as a hairdresser, but feels hopeless about getting work. Instead she has become pregnant again. Her neighbours, who have petitioned to have her rehoused, regard her pregnancy with anger. The social worker who has been alerted to the pregnancy wants Coral to go to a family centre, where she thinks that Coral will get support to work on her parenting skills. But Coral will not take up the offer, because she feels she will be stigmatised even more. John now hangs around the streets.*

Rachel *lives with her partner and their two children, George, aged 3, and June who is just coming up to her first birthday. Before having children, she was a full-time lecturer, but since George was born, she has worked part-time, three days a week. Going back to her job twice after maternity leave, arrangements for the care of her children have been a constant problem. Arrangements for George have changed on a number of occasions, including a move from childminding to a day nursery when his childminder had to give up due to ill health.*

Since June was born, life has become even harder. With two young children to think about, Rachel first looked for a childminder who could care for both and lived locally, so that George could continue attending the playgroup where he was happily settled. This proved impossible due to a shortage of baby places among local childminders. With the high price of private day nurseries, the only affordable option seemed to be to employ a nanny. The first one left after three months, without any notice. Renewed attempts to find a childminder failed, and a second nanny has been recruited: this one is again unqualified. Weekly costs for the nanny, who works three days, and George's playgroup fees are £125, which leaves no spare money for extra care so that Rachel can work on the Ph.D. she began before she had children and which she has one year left to complete. For Rachel, her determination to continue her career carries a price of constant anxiety about the quality and stability of care available to her children.

Margaret *and her husband who is a gardener live in a tied cottage on a small privately owned estate in the countryside. Margaret has triplets aged 18 months. She looked forward to having children but it took many years and eventually she received IVF treatment for infertility. Before the children were* born she worked as a shop assistant in a china shop, a low-paid job which involved travelling by bus to the nearest town, and she was glad to give it up. She is a devoted mother but had not anticipated the isolation she now feels. She has no transport and cannot visit relatives or friends or even shop without help. Her mother comes to stay occasionally although the cottage is small and there is not enough room.

Her husband helps as much as he can, coming home at lunchtimes and dropping in more often if it is urgent, for instance when the triplets caught a cold, and he does the weekly shop. But he is increasingly bitter, knowing that because of the tied accommodation he cannot afford to disagree with his irascible employer, nor can he easily seek another job in a town so that Margaret could get out and about on her own. Unless Margaret also worked their income would never be enough for a mortgage. So they both feel increasingly trapped by their circumstances, and the stress of the constant caring for the triplets is undermining the joy and pride they looked forward to in having a family.

Janis is a single parent with a ten-month-old baby. She is in her early forties, with a responsible and well-paid job as a manager in a large company. She has her own garden flat on which she still has 15 years mortgage owing. She has had a number of relationships with men, but values her independence and was wary about giving it up. She wanted a baby and was conscious that her biological clock was running out and that she could not leave it much longer. The father of the baby already had a grown up family and was reluctant to have another child. He made it clear to Janis that he would not support the baby, and indeed has now taken another job and moved away from the area.

Janis has bought a place in a private day nursery for her son, which costs £120 per week. Janis can afford this amount but there has been a breakdown with the nursery. Her son has a stomach malformation which means that he is often violently sick, and he will need an operation when he is older. The nursery cannot cope with him and have told Janis that she must find somewhere else. Janis has already taken a lot of time off work but her company is asking her to travel and has made little allowance for her domestic situation. She is afraid that she will be taken off the project in which she is involved and be sidelined into routine work, or else runs the risk of redundancy.

We have used these examples of six very different and individual families to illustrate a number of themes which we explore in this chapter. The first theme is the increasing diversity of family life, and the difficulty of assuming any kind of norm. The second theme is the continual underestimation by those delivering services to young children of the position of women in the labour force and women's wish and need to work. The third theme is the inseparability of children from their family circumstances. We are uneasy with the language of some of the educational debate which focuses on 'the child's learning' as if the family and the stresses and strains it experiences are no more than an inconvenient backdrop, a hindrance to efficient learning and the 'all-round' development of the child – issues we develop further in Chapter 6.

Most parents of young children, quite understandably, do not have the time or inclination to become involved in theoretical debates about early childhood services. Demands on their time and attention are heavy and constant, while needs are immediate and pressing. Parents have to get on and make the best of what there is. To a mother or father trying to juggle a job, the care of young children and the management of a home, talk of a 'comprehensive, integrated and coherent early childhood service' may seem incomprehensible and irrelevant. But we shall argue that the vision we outlined in Chapter 1 – of a **comprehensive, integrated** and **coherent** early childhood service, offering **equal access** to **high quality** services for **all young children from 0 to 6 and their parents** – would prove an attractive and highly relevant response to the needs of parents and their children. For a comprehensive, integrated and coherent early childhood service is in fact far better able to respond to the realities of contemporary early parenthood than the current fragmented and incoherent systems.

None of our six families has services which meet their needs. We do not claim that these six families are a 'representative national sample', but neither are they untypical. Many readers will readily identify with their circumstances and their experiences in trying to find appropriate services.

MEETING THE REAL NEEDS OF FAMILIES

The solutions that parents need, in their own interests and those of their children, are often unavailable. The services that are available are unsatisfactory in many respects. Parents, and in most cases we are talking in practice about mothers who usually have to manage relationships with services, have to fit their needs around what is available and what they can afford – and it is striking, if not surprising, how frequently cost comes up as an issue, either imposing a heavy drain on the incomes of young families or making services inaccessible. Parents often end up stitching together arrangements; too often, the results come undone at the seams.

Most families have a variety of needs. Families do not divide up neatly into those who need care while parents work, those whose children need socialisation and learning opportunities and those whose parents need support. Coral needs support and help as a parent and badly needs an opportunity to change her view of herself and bolster her self-esteem: John needs opportunities for relaxed play and socialisation and although aged 5, cannot yet fit into school, which would be a disaster for him. Hazel and Rachel want their children to enjoy the socialisation and learning opportunities at nursery class or playgroup: but they also need their children safely cared for while they and their partners are at work. Agnes needs care to enable her to study which, in turn, might provide an answer to her isolation; helping mothers and fathers to get qualifications, employment and a secure income, with the independence and self-esteem that follow, can often be the best way of supporting them as parents. But Agnes' children also need the chance to get out from their cramped home to meet and play with other children, in an environment where the needs of her children are appreciated and met. Margaret wants some kind of care for her triplets so that she can have a much-needed break, and needs transport to get there, and may well want to reconsider her ideas about having a job. Janis needs to work and support herself and needs skilled care for her son, who, as a single child, will also benefit from the company of other children.

Many families share the basic needs for care, learning, socialisation, health and support. But the form these needs take may vary. Parents' working hours vary in length and timing. Some, like Rachel, combine or would like to combine a job and studying. Some parents need little or no support, because they already have effective social networks of relatives and friends and fewer pressing problems. Some children and some parents, like Coral and John, need a lot of help, at least for a time.

Moreover, needs are not static; they vary over time. The birth of a second or third child creates new and more complex needs. Needs change as children get older. Parents' own circumstances change: they lose a job, take leave, re-enter employment, undertake a temporary period of study. Parents separate and 're-partner'. Children or parents may experience periods of poor health. Other family crises occur.

A comprehensive, integrated and coherent early childhood service would have individual services that are not only 'multi-functional' – able to address a range of needs for children and parents – but also flexible, adaptable to different and changing needs. To take an obvious example, an emphasis on age-integrated centres, taking children from 0 to 6 years, would enable the same service to take children across the age range as well as older and younger siblings. This is also why we argued, in Chapter 1, that a comprehensive, integrated and coherent early childhood service 'will challenge nursery classes and playgroups to evolve, exploring the potential for broader models of school-based and parent-run early childhood services', since in their present form they are usually neither multi-functional nor flexible, nor at all age-integrated.

CHANGING NEEDS

Demographic, economic and social trends affecting family life are creating the circumstances and needs exemplified by our six case studies. A well-established decline in fertility has reduced the number of larger families. Single-child families are common, and mothers on average are older (women's average age at first birth is now 28). The proportion of lone parents has increased rapidly, more than doubling between 1971 and 1991; Britain now has the highest level of lone-parent families in Europe. At the same time, 're-partnering' and step-families are becoming more common.

The consequences of these demographic trends are complex and far-reaching. Combined with increasing parental employment, discussed below, young children are less likely to have other children around with whom to play. Extended families are getting smaller, because over time smaller families mean fewer relatives. Social networks, of friends and relatives, are likely to be diminished. Families are more mobile. Increasing numbers of children live in homes without the presence of a man (although even when present, many men spend much of their time out at work). Children and parents increasingly experience changes in family life.

Poverty has grown rapidly throughout the whole of British society, but families with children have suffered worst: in 1979, one in ten children was living in a low income family; today, poverty affects one in three (Kumar, 1993). This has been accompanied by growing financial inequality. The bottom half of the population, who received a third of national income in 1979, now only receive a quarter. Nearly two-thirds of people live in households whose income is below the average (Central Statistical Office, 1995a, Table 5.21), a sharp reminder that society does not consist simply of a poor minority, candidates for a minimal welfare safety net, and a rich majority, who can make private arrangements for all their needs.

Since the mid-1980s there has been a rapid increase in employment among women with young children; by 1994, 46 per cent of women with a youngest child under 5 were employed and a further 6 per cent were looking for work (Central Statistical Office, 1995a, Table 4.5). Two-thirds of employed women with young children still have part-time jobs and many work very short hours. Moreover, many part-time employed mothers with young children work evenings, nights or weekends; for example, in 1991, 37 per cent of part-time employed women with a child under 5 worked evenings or nights compared to 5 per cent of all employed married women. In many households, therefore, managing employment and family life depends on the mother finding a job whose hours, both in terms of length and when worked, fit in with the limited care arrangements that are available, affordable and acceptable – which in most cases means sharing the care with a child's father (so working at times when he is at home) or relying on the willingness and availability of relatives (Brannen et al., 1994).

But this period of growth in maternal employment, since the mid-1980s, has seen full-time employment increase faster than part-time employment. There has also been a rapid growth in women resuming their employment straight after maternity leave (McRae, 1991). However, growth in maternal employment has not been uniform; there have been 'winners' and 'losers'. Employment is growing fastest amongst certain groups (for example, those with high levels of educational qualification, those living with partners and, among them, those with employed partners, white mothers, and mothers with only one or two children), and growing slowly or even, in some cases, decreasing among other groups (for example, those with no qualifications, lone mothers, mothers with non-employed partners, black mothers and mothers with three or more children) (Harrop and Moss, 1995).

At the same time, around 84 per cent of fathers with young children are employed, with a further 11 per cent looking for work; only 5 per cent are 'economically inactive' compared to 41 per cent of mothers. The high level of employment among fathers of young children has fallen only slightly since the mid-1980s, illustrating that mothers' employment supplements, rather than replaces, fathers' employment. Moreover not only do nearly all fathers work full-time but many work very long full-time hours: the hours of work of British fathers actually increased during the 1980s and they work the longest hours in Europe while British mothers work the second shortest hours in Europe (EC Childcare Network, forthcoming).

Present trends mean more 'dual earner' families – but also more 'no earner' families (because of low employment rates among lone mothers, whose numbers are increasing, and among mothers whose partners are not employed). There is a process of polarisation underway among families with young children, as employment grows fastest among more advantaged mothers. This process has enormous implications for many aspects of family life and childhood, not least differences between families in income and how children are cared for. If present trends continue, children with a mother at home full-time will not only be a diminishing minority but will be increasingly concentrated in the most economically and socially deprived families.

But it is not just the amount of employment that is changing; it is the nature of employment itself. New technology and growing competition, deregulation and increasing flexibility in the labour market open up new opportunities for some workers, especially those with valued skills and expertise. But they also bring increased insecurity and intensification of work for many others, producing what one commentator has described as a 'thirty, thirty, forty society'. The first 30 per cent are the unemployed and economically inactive: 'this 30 per cent, with their children poorly fed, their families under stress and without access to amenities like gardens are the absolutely disadvantaged' (Hutton, 1995a, p. 106). The second 30 per cent are the marginalised and the insecure, defined not so much by income but by their relation to the labour market: 'people in this category work at jobs that are insecure, poorly protected and carry few benefits . . . (and) includes the growing army of part-timers and casual workers' (ibid., p. 106) The remaining 40 per cent are relatively privileged, workers both full-time and part-time, in relatively secure jobs. Arguing that the impact of growing inequality and insecurity is pervasive, Hutton concludes:

> The fact that more than half the people in Britain who are eligible to work are living either on poverty incomes or in conditions of permanent stress and insecurity has had dreadful effects on the wider society. It has become harder and harder for men and women in these circumstances to hold their

marriages together, let alone parent their children adequately, as the hours
of work in which a decent wage can be earned grow longer and longer.

(ibid., p. 109)

Of course, the consequences of these and other changes will not be uniform
across all families, nor are social, economic and demographic trends uniformly
adverse in effect; there are always gains as well as losses, winners as well as
losers. But added together they suggest many parents with young children are
under great pressure, whether from low income, unemployment, insecure
employment, working too many hours, coping with difficult transitions or
bringing up children single-handed or with too little contribution from their
partner. They also suggest that opportunities for children and parents are
becoming more, rather than less, unequal.

It would be foolish to suggest that early childhood services, however
comprehensive, integrated and coherent, were a cure-all for these ills. They
cannot make good the corrosive effects of poverty and insecurity, or the
debilitating consequences of overwork. As we argued in the first chapter, they
should never be considered in isolation.

But a comprehensive, integrated and coherent early childhood service can
contribute to improving the quality of life and opportunities of parents and
children. It can ensure safe, secure and accessible care for children to enable
parents to work or study. By so doing, it can offer parents, especially mothers,
more opportunities in the labour market, not tying them to jobs that 'fit in'
with the availability of fathers or relatives to care for children. It can also
remove one barrier to employment for lone parents and other less advantaged
parents – although other barriers also need removing, including low skill
levels.

A comprehensive, integrated and coherent early childhood service can
provide learning opportunities for children, offering experiences that are
unavailable at home (this is not an implied criticism of homes and families,
only a recognition that services and families can each provide children with
unique experiences and relationships, and should be regarded as
complementary to each other in ensuring that children have a good upbringing
and develop their full potential). It can extend opportunities for children to
meet other children and other adults, including men. It can provide
opportunities for parents to meet other parents and so extend their social
networks and, consequently, their informal support resources. It can provide
an element of continuity in the lives of children and parents in an increasingly
turbulent and uncertain world.

WHAT DO PARENTS WANT?

We have argued so far that our vision of a comprehensive, integrated and
coherent early childhood service fits well with the needs of parents and
children. But does it square with what parents themselves say about services?

First, most parents (or again, in practice, usually mothers, since fathers' views are seldom sought) want a service. In a 1990 government survey in England (Meltzer, 1994), 84 per cent of mothers with children under 5 said they preferred their children to attend 'a day care service or nursery school or class' (a category which includes parent and toddler group). Second, many mothers already using one of these 'day care' services would have preferred their child to be in another type of service – half of the mothers using playgroups and parent and toddler groups and over a third among mothers using day nurseries. The highest level of satisfaction was with nursery education, where only a fifth of mothers said they would have preferred an alternative service for their child; nursery education was the main preferred alternative for dissatisfied playgroup and day nursery users. Third, many mothers using 'day care' services expressed a preference for their children to attend for longer periods each week. Half of the mothers whose children used playgroups, day nurseries or parent and toddler groups said they would prefer their children to go more days each week (a majority of children in each case attended for 3 days a week or less); while two-fifths of mothers whose children attended playgroups and nursery education (most of whom only got half-day attendance for their children) and nearly two-thirds of day nursery users wanted a later finishing time.

The survey also asked parents their reasons for sending children to particular types of 'day care' service. In every case, 'to play with others' was the first reason given; socialisation, therefore, was the first and foremost need that parents looked to services to meet. But the next two reasons varied according to type of service – to 'develop skills' and 'be independent' for playgroups and nursery education, 'mother: work' and 'mother: other' for day nurseries. This reflects the fragmentation of present services, where playgroups and nursery education are geared to socialisation and learning but not care, while the primary function of day nurseries, at least those provided privately, is conceived of as 'child care for working parents'.

A less specific, but broader, picture of 'parents' views' is provided by a report from the Early Childhood Unit at the National Children's Bureau (Elfer, 1994). The Children Act 1989 requires local authorities to undertake reviews of 'day care' services every three years. The NCB report examines the results from consultations with parents undertaken as part of the first round of these local authority reviews in 1992. The sources vary from formal surveys to informal community based exercises, but all point to certain broad conclusions:

• Parents want more services and much of the feedback 'referred to a lack of flexibility in services to meet the multi and various needs of families' (p. 5).

• Parents want provision that will promote the educational and social development of children, but many also want more care, so that 'whilst the educational component of services is clearly very important to parents, it is by no means the exclusive preoccupation of families' (p. 5).

- Parents want reliable standards, covering issues such as curriculum, activities, staffing, physical environment and parent involvement.

- Parents want services which are affordable – 'many parents expressed anxieties about the cost of services' (p. 6) – and geographically accessible – 'getting children to and from different services and making these arrangements work so that they fitted in with the timetable of the services and the timetable of parents involved many families in impossibly complicated arrangements' (p. 6).

The author concludes that 'parents want *more* provision of *reliable quality, lower cost* located *near where they live* (or work) and that are *flexible*, i.e., can respond to different kinds of family needs (needs of working parents, social/educational needs of children and the play/leisure needs of children)' (p. 8, original emphasis).

Parents may not be articulating an explicit demand for a 'comprehensive, integrated and coherent early childhood service'. It would be surprising if they were, given the lack of vision at a public and political level and the consequent low level of public discussion. When it comes to early childhood services, Britain suffers a poverty of expectation and a low level of awareness of issues, arising from years of neglect and indifference. Yet whether we consider individual cases, broad trends or attempts to tap into what parents want for their children and themselves, the evidence points to a need for and a preference for services which can best be provided within the system of early childhood services that we envision.

3

What Have We Got?

*The Government believe that in the first instance it is the **responsibility of the parents** to make arrangements, including financial arrangements, for the day care of pre-school children.*

(Memorandum submitted by the Department of Health and Social Security to the House of Commons Education, Science and Arts Committee, 29 June 1988; our emphasis)

*Part III (of the Children Act) also introduces the review duty under which local authorities . . . are required to review and report on the **day care** service in the area used by children under 8. This new duty, the general duty to provide **day care** for children in need (section 18) and the modernised registration system in Part X of the Act to regulate independent **day care** services and childminding used by children under 8 give local authorities for the first time a clear function to oversee and co-ordinate these services . . . in the case of day care and education services for young children the importance of **co-ordination** between different local authority departments – particularly if not exclusively social services and education – has long been recognised.*

(Volume 2 of The Children Act 1989 Guidance and Regulations, Department of Health 1991; our emphasis)

*In my view, (nursery education) should be regarded as a great benefit for children between the age of **three and five**, enabling them to learn better attributes and perhaps to start some of the early learning processes. **In no way should it be regarded as a mechanism to enable women to work.***

(Angela Rumbold, Minister of State, Department for Education, Parliamentary debate, 4 February 1991; our emphasis)

*The Prime Minister's commitment is to provide, over time, good quality pre-school places for all **4 year olds** whose parents wish them to take it up. There are no plans as yet to extend the commitment to younger children.*

(Eric Forth, Minister of State, Department for Education, written answer to Parliamentary Question, 21 February 1995; our emphasis)

Table 1. The current range of services in Britain for young children

Type	Administration	Values – Philosophy	Staffing
Publicly Provided Services			
Nursery Schools	Education	'To enlarge a child's knowledge, experience and imaginative understanding and thus his awareness of moral values and capacity for enjoyment; and . . . to enable him to enter the world after formal education is over as an active participant in society and a responsive contributor to it.'	Nursery Teachers Degree, PGCE
Nursery Classes (attached to primary schools)	Education		Nursery Nurses
Reception Classes	Education	Introduction to formal schooling, and the National Curriculum	Primary Teachers, Degree, PGCE
Day Nurseries	Social Services	Day care services emphasising the care and protection of vulnerable children.	Nursery Nurses (NNEB)
Family Centres	Social Services	Emphasis on a programme of work involving parents and children. Usually compensatory.	
Combined Nursery Centres	Social Services/ Education	Vary widely in their emphasis and approach, but usually include a combination of care and education.	Nursery Teachers and Nursery Nurses
One O'Clock Club	Leisure/ Social Services	Recreational emphasis – frequently non-directive play, with mothers or carers present.	Play Leaders often qualified
Playcentres	Registration Duty of Social Services if parents leave their children		
Voluntary Services			
Playgroups (may also be private)	Registration and inspection duty of Social Services. Majority affiliated to Pre-School Playgroup Association (PPA)	Loosely modelled on nursery education. Parents committees manage the groups and parents often help on a rota basis. The emphasis is on *play* as the tool for learning. May provide opportunity groups for children with disabilities. Emphasis on parental development and support.	Play Leaders PPA trained Volunteers
Voluntary Nurseries Family Centres Family Support Centres	Registration and Inspection duty of Social Services	Centres generally established by voluntary childcare organisations focusing on community development or 'self-help' centres that have grown out of voluntary community groups.	Social Workers, Nursery Nurses (NNEB) Volunteers

Ratios	Age	Opening Times	Access	Charge	% Attendance
1 to 23 (Teaching) 1 to 13 (Overall)	3 to 4 years	Part-time (Sessional) 2.5 hours	Self-referral; applications considered by individual schools	Free	26% of 3 to 4 year olds
1 to 30/40	Rising 5s (Reception Class)	School Day 9 a.m. – 3.30 p.m.			21% of 4 year olds
Recommended 1 to 5 (2–5)	0 to 5 years	Full-time, though sessional care common	Generally criteria based on need	Usually means tested	0.9% of 0 to 5 year olds
1 to 3 (0–2)		Varies			(See family centres – Voluntary Sector)
1 to 3 (Children with special needs) 1 to 2 (0–2)		Full-time			No national data – 40 groups are members of National Association
2 – ?	0 to 5 years	Sessional Extended Day	Self-referral, although may be changed to 'children in need'	Covers food costs	No figures available
1 to 8	2.5 to 5 years	Sessional; varies but usually between 5 and 15 hours per week	Self-referral	Average £7.50 per 2.5 hour session	60% of 2.5 to 5 year olds
Recommended the same as for day nurseries	0 to 5 years	Flexible – may offer sessional, full day or out of school	Self-referral based on catchment areas or targeted to 'children in need'	Minimal charge to cover costs or free	Unknown – but 500 centres belong to the Family Centre Network

Table 1. The current range of services in Britain for young children *(cont'd)*

Type	Administration	Values – Philosophy	Staffing
Specialist Resources			Volunteers
Toy Libraries	Play Matters (National) Toy Libraries Association	Lend toys, at minimal cost, to children and families. Undertake community work.	
Out of School (May also be private)	Kid Club Network (Education/ Youth Services/ Leisure) Registration and Inspection duty of Social Services for 5–8 (Children's Act 1989)	Promotes play/care services for children before and after school and during school holidays.	Play Leaders Volunteers
Parent–Toddler Groups	Often supported by the PPA	Often self-help initiatives that offer a drop-in service for parents to meet and toddlers to play. Parent must be present.	Volunteers
Private Services			
Childminders	Registration and Inspection duty of Social Services	A private arrangement between parent and childminder offering full day care in a childminder's home. Emphasis on 'extension of home' and individual care.	Women at home may have short vocational training
Nannies	Private or registration duty of Social Services if carer is involved with 3 families or more (Children's Act 1989)	Day care for children within their own homes provided by a carer who comes to the home. Emphasis on individual care.	Nursery Nurses or Untrained
Nurseries	Registration duty of Social Services	Day care for working families or students. Educational content and quality of care can vary enormously. Emphasis on group care. Profit driven.	Nursery Nurses PPA or Untrained
Nursery Schools	No requirement to register nor inspection necessary, other than school inspection if part of a school	Varies. Often emphasis on formal education, the 3 'R's. Profit driven.	Teachers Nursery Nurses

Ratios	Age	Opening Times	Access	Charge	% Attendance
Not applicable	0 to 5 years	Varies	Self-referral	Minimal charges; 10p for toys	No national figures available
1 to 8	3 to 8 years	Out of school hours	Self-referral, often based on catchment areas	Varies	No figures available
Varies	0 to 5 years	Generally one or more sessions per week	Self-referral	Minimal to cover costs	No figures available
Registration generally 1 to 3 under 5 years inc. own children	0 to 5 years	Full day	Self-referral; private arrangement; based on ability to pay	National Childminders Association guidelines £50–£90 per week	7% of 0 to 4 year olds
Varies according to family size	0 to 5 years	Full day	Private arrangement; based on ability to pay	Varies	No figures available
1 to 3 0–2 1 to 4 2–3 1 to 8 3–4	0 to 5 years	Full day	Private arrangement; based on ability to pay	£50–£200 per week	2.9% of 0 to 4 year olds
Varies	2 to 5 years	Varies	Private arrangement; based on ability to pay	£50–£200 per week	1.45% of 0 to 4 year olds

Having set out our vision of a comprehensive, integrated and coherent early childhood service, open to all children from 0 to 6, and how this might dovetail with the realities of present-day family life, in these next two chapters we look at the services we actually have from a national and local perspective. First, in this chapter, we review the current range of services in Britain for young children. Because the present compulsory school age, and start of primary school, is at age 5, we have focused on services for children under this age although in our vision for an early childhood service we have covered children up to 6. In Chapter 4 we look at what happens on the ground in a given locality.

Britain certainly has great diversity in its services. In Table 1, we compare over a dozen different types of service across their main features. A first level of classification is between services that are currently labelled as 'day care' (mainly *day nurseries, playgroups* and *childminders*), and which operate within the welfare system (i.e. under the oversight of social services authorities) and those labelled as 'early years education' (mainly *nursery schools, nursery classes* and *reception class provision for 4 year olds*), which operate within schools and the education system.

In Table 1, however, we have organised the different types of service according to who provides them, dividing them into three main categories: publicly funded *and* provided; voluntary, non-profit organisations, which may in some cases receive some public funding; and private. Even with this apparently straightforward classification, the three main categories cover increasingly diverse situations. Nursery classes may be on offer in schools provided by local authorities or in 'opted-out' grant maintained schools. Local authority Social Services Departments may sell places in publicly funded and provided day nurseries to employed parents as a method of revenue-raising. There has been increasing emphasis in recent years on local authorities purchasing places for children 'in need', for whom they have a duty to provide, in the voluntary and private sectors. Voluntary organisations vary from large, long-established national children's charities to small local committees running one part-time playgroup. While in the private sector, individual family day carers, looking after 2 or 3 children in their own home, co-exist with, for example, the proprietor of a single private day nursery and limited companies running expanding chains of nurseries as a big business.

PUBLICLY PROVIDED SERVICES

Education system

There are three kinds of publicly funded and publicly provided education services for children under 5 years: *free-standing nursery schools; nursery classes attached to primary schools;* and *reception classes in primary schools which admit 4 year olds.* As we shall describe in Chapter 5, nursery education was originally seen as a 'free-standing' service, independent of primary schools, and most of the literature up to 1960 refers to *nursery schools*. *Nursery schools* have their own management, usually a supernumary headteacher and a teaching deputy headteacher (although in many local authorities this post is now being phased out), together with secretarial assistance. They may also have their own governing body, but this is not a formal requirement.

Nursery classes now provide for far more children than nursery schools; in 1993, for example, they accounted for 80 per cent of places in public nursery education in Britain (see Table 2). They are a slightly cheaper option, partly because they belong to the management of the school and do not have supernumary staff. They have been seen increasingly not only as a preparation for primary school but as a way of attracting pupils and maintaining or increasing pupil numbers in the primary schools to which they are attached.

Reception classes frequently admit children aged 4. There has been considerable criticism of this practice, on the grounds that many reception classes are not geared to meet the needs of 4 year olds. Even so, there are more 4 year olds attending *reception classes* than *nursery schools* and *classes*.

While most under 5s attend *reception class* on a full-time basis (91 per cent in 1994 in England), 90 per cent of under 5s in *nursery school* or *class* attend part-time (Department for Education, 1995, Table 1).

Social services

Social services departments have traditionally provided *day nurseries*. Like *nursery schools*, the function and clientele of these *day nurseries* have varied according to current social and political concerns. After the Second World War, a main group of users were single parents with a job. In the last 20 years or so, local authority *day nurseries* have focused increasingly on distressed or disorganised families. Many have changed their name, along with their function, and are now called *family centres* or *therapeutic family centres*, where parents, usually mothers, receive some guidance about childrearing alongside activities provided for their children.

In the last five years, a few local authorities, prompted by economic concerns, have redesignated their *day nurseries* yet again. As well as offering a service to children referred by social workers as being 'in need', they also offer a service for some working parents. In these cases, a proportion of places are sold on a 'first come, first served' basis to anyone in the locality able and wishing to purchase a place. The conflict of aims – welfare for children 'in need' and revenue raising for working parents – has sometimes proved problematic (Penn, 1990).

Education and social services

There have been a number of attempts to bring education and social services provision together under one roof, but without relinquishing any of the functions or administration of either of them. These *combined centres* were reviewed by Elsa Ferri and her colleagues (1981), who noted unresolved inequalities and other differences between the two types of provision which made it difficult for them to operate harmoniously. More recent reports such as that of Ball (1994) have recommended them as a way forward.

Leisure

There are a number of services for young children attached to parks and recreation facilities. They vary considerably in type. *One o'clock clubs*, for example, are playcentres for pre-school children based in parks. Mothers or other carers (e.g. relatives, childminders) stay with their children.

VOLUNTARY SERVICES

Playgroups are the most widespread service for young children and more children under five attend this service than any other. Most commonly they operate for 12–15 hours a week, although some are open as little as 5 hours a week (e.g. 2 mornings a week); in recent years, however, there has been growth in playgroups offering extended hours or full day care of up to 35–40 hours a week. Many playgroup places are shared between 2 children (the Pre-school Learning Alliance estimates that, in 1993, on average there were 1.8 children using every 1 place; a government estimate, for 1990, arrives at a rather lower figure of 1.3 (written answer to Parliamentary Question by Eric Forth, Minister of State, Department for Education, 21 February 1995)). The majority of children at *playgroups* attend for only 2 or 3 part-time sessions a week (between 5 and 9 hours) (Meltzer, 1994).

Most *playgroups* are organised on a self-help basis, run by parent or local community groups, and depend entirely on parent fees and fund-raising. However, a minority get some public subsidy, usually a small amount. Some *playgroups* are run privately, for profit, while a small and decreasing number are provided and funded by social services departments.

Voluntary or community nurseries have been established by small, local non-profit organisations to meet local need and demands, especially from working parents. In contrast, large, often national, voluntary organisations (e.g. Barnardos, National Children's Homes, the Children's Society) run *family centres* in areas of high social need. Their purpose has been to provide a mainly welfare or community development role, rather than a service for working parents.

There are a variety of more specialised services. The term *crèche* covers a wide range of provision. It may be provided as an adjunct to another service to enable parents to use that service (e.g. a college, sports centre, shopping centre) or in its own right. It may be a one-off arrangement (e.g. providing care for children whose parents are attending a conference) or it may operate on a regular basis.

Parent and toddler groups offer short sessions to enable parents (nearly always mothers) and their young children to meet up together; parents stay with their children. They may be free-standing or attached to *playgroups* or *family centres*. They provide opportunities for socialisation for parents and young children, and more generally are considered as support for young women with very young children who are considered too young to be left in group care.

PRIVATE SERVICES

Private providers rely wholly or largely on fees paid by parents, and operate on a for-profit basis. 'Profit' in this context can vary considerably, from substantial sums made by companies running a chain of centres to a small weekly income for a childminder with 1 or 2 children. Local authorities pay the fees of some children attending some private services, although the number of children involved and the contribution to total income is small (Government statistics for England in 1994 (Department of Health, 1995, Table 8) show 21,400 children placed by local authorities with voluntary or private day nurseries, playgroups or childminders, less than 3 per cent of the places available in these types of provision; even allowing for the official statistics substantially under-reporting local authority placements, the proportion is unlikely to be more than 5 per cent).

Childminders look after children in their own homes, while *nannies* (also *mothers' helps, au pairs*) look after children in the children's own home. *Private day nurseries* have their own premises. These services mainly provide for working parents. *Childminders* and *private day nurseries* have to be approved and regularly inspected by local authority social services departments; there is, however, no regulation of *nannies*.

Private nursery schools and classes offer a private education to young children, but may also provide care facilities suited to working parents. The situation is complicated because some services that call themselves *private nursery schools* are in fact, legally, *playgroups* or *day nurseries*, and are regulated by social services departments and fall within the welfare system. There is another group of services, which may call themselves nursery schools which are regulated by education rather than social services by virtue of being attached to a private school taking children of compulsory school age.

STOCKTAKING

Table 2 shows the number of places provided in 1993 in most of these different types of provision in Britain, that is excluding Northern Ireland. The main types of provision excluded are out-of-school provision for children under 5, family centres, services attached to parks and recreation facilities, parent and toddler groups and nannies. For the last three of these services no official statistics are available. The official statistics on family centres are limited to those provided by local authorities (450 in England in 1994) and give no information on the number of places or children attending; those for out-of-school services provide no age break-down for places provided, or of children attending, making it impossible to say what proportion of places are for children under 5 (Department of Health, 1995, Tables 6 and 7).

For the services included in Table 2, there were 1,566,009 places in 1993, equivalent to 42 per cent of the under-5 population. The largest number of

Table 2. Places for children under 5 in services in the education and welfare systems, Britain, 1993

Type of service	Number of places	
Within the educational system:		
(a) Maintained schools		
Nursery schools	46,534	
Nursery classes	187,090	
Reception classes	337,735	
(b) Independent schools	39,600	
Total		*610,959*
Within the welfare system:		
Local authority day nurseries	27,670	
Private nurseries	123,960	
Playgroups	464,830	
Childminders	338,590	
Total		*955,050*

Source: National Children's Bureau 1995, compiled from official statistics from various government departments.

Note: Official statistics for maintained schools give the number of pupils attending; the number of places has been calculated on the basis that two part-time pupils occupy one place.

places (30 per cent) were in playgroups, followed by reception classes and childminders (22 per cent each); then come places in maintained nursery education, schools and classes (15 per cent), followed some way behind by voluntary and private nurseries (8 per cent). Lowest levels of provision were in private schools (3 per cent) and local authority day nurseries (1 per cent).

Three points should be made about this snapshot of provision for children under 5 in Britain in 1994. First, the number of children attending services is higher than the number of places, because so much nursery education is attended on a part-time shift basis (so that the 233,624 places in maintained nursery schools and classes are used by 416,533 children) and many playgroup places are used by more than one child (see above for estimates), as are many places in local authority day nurseries. This is only partly offset by there being fewer children at childminders than there are places, implying considerable vacancies; the government has estimated that in 1990 in England, there were 180,000 children attending childminders (written answer to Parliamentary

Question by Eric Forth, Minister of State, Department for Education, 21 February 1995), at a time when there were 205,500 places (Department of Health, 1995, Table 2).

Second, attendance is not evenly distributed over the country; there are large local differences both in overall levels of provision and in the mix of services available. For example, the proportion of 3 and 4 year olds attending public nursery schools and classes in English local authorities in 1994 varied from none to 58 per cent; 14 local authorities provided for less than 10 per cent of their children while 15 provided for more than 50 per cent (Department for Education, 1995, Table 3). Playgroup places as a proportion of the 0–5 age group varied from 2 per cent in one English local authority to 26 per cent in another local authority, with 15 having less than 5 per cent and 9 having over 20 per cent (Department of Health, 1995, Table E); not surprisingly, local authorities with the high levels of nursery schooling usually have low levels of playgroup provision and vice versa (Owen and Moss, 1989). A quick browse through the official statistics will show similar local variations for other forms of provision.

Finally, most places for children under 5 depend on parents' fees, being in the voluntary and private sectors. In Table 2, 61 per cent of places are in voluntary and private services which rely on fee income. But in a small proportion of cases, these fees will be paid or part subsidised by local authorities, purchasing places for children they consider to be 'in need'. Overall, therefore, about 60 per cent of places will rely wholly or mainly on fees paid by parents.

The introduction of vouchers for 4 year olds will make only a limited impact on this situation, because public funding is unevenly spread over the age range, being at its highest level for 4 year olds. In fact, the great majority of 4 year olds (nearly 80 per cent according to the government's own estimates) already attend publicly funded provision, mainly in schools. The younger the age group, and especially for under 3s, the more parents must pay for any service they want.

Over the years, the proportion of fee-paying places has increased. In the United Kingdom (including Northern Ireland) in 1985, they accounted for 57 per cent of places; in 1993, for 61 per cent (Central Statistical Office, 1995a, Tables 3.2, 3.3). While there has been some expansion in places in publicly funded education for children under 5 during this period (places up 24 per cent) and virtually no increase in playgroup provision, the fastest growth has been incurred in three private sector services – private day nurseries (up 338 per cent), childminders (up 124 per cent) and private schooling (up 43 per cent).

RANGE OF DIVERSITY

So far we have laid out the different types of services and the different types of providers. We have also shown that levels of provision vary between local authorities. But there are many other differences. In the second half of the chapter, we consider some of the main parameters of diversity.

Legislation

Services for young children broadly fall within two systems: welfare, which covers 'day care' services, and education, which covers 'early years schooling'. While there are many differences between services in each of these systems, many of the most basic differences are because of this fundamental division. As an obvious example, the systems are covered by quite different laws. 'Early years schooling' is subject to various parts of education legislation, while 'day care services' are mainly covered by the Children Act 1989. This welfare legislation, for example, covers a public duty to regulate 'day care' services in the voluntary and private sectors and a public duty to provide 'day care' services, but only for children defined by welfare authorities as 'in need'.

Administration

Local authority *education departments* are directly responsible for *nursery schools*. They are also responsible, within the limits of school governance of primary schools, for *nursery classes* and *reception classes* in schools which are not grant-aided. Since the Education Reform Act does not refer to children under 5, there is some leeway in how the requirements of the Act are framed in relation to nursery education, especially in respect of finance and governance. Nursery classes generally come under the remit of the primary school and are subject to its governance and budgeting. The 500 or so nursery schools in England have generally adopted a system of governance similar to primary schools with a part elected, part nominated governing body, but budgetary responsibilities remain with local authorities. Education provision for children under 5, like other education services, is inspected independently by OFSTED according to nationally agreed criteria which in part reflect the National Curriculum and the inspection criteria used for primary schools. These are currently in the process of being revised.

In addition to a duty to provide non-education services for young children 'in need', local authority *social services departments* are responsible for regulating most voluntary and private provision. Local authorities set requirements for these services, which mainly deal with health and safety and staffing. There are few educational criteria and the staff carrying out initial registration and subsequent annual inspections are unlikely to have an educational background. There is little liaison nationally or locally between education and social services inspectorates, and on present criteria it is likely that a nursery school would fail a social services inspection and vice versa.

Local authority *leisure services* have been increasingly privatised, and the limited early years services which some of them provide have been circumscribed by competitive tendering. For example, many leisure centres which now have to be self-financing provided crèches or holiday playschemes and it has become more difficult to subsidise such services. However, all services for young children provided by leisure departments have to be registered and inspected by social services.

Local authority *personnel* and *economic development* departments may also be responsible for developing early years services, usually as a means of supporting the entry and retention of women in the labour force. The concern may be with the authority's own workforce or, more broadly, with labour supply and economic development in the local authority's area. Sometimes these departments run their own *day nurseries* or they may sub-contract them to private providers. Overall, the rationale for and expectations of this provision may be very different from education, social services or leisure departments.

These administrative divisions at local level are replicated nationally. The Department for Education, the Employment Department (both now combined in the new Department for Education and Employment), the Department of Health, the Department of the Environment, the Home Office, and the Welsh, Scottish and Northern Ireland Offices all have some interest in services for young children. The extent and nature of that interest varies considerably.

Admissions

Where resources are scarce and do not meet demand, admissions policies are critical – they are the rationing system used to share out provision. Once again, there are major differences between services. Education services are founded on the basis of equal entitlement to services; the lack of equal access to nursery education, because of insufficient places, is a matter of concern to many educational administrators. In principle any parent may apply for nursery education, assuming of course that their local authority provides the service in their area. The final selection is usually left to the school, often on a 'first come, first served' basis. Admissions are termly or annually in September, depending on local policy on school admission.

Social services provision, by contrast, is targeted on children and families deemed to be 'in need' by social workers, and is intentionally only available for a small minority of the population. Access is usually determined by assessment: the circumstances of the family are investigated, admission criteria related to some concept of need are applied and the most urgent cases will get priority for places as they come up. This process of admission, combined with low levels of provision, mean that *day nurseries* and *family centres* provided by social services and the larger voluntary organisations will often have high concentrations of distressed and distraught children from very disadvantaged and precarious families.

In contrast, again, leisure services provision is based on the principle of user choice. In other words it is up to the user whether or not they make use of the service. They are therefore neither universal nor targeted.

Some voluntary sector services operate on a neighbourhood and 'first come, first served basis'; others may rely on a referral basis, taking children on the basis of need. In the private sector, admission depends both on the availability of services and, above all, on parents' ability to pay.

Values and philosophy

These different approaches to admission reflect the very different philosophies and value systems that underpin different services for young children. Recently, we asked a group of *day nursery* staff from inner city local authorities to sum up the principles which informed their work. We then asked a group of teachers working in *nursery schools and classes*, in a similar inner city setting. Their replies are given in Fig. 1.

While there are some common grounds informing both sets of principles, they also reveal differences in emphasis and orientation. For teachers in *nursery education*, the main aim is to promote children's learning, but with an exclusive focus on 3 and 4 year olds; the child's paramount need is to learn and master basic linguistic and numerical skills and the teacher's main task is to teach. The curriculum is central to this purpose, and is extremely sophisticated; it is divided into 8 basic areas, subdivided into many parts, each with many ideas about practice, and is dovetailed into the National Curriculum. Effectiveness is conceived in terms of developmental outcomes for children.

Day nursery staff

- encourage high standards of professional practice in working with parents
- provide a safe, secure environment
- use a key worker system to identify needs
- provide a wide range of facilities appropriate to the needs of children and families
- recognise and support the skills of staff
- provide clear procedures and guidelines
- provide a stimulating environment to realise a child's full potential
- provide an equal opportunity based and non-discriminatory service
- promote good childcare practices
- provide good care and education for children under 5
- provide a community-based service
- provide a service where learning is fun and purposeful
- meet individual needs in partnership with parents and carers

Nursery education teachers

- provide highest quality teaching and learning
- develop language
- develop physical skills through the use of appropriate equipment
- provide an enriching learning environment
- develop a curriculum with an emphasis on speaking and learning
- learn to be an independent person
- provide a stimulating and challenging environment for children
- help the children to experience caring, sharing and respect for others
- promote equal opportunities
- educate parents
- help families to feel valued so that they can enhance the education of their children

---

Figure 1. Principles informing work of staff in different services

By contrast, the *day nursery* staff have a more diffuse view of their purpose – caring for children, promoting children's development, supporting parents, providing information – and they see themselves as having many tasks. For them, the paramount need is to ensure children feel safe and secure and are free from harm. The curriculum is peripheral; learning is achieved through providing basic play materials and the organisation of these materials. Effectiveness is a matter of child, parent and staff satisfaction and social work assessment.

These differences in philosophy and principles relate specifically to staff in social services *day nurseries* and education *nursery schooling*. Other services would show other differences.

Staffing

Staffing is discussed in more detail in Chapter 7; here we summarise differences on a few salient dimensions (for a full summary, see Table 4 in Chapter 7). At least 200,000 people, almost all women, work in one capacity or another in services for children aged 0–5. This figure includes teachers, nursery nurses in 'early years education' and 'day care' services, playgroup workers and childminders, but excludes workers in a variety of other services including reception classes, parent and toddler groups and nannies. With the exception of teachers, who make up less than 5 per cent of the workforce, most workers if they are trained will have had two years post-16 vocational training with an academic transferability of approximately 1 A level. The overwhelming majority of workers are untrained, or will only have *ad hoc* local training which carries no academic transferability. The level of complexity and stress of the work does not relate directly to the level of education of the staff; the most distressed children, those assessed as 'in need', are referred to social service *day nurseries* and *family centres*, which are unlikely to employ teachers.

The ratio of staff to children varies less with children's age than with type of service. Children of the same age can experience very different ratios. Within education services, the ratio is 1 adult to 13 children in *nursery classes* and *nursery schools*. But staffing levels in *reception classes* are poorer, and can be as low as 1 adult to 30 or more children. This difference in resourcing is reflected in the government's proposed voucher scheme for 4 year olds; the voucher, worth about £1,100, is intended to be exchangeable for a **part-time** place in nursery education or a **full-time** place in a reception class.

In 'day care' services, regulated by local authorities, different standards apply. In all centre-based provision (*nurseries* and *playgroups*) there should be 1 adult to 8 children aged three to five, 1 adult to every 5 two year olds and 1 adult to every 3 children under two. *Childminders* are restricted to 3 children under five years old, including their own.

Crude and inflexible measures of staffing ratios can be misleading. The level of staffing might more appropriately vary at different times of the day, and should ideally depend on many factors, including: the age of children; the extent of special needs; staff levels of training and experience; the specification of the work (for example, whether it involves an element of working with parents); how much non-contact time is included in working hours; the opening hours of the service; and the availability of auxiliary staff such as secretaries, cooks, cleaners and janitors (McGurk *et al.*, 1995). Although it is sometimes assumed that adult–child ratios are a critical factor in maintaining standards, the complexities of staffing issues means there can be no simple relationship between numbers of staff and quality of provision.

Ages of children

Education services for young children provide almost exclusively for children over 3, and indeed most services are for 4 year olds. The same is true of *playgroups*, although this type of service also takes some 2 year olds (partly because they have been 'squeezed' out of providing for 4 year olds by schools). The great majority of services for young children – in schools and *playgroups* – are highly age segregated, providing for only 1 or 2 years of the under 5 age range.

Services that may provide for the full age range, offering the possibility of 'age integration', are mostly to be found in the voluntary and private sectors, in particular *day nurseries, childminders* and *nannies*. The only exceptions are social services *day nurseries* and *family centres*.

The net result is that attendance at services increases with age, with a particularly large jump at 3 (Meltzer, 1994, Table 4.1).

Hours of attendance

Most provision in services for young children is only available on a part-time basis, and for quite short part-time hours. *Nursery schools* and *nursery classes* are open during term times only and for school hours. Moreover, nearly all operate a shift system, in which a place is used by one child in the morning and another in the afternoon; average attendance in these part-time places, which account for nearly 90 per cent of children in nursery education, is around 12–15 hours a week, in term time only. *Playgroups* also operate school terms, but are mainly open for shorter hours than schools, many during the morning only and some for less than 5 days a week. Even then, many places are shared so that most children attend for less than 10 hours a week.

Social services *day nurseries* and *family centres* are open for about 10 hours a day, throughout the year, but again in practice many take children on a part-time basis, spreading the service around a wider range of children. Voluntary and private *day nurseries, childminders* and *nannies* are the only services which mainly take children for a full day and throughout the year, and indeed are specifically geared to meeting the needs of working parents.

Although there have been some attempts to combine care and education – for instance, offering care before and after the school day – there are in operation very few publicly funded integrated services providing for a range of needs of children and parents and offering parents, whether employed or not, choice in hours of attendance. Private nurseries are much more flexible in this respect (Penn, forthcoming).

Costs and funding

There are large variations in the annual cost of different services. One reason for this is the different times that different services are open and that children spend at different services. However, even if comparisons between different services are made on a comparable basis, by using the cost per child hour, differences remain large. For example, an analysis conducted by one local authority of services within its area found that the cost per child hour was £5–£6 in a nursery class, £2.50–£3 for 4 year olds in reception class, £2–£3 for a day nursery and £0.60–£1 for a playgroup (Alexander, 1995). A survey in 1994 of its membership by the National Childminding Association found that average hourly fees across the country were £1.60 an hour per child (Thompson, 1995).

There are substantial cost variations between individual services; for example, the childminding survey revealed that costs varied from £1.10 an hour to £4 an hour. There are also geographical differences. For example, costs in London for all types of provision are likely to be higher than elsewhere. A 1995 survey of the net weekly pay of daily nannies showed an average of £150 a week in Central London compared to £110 in rural areas (Nursery World, 1995); the actual cost per child per hour for nannies is however difficult to calculate, since there is no information on average hours of work or the number of children that each nanny cares for (the cost per child hour will be much lower if a nanny cares for 2 children rather than 1).

Overall, there is a close relationship between the costs of different types of provision and staff wages, conditions and levels of training (see Table 3 in Chapter 7). In other words, the lower the cost of the service, the lower the pay and the level of training and the poorer the conditions. This close relationship is not surprising since staff costs account for a large proportion of total costs.

There are also large differences in how services are funded. Nursery education, reception classes and local authority day nurseries are largely or wholly publicly funded; parents pay nothing or only a small contribution. Other services, that is most voluntary and private sector 'day care' services, rely wholly or mainly on parents' fees. As already noted, more than half of all places in services for young people depend wholly or mainly on parents' fees, a situation in marked contrast to other important services for children, such as primary or secondary schooling or health services.

The funding of many services therefore depends not on what children need, but on what parents can afford to pay – in other words, on what the local market can bear. Because many parents using playgroups, day nurseries or childminders could not pay the fees needed to fund a workforce that was appropriately trained and paid, many workers in these services are poorly trained and poorly paid. We discuss these staffing issues further in Chapter 7, while the issue of costs and funding is considered further in Chapter 10.

Currently, early childhood services are inequitably distributed and incoherent; they do not meet the needs of children and parents. Few services are multi-functional, flexible, able to cover the full 'early years' age range, providing for a range of needs of children and parents and offering parents, whether employed or not, choice in hours of attendance. Instead, children and families are separated out into different services and different systems – 'child care' in the welfare system for children with employed parents, 'day care' also in the welfare system for children and families considered to be 'in need', 'early years schooling' in the education system for many 3 and 4 year olds and so on. Despite diversity of services, choice is in practice limited, by the patchy availability of service, by what families can actually afford, and by the inflexibility of so many services on offer. In the next chapter we focus on one particular location to see how these shortcomings are manifested in practice.

4

Why This Won't Do

Pinker Estate is a large council estate on the edge of a northern city. By some standards it is well served: there is a nursery school, a nursery class, a family centre, a private nursery, a playgroup, and childminders – a diversity of provision and an apparent choice for parents. In practice there are many shortcomings.

Morgan Place Nursery is a 60-place nursery school staffed by a headteacher, a deputy headteacher, 2 other teachers, 5 nursery nurses and a bilingual assistant and a secretary. The nursery is well-equipped, and all the records are computerised. The nursery sessions are part-time, and parents do not or will not use the afternoon sessions – there are always vacancies. Some of the children, particularly those from the Muslim community, do not attend regularly, although no one seems to understand why this is so. The nursery school opens at 9 a.m., and at 11 a.m. they begin to tidy up and get the children ready for going home. By 11.45 a.m. the nursery is pristine and every child is decanted out of the building. There is a one and a half hour lunch break after which at 1.15 p.m. someone unlocks the door again to let the children in for the afternoon session. By 3 p.m. the nursery has closed again. In October the nursery is half empty and one of the rooms is closed off. This is because the nursery admits children gradually, so gradually that the other room is not brought into use until nearly the end of the first term. Since this authority also admits to school children aged four on a termly entry, the same slow and inefficient process is repeated each term.

The other school on the estate is a primary school. Although it was being built to serve the estate, many of the children who attend Loretta JMI school come from outside the area because it is a denominational school. Despite the other provision already existing, the headmaster decided it would be a good idea to open a part-time nursery class. He and the other school staff see the nursery class as an extension of the work they are doing, as a means of improving SATs and thereby enhancing the school's reputation and popularity. He exerts pressure on local parents to use the nursery class as a means of guaranteeing a place in the primary school; some children in the class have been taken away from Morgan Place School by their parents.

As well as the nursery class, Loretta has a reception class with 33 children, one teacher and a part-time helper. It takes children in the year they are five, so some starting in September are only just four and a few start in without any previous experience in a nursery or playgroup. The children in the class, mainly 4 year olds, have to line up, attend school assembly, use the same playground and equipment as other children, and eat their dinners in the school hall alongside the older children. All the children wear uniforms and discipline is firm. Nursery and reception class children, like all the other pupils, receive standard school termly reports covering their progress on curricular areas, indicating those areas where parents should help more, and noting both authorised and unauthorised absences. The school pays no attention to the views of other service providers about new pupils, nor does it liaise with any other early childhood services on the estate, but administers its own baseline assessment tests to children on admission.

The Circus is a 40-place family centre near the nursery school which takes children referred from the social work department. It is open from 8 a.m. to 6 p.m. throughout the year. There is an officer in charge, a deputy, 8 nursery nurses, and a cook, but no secretarial help and the OIC keeps all the records by hand; her case notes and letters are also written in longhand.

There is no connection between the nursery school admissions, the nursery class admissions and the social work admissions; they operate in ignorance of one another, although some of the same children feature on all lists. At The Circus, there is a long and urgent waiting list of referrals, so much so that every case is reviewed after 3 months, and if the child's circumstances are judged to have improved, the child is required to leave and cede the place to the next referral. But the referrals take time to organise, there is a great deal of paperwork, and there is usually a gap of several weeks, or even months, between one child leaving and the next coming.

Children are bussed in from other areas, and do not necessarily come from the local area. Some of the mothers are also told by the social workers that they must attend the family centre with their child. When they get there neither the staff nor the mother knows what to do. Often there is an embarrassed and demoralised mother shadowing an equally embarrassed young nursery nurse with a child who is playing them both up. The family centre staff feel under pressure, since they are dealing with resentful mothers and extremely difficult children who no sooner settle than they are out. There is a high rate of staff sickness. Because of this the officer in charge has reduced still further the hours the centre is open, takes less children and closes altogether for one day a week, offering a 'drop-in' instead. Sometimes mothers come to this and sometimes not.

The children gradually arrive after 9.30 a.m. and have left by 3 p.m. on the four days the service is provided, although some of these children, for transport or other reasons, only come for one or two days. The attendance rate is poor, and often children do not turn up on the days which they are allocated. Despite the fact that these are distressed children, who find it difficult to make relationships, the groups of children vary daily. Even at the busiest time of day there could be as few as 14 children and as many as 7 staff.

The OIC is a nursery nurse, and she used to work in a nursery school. She has arranged The Circus to look like a nursery school; she has opened up the small group rooms and has improved the range of activities, with children free to move and choose from amongst a range of toys, games and books. Although she knows the headteacher at the nursery school, there is no collaboration or discussion or sharing of curriculum planning and materials between them. They operate completely independently of one another.

The Talkplace is a 50-place private nursery. It is a lively busy place open from 8 a.m. to 6 p.m. throughout the year for children 0–5. It is a workplace nursery which services the local hospital. It has an enthusiastic and committed owner/officer in charge, who is a psychology graduate, but not a trained teacher. The staff are all nursery nurses, but they get paid considerably less, and have poorer conditions of employment than nursery nurses in either the nursery school or the family centre.

Talkplace is purpose built, but considerably smaller than the nursery school or the family centre, with more restricted outside space, and very limited facilities for staff, who share the owner's office as their staffroom. Talkplace pays a subsidised rent for the premises, but all other costs, including staff wages and any in-service training, have to be covered by fees. The charge is £80 per week (more for babies) a price which is affordable only by those families where there is one child and two parents are in work earning a reasonable salary. There are never vacancies, and few absences. The catchment is drawn from far afield; no one who lives on the council estate can afford to use the nursery. Talkplace has no contact with either the nursery school or the family centre.

The hospital also has in its grounds, in the building next to Talkplace, a **referral and assessment centre** for children with disabilities. Children who are diagnosed as having a problem are referred here through their health visitor and their GP, where they are assessed and prescribed treatment programmes by paediatricians, psychologists and physiotherapists. The playroom at the centre is staffed by nursery nurses. The children may attend the centre for two or three years, on a sessional basis until they are of school age. There are no regular or formal links or indeed any contacts with any of the preschool services on the estate, other than through the health visitor or GP.

St Thomas Playgroup operates in the church hall for two hours on Monday and Wednesday mornings. The hall is cluttered with old chairs and tables which have to be set to one side by the playgroup leader and her helper. The hall floor is splintery and the playgroup has to put down mats to cover it, then roll them up again at the end of the session. The registration officer also insists that the big old-fashioned radiators are covered up, and the playgroup is having a jumble sale to raise the money for a grille – in the meantime they cannot use that part of the room. The playgroup leader keeps the accounts and pays herself £2 per hour. She is helped by a rota of volunteers, not all of whom turn up regularly. She has a playgroup training but has no other childcare or education qualification.

The playgroup is registered for 16 children although only 14 come. Since the church is half way up a hill some distance from the estate, few of the estate mothers use it; the playgroup catchment is drawn from the families who use the church. The playgroup keeps a register of attendance, but there are no other written records nor any information about the background of the children. There is no contact with any of the other providers.

There are two childminders on the estate, and their business is irregular. Since they charge the going rate of £50 per week it is not surprising on this low income estate, that they are not used by local people, The family centre suggested that they come and visit and use the drop-in crèche, but they are reluctant to do this, because of its reputation as a place where social services send you if you mess up your life. The local branch of the National Childminding Association meets outside the area and these childminders are not members, although they attend the Christmas fair and party.

LESS THAN THE SUM OF ITS PARTS

There are many examples of good individual services: vibrant and lively nursery schools and classes; family centres that offer invaluable support to families at times of stress; busy well-attended playgroups operating in good premises; community day nurseries offering an affordable, local service; childminders integrated into their local community. But Pinker Estate does provide a not untypical example of how, *in toto*, current services fail children, parents, local communities and their own staff and are far away from achieving our vision of a comprehensive, integrated and coherent early childhood service. Today's whole is less than the sum of its parts; our vision is that it should be more.

The present hodgepodge of provision fails to deliver flexible, multi-functional and equally accessible services. There is a diversity of services – but uniformity in their inflexibility and narrowness, and access that is limited in a number of ways. Unusually on Pinker there is not an absolute shortage of places; there are as many places as there are children. But the children do not fit into the places available.

There is an excess of part-time services for children aged 3 and 4, but only one centre-based service for children under 3 which most parents cannot afford. Similarly most of the services are part-time and the only ones which are not are again too expensive. Children come from communities outside, where there are fewer places, and use up places which exist in the area. Some of the services, the reception class and the family centre, are of questionable quality because they operate so inappropriately for the children who attend.

SEGREGATION AND LACK OF COHERENCE

Instead of an integrated early childhood service, there are segregated services for young children. The services operate in isolation from one another; they are administered separately and often without reference to one another. They have different catchment areas. They have different philosophies and objectives; consequently, they strive to meet different needs for different groups of children. *The Circus* on Pinker Estate provides a service for social work referrals, but drawn from far and wide; it congregates children and families with high social needs and segregates them from other families. *The Talkplace* and the two *childminders* are for working parents, but for those who can afford them and, in the case of the private nursery, for the employees of a particular workplace; in practice, they are not community services – they are in a community, not for a community. This leaves *Morgan Place Nursery School, Loretta Nursery Class* and *St Thomas Playgroup* each providing similar short hours for a similar age group, offering little either to working parents or to parents in need of extra support or indeed for children who would like more opportunity to play and socialise. *Loretta Nursery Class* is used to pressure parents into attending the school, and the highly focused educational goals of the school means that the needs of 4 year old children in the reception class are misunderstood or ignored.

The end result is that children who may come from the same community are segregated according to whether or not their parents are in work; whether or not their parents are in well-paid jobs or jobs where employers subsidise a nursery or some other type of service; whether or not they or their families are deemed to have some special need; and whether or not they have put down their names for school early enough. There is no provision on the estate which can offer a flexible and comprehensive service to any child and family.

The other striking feature of the current situation, exemplified by Pinker, is the total lack of coherence. Some differences between services are necessary and justifiable if an early childhood service is to be more than a uniform system of identical centres. But too many differences in the present set-up are neither necessary nor justifiable, and lead to inequality, inefficiency and inflexibility. Not only are there fundamental differences in the legal and administrative frameworks, producing in effect at least two systems of provision, but there are further differences in a wide range of policies and practices, both between services in the two systems and between services within the welfare/day care system: admission policy; hours of opening; age range of children catered for; funding; cost to parents; training, pay and conditions of workers; environment; standards and regulation. None of these differences can be easily justified, and owe more to historical accident than to contemporary needs.

Underlying this lack of coherence and segregation of services is the absence of any shared concepts, objectives or visions. This applies whether we look at the level of individual services, individual local authorities or at national government level. The services on the Pinker Estate can be seen as a microcosm of the wider national failure to adopt a shared and holistic approach to young children and their families, and develop services that reflect that approach through flexible and multi-functional operation.

DISCONTINUITY, WASTED RESOURCES AND UNDERFUNDING

The Pinker Estate illustrates vividly three other defects of the current situation. First, a large degree of discontinuity is built into the system. The main services on offer are nursery class or playgroup; children today usually go for a year to one or other before being moved on into reception class when still only 4. In a substantial number of cases, children will find themselves moving from home to playgroup to nursery class to reception class – all in the space of less than 24 months.

Playgroups and nursery classes and schools take a narrow age range of children, for a short period of time. Each prepares for the next stage, in a hierarchy which assumes that primary school is the ultimate and highest goal. Moreover, as more parents go out to work, discontinuity over time is increasingly combined with discontinuity in the course of the day, as parents have to construct elaborate multiple arrangements to ensure their child gets some time at a playgroup or nursery class. The alternative, if affordable, is a full-day private nursery which often means taking children away from their local community and the children with whom they will be going to school.

Second, there is a great waste of resources. *The Morgan Place Nursery School* like other nursery schools and classes is only in use by children for 5 hours a day, 40 weeks a year; for part of the year, it is half empty. Similarly the playgroup is open only a few hours a week, while the family centre is also under-utilised. Only the private day nursery is in full use, but that is only achieved through operating across a very large catchment area.

At the same time, there is a pervasive sense of under-funding around much provision. The poor physical environment at *St Thomas Playgroup* is all too common among playgroups. The childminders also live in cramped circumstances, and cannot offer a rewarding physical environment unless they make a very determined effort to use local parks. They must buy their own toys and equipment, as must the playgroup which has to rely on fundraising events such as jumble sales. The family centre does its best with a budget of less than a £1,000 per year to pay for all consumables and new equipment, although the nursery school does on occasion offer it furniture it would otherwise throw out.

The workers too are underfunded, an issue we develop in Chapter 7. The fees charged by the childminders may be enough to deter some parents, but they do not provide a decent income, especially when work expenses and the absence of benefits such as paid holidays and superannuation are taken into account. The same is true for the playgroup. Any improvements in either service – better environment, training, pay or pension arrangements, for instance – must be paid for by the workers themselves, who can only find the money by raising the fees they charge parents. Elsewhere, many staff in private day nurseries are paid wages that are low in absolute terms or in relation to the demands of the job, have a low level of basic training and have little or no access to further training or regular periods of non-contact time when they can pursue training, prepare and reflect on their work and so on. Perhaps only nursery education can be said to be reasonably resourced – but then this relatively well-resourced service is available to children on a very restricted basis.

There is also wasted information and skills. Because there is no regular dialogue about methods and activities, no exchange of ideas or of information or of resources, each of the services must reinvent the wheel. Staff are isolated and do not discuss and develop their approaches outside their own service, and do not undertake any in-service training in common. A child can go through the same project theme on 'buses' at the playgroup, the nursery school and again in the reception class. Parents too have to go through the same rigmarole of giving information and personal details at each of the places they use, a distressing affair for parents whose children have a health problem or who are themselves under stress.

The net result is that despite the undoubted diversity of services, on Pinker Estate and elsewhere, the choice available to parents is in practice very limited. Parents can neither choose freely between services nor negotiate easily over many aspects of the services they use – instead the options are too often to take it or leave it. In this case, diversity of service comes at the expense of flexibility of service; the children and parents on the Pinker Estate might well be better served by fewer but multi-functional services, responsive to the needs of local families, less choice *between* services and more choice on offer *within* individual services.

A NATIONAL FAILURE

We have taken a very local example to illustrate what we see as the fundamental defects in the present situation of services for young children and to show just how far what we have falls short of our vision of a comprehensive, integrated and coherent early childhood service. We do not want to leave the impression that we blame local services for the current state of play. Indeed, the many good things to be found in the British situation (and we give some examples in Chapter 8) have been due to local initiatives taken by local authorities and local, and sometimes national, organisations – despite, rather than because of, national policy.

As we have already indicated in the preface, successive governments bear much of the responsibility for the critical situation we are in. Nobody would argue that central government should deliver services or even try to plan them at a local level; these are clearly tasks for locally-based organisations and local authorities. We would argue, however, that central government has a vital role to play in creating a framework – including legislation, administration, finance and infrastructure – that will enable the planning and development of a system of good, local services. Even more fundamentally, we would argue that central government should provide a clear sense of direction for the development of services through a national policy that sets out principles, objectives, priorities and targets for services. But in the case of Britain there has been no national policy on early childhood services, not even an attempt by any government to review existing provision and different options.

It need not be this way. Other countries have transformed their services as the product of comprehensive review, identification of the key issues to be resolved and widespread discussion of how best to do this. We review examples of efforts to reform early childhood services and put forward our own proposals in the final chapters. In our next two chapters we focus more closely on nursery education, as the service which, if transformed, could play a major role in a comprehensive, integrated and coherent early childhood service.

5

A Historical Perspective on Nursery Education

If left to their own impulses, (children) fill the air with perpetual questionings. Every new thing being a mystery to them, their demands for information are co-extensive with novelty . . . rational children (should not be) stinted, rebuked or dispirited . . . (but allowed) a continuous elastic spirit, ever inquiring and ever extending to others the fullness of its own aspirations

(Robert Owen, 1836)

Man as a child resembles the flower on the plant, the blossom on the tree; as these are in relation to the tree, so is the child in relation to humanity, a young bud, a fresh blossom

(Friedrich Froebel, 1897)

As ratepayers and citizens fathers and mothers have a right to send their children to the nursery as to (primary) schools. There are many today who do not begin to realise the meaning of collective buying and collective organisation and who cannot, therefore, imagine that the pleasures and comforts of the well-to-do can ever come within the reach of the poor. Yet it is just this new idea, viz., that all can share the good things of life . . . that is at the root of the open air Nursery School.

(Margaret McMillan, 1918)

It is a great mistake to think of the Nursery School idea merely – or even indirectly – in terms of health, or to be satisfied with leaving its practical development to a few enthusiasts or to the most provident local authorities . . . it belongs fundamentally to the question of whether a civilised community is possible or not.

(Education Enquiry Committee, 1929)

The nursery school is an excellent bridge between the home and the larger world. It meets certain needs which the home either cannot satisfy or cannot satisfy in full measure, and it prepares the child for his later life in school in a way which nothing else can do . . . experience has shown that it brings the child such a great variety of benefits that it can be looked upon as a normal institution in the social life of any civilised community.

(Susan Isaacs, 1954)

Nursery education in Britain, more than any other kind of service to young children, has been the subject of intense discussion, debate and theorising for more than a century. Over this time, the visions and practices of nursery education have been frequently revised and reflective of their wider societal and political contexts. In this chapter, we look at these changing ideas and assumptions about nursery education – about who it is for, how it is delivered, what its content is, who delivers it and how it relates to other educational stages. This history suggests that there is no one immutable concept of nursery education. Indeed, viewed from this historical perspective, our idea that nursery education should be transformed to form an important part of a comprehensive, integrated and coherent early childhood service, reflecting contemporary needs and conditions, is itself repeating history!

PUBLIC ATTITUDES TO NURSERY EDUCATION

Nursery education has had its articulate advocates in the UK for nearly 180 years. However, views about the form it should take have varied according to social and economic conditions, and have reflected the views of the time about the roles of men and women and the nature of childhood. Many, if not all, of the main writers considered their arguments undeniable, and concluded that a breakthrough was imminent.

Compulsory schooling was introduced in 1870. As Britain rapidly changed from an agricultural to a primarily industrial economy, the early infant schools soon took on a secondary role, providing care – of a sort – for the younger children of factory parents who might otherwise have kept their older children from school to look after the younger ones. Deasey (1978, p. 62) quotes this account of an infant school in 1876.

> My mother and I were somehow led by somebody into a classroom. It seemed an enormous apartment, and was filled with babies arranged in galleries almost to the ceiling, as I thought – all steaming, murmurous and palpitating with suppressed and uneasy life, in an atmosphere thick with dust and smelling acridly of chalk, varnish and dirty clothes . . . one of the babies at the top of the gallery fell off his seat and rolled right down one of the gangways to the floor at the bottom, raising a dreadful succession of thuds and screams. The teacher went on writing, with just the merest lift of the head. 'It serves you right' she said. 'You're the worst wriggler in class. How often have I told you to sit still and keep your arms folded? And now you see you are punished for your disobedience.'

By 1900 more than 50 per cent of 3 and 4 year olds, and many 2 year olds, attended infant schools. This situation was regarded as profoundly unsatisfactory by many professionals, and Katherine Bathurst, an Inspector with the Board of Education, in 1905 issued a famous report criticising the system, calling for 'national nurseries', and arguing that in a male-dominated education system the needs of young children were continually overlooked.

> Surely in this matter I may expect the support and sympathy of the women of this country - little children require nurses rather than teachers, and lady doctors rather than inspectors. By placing the infant schools entirely in the hands of men inspectors, the whole atmosphere has been made into a forcing-house for the schools for older scholars. Even where kindergarten methods are better understood, the teachers are hampered and hindered by a masculine love of uniformity and order.
>
> (quoted in Van der Eyken, 1973, p. 120)

Bathurst gave voice to the idea that very young children in the public education system should have separate facilities and a different style of teaching from older children. The notion of nursery schools then began to appear in official reports and documents. Provision for nursery education was incorporated into the Education Act 1918, although on an optional basis. This legislation inspired Grace Owen, a well-known protagonist of nursery education, principal of the Mather Training College in Manchester and secretary of the Nursery Schools Association to write that 'the decision to make Nursery School the foundation of England's system of education is one of far reaching importance' (Owen, 1928, p. 11).

In 1919 the embryo Labour Party came out in favour of nursery education, and issued a pamphlet advocating universal nursery education (Van der Eyken, 1973). A decade later, in 1929, came a special report, *The Case For Nursery Schools*, from the Education Enquiry Committee. Like the more recent National Commission on Education, the Committee was an august self-constituted body set up to investigate the state of the nation's education, and included such luminaries as Percy Nunn and R. H. Tawney. Its report concluded that 'the Education Act (1921) should be amended in such a way that it would be compulsory for every local authority to provide the number of Nursery Schools required to meet the needs of their district' (Education Enquiry Committee, 1929, p. ix).

In 1931 the Consultative Committee on the Primary School, commissioned by the government, again recommended nursery schooling. The Committee took evidence about how nursery and infant schooling should be organised from Cyril Burt and Susan Isaacs who argued that young children were characterised above all by the intensity of their emotions. Nursery schooling in their view enabled children to become more detached from their mothers, and learn to play with other children. This was particularly important where the home environment was not secure: 'the more orderly environment of the nursery school, with calm dispassionate treatment, may save the child from the permanent ill-effects of an unwholesome environment at home' (quoted in Van der Eyken, 1973. p. 245). The Committee's report called for more research into children's behaviour at nursery school and how this related to their behaviour at home.

The demand for nursery schooling receded in the face of the 1930s recession. But during the Second World War many new day nurseries opened. As Riley (1983) has convincingly argued, they were not good nurseries. They were opened in a hurry and without forethought. There was muddled administration and continual arguments between ministerial departments, employment, education and health, as to who should carry oversight for them and ensure their standards, and who should fund them. Young mothers too did not like working long hours in heavy industry and leaving their children in what were often grimly institutional settings. It was with some relief after the war that many of them were closed. This was partly due to a muddle over who should continue to fund them, partly a matter of deliberate policy in changed conditions.

> The Ministers concerned . . . are of the opinion that, under normal peacetime conditions, the right policy to pursue would be positively to discourage mothers of children under two from going out to work; to make provision for children **between two and five** by way of nursery schools and nursery classes; and to regard day nurseries and daily guardians as supplements to meet the special needs . . . of children whose mothers are constrained by individual circumstances to go out to work or whose home conditions are in themselves unsatisfactory from the health point of view or whose mothers are incapable for some good reason of undertaking the full care of the child.
>
> (Ministry of Health, 1945, our emphasis)

Although many of the war nurseries were closed down, in the 1940s there were again official recommendations to open more nursery schools. The Education Act 1944 left it open to local authorities to have regard 'to the need for securing that provision is made for pupils who have not attained the age of five years by the provision of nursery schools or, where the authority considers the provision of such schools to be inexpedient, by the provision of nursery classes in other schools' (p. 4).

There were two separate arguments advanced for nursery education. The first was the need for children to learn how to co-operate. The British Medical Journal in 1944, in an editorial, expressed concern that

> in the years from two until five the battle between love and primitive impulse is at its height . . . Winnicott, Buhler, Isaacs, Bowlby and others all note the turbulent characteristics of the age . . . Destructive impulses let loose in the war may serve to fan the flame of aggression natural to the nursery age . . . the Age of Resistance may thus be prolonged to adult life in the form of bitterness, irresponsibility or delinquency.
>
> (quoted in Riley, 1983, p. 1)

The second argument in favour of nursery education related to concern about the low birth rate. There was a huge literature, in 1945 and 1946, which argued 'for nursery schools, after-school play centres, rest homes for tired housewives, family tickets on trains, official neighbourhood babysitters . . . a revolution in domestic architecture towards streamlined kitchens, and more communal restaurants and laundries' (Riley, 1983, p. 167).

The 1949 Royal Commission on Population took evidence from a wide variety of organisations about the need for nursery schooling. They concluded that a package of measures which included nursery schooling should be provided to encourage mothers to have families: the general aim should be to 'reduce the work and worry of mothers with young children'. The evidence to the Commission included a statement from the Hygiene Committee of the Women's Group on Public Welfare: 'we cannot afford not to have the nursery school: it seems to be the only agency capable of cutting the slum mind off at its root and building the whole child while there is yet time' (quoted in Riley, 1983, p. 171).

The message from the Commission was overlooked. It was nearly 20 years before the case for nursery education was restated in an official report; but again the grounds had changed. The concern of the Central Advisory Council on Education (1967) in their report, *Children and Their Primary Schools*, was social inequality. The Plowden Report (so named after the Council's chairwoman Bridget Plowden) argued that policies should positively intervene against disadvantage, and prioritise resources to those most in need. Nursery schooling was an important part of this strategy, an inoculation against disadvantage. Children in socially deprived neighbourhoods 'need above all verbal stimulus, the opportunities for constructive play, a more richly differentiated environment, and the access to medical care that good nursery schools can provide' (p. 63).

This report was strongly influenced by Bowlby's ideas about mothering (see below). The members of the Council were convinced that children should be at least three before entering nursery, and decried the practice of admitting children at a younger age. They also felt that mothers should not be tempted to leave their children for more than a short time. Before Plowden it was generally assumed that most nursery schooling would be full-time, like ordinary schooling. The Central Advisory Council, however, took the view that nursery education should be part-time, a recommendation which has haunted nursery education ever since.

It is generally undesirable, except to prevent a greater evil, to separate mother and child for a whole day in the nursery. We do not believe that full-time nursery places should be provided even for children who might tolerate separation without harm, except for exceptionally good reasons . . . But some mothers who are not obliged to work may work full-time, regardless of their children's welfare. It is no business of the educational service to encourage these mothers to do so. It is true, unfortunately, that the refusal of full-time nursery places for their children may prompt some of them to make unsuitable arrangements for their children's care during working hours. All the same, we consider that mothers who cannot satisfy the authorities that they have exceptionally good reasons for working should have low priority for full-time nursery for their children.

> (Central Advisory Council on Education, 1967, pp. 127–8).

It is worth noting that, despite the caveats, the Plowden Report estimated that 15 per cent of 3 and 4 year olds would require full-time nursery education, a figure which has still not been reached!

The conclusions of this report have profoundly shaped the delivery of nursery education in the UK. While many other European countries continued to view nursery education as a full-time service largely separate from primary schooling, in the UK part-time nursery classes attached to primary schools became the norm. Since Plowden recommended that the primary schools should utilise 'discovery' methods of teaching and a 'free curriculum', as nursery schooling had long since done, and that most access to nursery schooling should be limited to children aged 3–4 on a part-time basis, it made sense to see nursery education as part of primary schooling, and to emphasise the continuity between them – a reversal of the position espoused by Katherine Bathurst at the turn of the century and by subsequent reformers.

The recommendations of the Council were sanctioned by Margaret Thatcher, then Minister for Education, in the 1972 White Paper, *Framework for Expansion*, followed in 1973 by a Circular on Nursery Education (Department of Education and Science, 1973). The White Paper and the Circular referred to Plowden, and accepted its arguments for nursery education unquestioningly. The Circular stressed that 'nursery education is particularly valuable as a means of reducing the educational and social disadvantages suffered by children from homes which are culturally and economically deprived' (p. 3).

While Plowden had been relatively open-minded about where nursery education was to be sited, the Circular took a clear position. It stressed the desirability of nursery classes as opposed to nursery schools.

> There are educational advantages in enabling most children attending school below the age of five to do so at the school they will attend after five. This avoids a change of school and enables educational development to be planned as a whole from three or four to the beginning of the junior- or middle-school course. This avoids a change of school and enables educational development to be planned as a whole . . . Nursery provision within primary schools is also more economical to provide and maintain than separate nursery schools. For these reasons, although nursery schools already in existence or at an advanced stage of planning should continue, it is recommended that most additional places should be provided in units attached to primary schools in so far as their sites allow.

> (p. 5)

The White Paper and the Circular predicted a steady increase in nursery education over a 10-year period in order to make two years' nursery education available for children whose parents wanted it, from the beginning of the term after their third birthday until the term after their fifth birthday.

Although the objective of part-time nursery class provision has been implemented, the 10-year expansion target was not and has never been. Within four years, the English Departments of Health and Education (1976) were convening a Conference on the theme of 'low cost day provision for the under-fives'. In 1977, the National Union of Teachers, drawing attention to the failure to implement the White Paper policy, argued in a pamphlet *The Needs of the Under Fives* that 'now more than ever there is a need to improve the level of nursery education' and defined the aims of nursery education as 'firstly the satisfaction of the needs of the child and the development of full potential and, secondly, by early intervention, ensuring that every child obtains the best possible start in his educational life' (National Union of Teachers, 1977, pp. 7–8).

Three years later, in the report of an influential research study commissioned by the Department of Education, Jerome Bruner questioned

> whether the pre-school out-of-home care for the child has kept pace with our knowledge of early human development . . . the lesson of importance of early childhood is surely that we do all in our power to assure that the young get off to a healthy and competent start before they enter school . . . it must be taken as a given in any national policy that the care of the young should be as thoughtful and as considered as it can be made to be.
>
> (Bruner, 1980, p. 10)

The 1980s brought a further shift in views about nursery education, this time in response to a growing emphasis on the process of schooling and the development of the National Curriculum. The Education Select Committee of the House of Commons asserted that 'education for the under fives can not only enrich the child's life at the time but can also prepare the child for the whole process of schooling . . . there should be steady expansion until all 3 and 4 year olds whose parents desire it have access to places' (Education, Science and Arts Committee, 1988, para 9.5). Instead of being seen as an aspect of social policy, nursery education was viewed more narrowly as an opportunity for individual children to improve their learning competencies in line with the National Curriculum. In 1989, HMI issued a booklet, *The Education of Children Under Five*, which attempted to define the underlying principles of the education of young children, and illustrate these principles with good practice, concluding that 'the nine areas of learning and experience discussed in *The Curriculum from 5–16: Curriculum Matters* are widely recognised as essential for all children including under fives' (Department of Education and Science, 1989, p. 9).

A year later, the Rumbold Committee of Inquiry, set up to consider the quality of educational experience offered to 3 and 4 year olds, issued its report,

Starting with Quality (Department of Education and Science, 1990). The report stressed the need for a quality nursery curriculum which promoted early learning. This was defined as 'aesthetic and creative; human and social; language and literacy; mathematics; physical; science; spiritual and moral; technology' (p. 14). Around this time, also, a group of early years educators further defined and encoded what they saw as the relevant areas of the early years curriculum, and published a widely distributed booklet giving details of how this curriculum might be applied (Early Years Curriculum Group, 1992).

Most recently, the National Commission on Education in their report *Learning to Succeed* yet again stressed that nursery education was being unwisely ignored. Like other commentators in the 1980s and 1990s, they remarked on the adverse effects of admitting children early to school, instead of offering nursery schooling. They argued for expansion of nursery education and revived the notion of nursery education for priority areas first, arguing that the cost of expansion would be mitigated by avoidance of remedial costs in adolescence while stressing the hidden cost of taking no action.

> We are persuaded that the gains made by children who receive high quality pre-school education will reduce the need for remedial education at a later stage, help to ensure that we do not waste talent, and perhaps also reduce the social costs which arise from youth unemployment and juvenile crime.
>
> (National Commission on Education, 1993, p. 137)

This ambitious claim that nursery education not only prevented school failure, but might circumvent life failure, was taken further in the report of the Royal Society of Arts, *Start Right: the Importance of Early Learning*, published soon after. The author, Christopher Ball, argued for part-time nursery education for 3 and 4 year olds, which could be part-funded by offering part-time nursery education, rather than full-time schooling, to 5 year olds and raising the compulsory school age to 6.

> This report presents a challenge to the nation – to parents, educators, employers, parliament – indeed to our society as a whole. It demonstrates the importance of early learning as a preparation for effective education to promote social welfare and social order, and to develop a world-class workforce.
>
> (Ball, 1994, p. 6)

These are just a few selections from the plethora of public and published statements over this century about the importance of providing nursery education. Although all the documents quoted support the expansion of nursery provision (and there is another literature altogether which explores concepts of need, demand for and practices of 'day care'), the ideas about what nursery education is for, the format it should take, and what it can accomplish differ considerably. It is worthwhile considering some of these ideas in more detail, to emphasise how much the context of the time has influenced the idea of nursery education.

THE EARLY FOUNDERS OF NURSERY EDUCATION

In 1816, **Robert Owen** founded an infant nursery in New Lanark, Scotland, which soon had visitors flocking from all over the world. This was partly because Owen claimed the substantial profits of his cotton mills were due to the rational and sensible education he offered the children of his workers. He was offering a practical as well as a radical solution to the problems of industrialisation. His workplace nursery offered places for children aged 12–18 months upwards, while their mothers and fathers were at work. His emphasis was on the freedom of the child from any restraint, a stimulating curriculum which included singing and dancing (he employed a small group of musicians to play to the children from a musicians gallery), and methods which insisted on the children's need to explore and create for themselves: 'the children were not to be annoyed with books, but were to be taught the uses or nature of common things around them by familiar conversation when the children's curiosity was excited so as to induce them to ask questions' (quoted in Silver, 1969, p. 65).

He took the resources of the nursery seriously. Amongst many other items, the accounts record the purchase of a small crocodile, to illustrate – vividly – the richness of the natural world. But above all, he emphasised the *irrationality of anger* and the importance of happiness. A fundamental tenet of his school was that 'each child is told in language he can understand that he is never to injure his playfellows but on the contrary he is to contribute all in his power to make them happy'. He believed parents should be fully aware of what he intended, and at the beginning of his experiment gave lectures – at which attendance was probably compulsory – to his workforce, urging them not to think him crazy, but to try to understand the rationale for the ideas he was putting forward. He claimed that after a while not only had he gained the affection of the children but he had secured 'the hearts of all the parents who were highly delighted with the improved conduct, extraordinary progress and continually increasing happiness of their children'. The teachers he employed (men as well as women) had to have 'a great love for and unlimited patience with infants'.

His visionary view of education inspired generations of activists but his humane objectives could not be sustained in the rapid and greedy industrialisation of Victorian times (Silver, 1969). His vision faded from the public view, as did the idea of nursery education as a popular cause for the benefit of all and a distinct phase with its own relaxed methodologies and separate from formal schooling. However, the idea of infant schools as part of the school system, but also as a solution to the problems of rapid industrialisation and working mothers, did endure. Both in the UK and in America the early infant schools were explicitly for childcare as well as education; in 1871–72, 18,755 children *under* three attended infant schools in Britain, as well as 25 per cent of 3–5 year olds; as described earlier in the chapter, the proportions were considerably higher by the end of the century.

A contemporary of Owen, **Friedrich Froebel** (1782–1852) took a different line on nursery education, and developed the idea of 'kindergartens'. He was a German steeped in romantic German philosophy, in which all events could be explained by a single mystic holistic explanation: 'the condition of child education is none other than comprehension of the whole nature and essence of humanity as manifested in the child' (Froebel, 1897, p. 7). It is difficult now to appreciate his originality and radicalism, but he was writing at a time when the main childrearing manual of the day in Germany, *Medical Indoor Gymnastics*, which ran to 26 editions and which was also widely available in England, stressed the need to make children obedient and to keep their bodily posture upright. The author of this book, Daniel Schreber, also patented an iron crossbar to keep the back straight and prevent the child from leaning from side to side, and a kind of iron helmet to hold the head in the right position.

Froebel proposed that, like buds or new leaves, young children 'unfurl'. As Steedman (1990, p. 82) points out, Froebel's metaphor of the 'garden' was central to his philosophy.

> The 'child-garden' would allow the developing child to be active in a fitting way, and activity would permit the flowering of inborn capacities. But although space, clean air, brightness and movement were specified as absolute needs of children, Froebel's 'garden' of children was not necessarily either a physical space or an actual garden. Rather it was an organising metaphor for a particular kind of relationship between the child and the universe.

Kindergartens provided an environment where children's 'inmost nature' could safely but freely develop under the watchful eye of suitably trained women or 'mother made conscious' as he described his nursery teachers. In comparison to Robert Owen, his view was deeply conservative. He believed in the sanctity of the family, the necessity of a motherhood devoted exclusively to rearing children, and saw nursery education or 'kindergartens' as a way of enhancing, supporting and giving credence to motherhood as well as to childhood. This was a welcome message to the new middle class women for whom working was not respectable. Froebel considered it a useful and natural role for women to fulfil their innate 'educational mission' to work with young children. The first kindergarten was set up in Britain in 1851, and the Froebel Society, dedicated to publicising his ideas, was established in 1874. They launched the Froebel Training College in 1876 in London.

His emphasis on the importance of play in childhood and the series of manuals on how to teach young children was a useful starting point for other more radical reformers. One of these was **Margaret McMillan**, who was a member of the Froebel Society for many years – but whose own agenda was very different. She was a Christian Socialist who, like Robert Owen, was shocked and horrified by the condition of the poor, and considered their treatment inhuman. A member of the School Board in Bradford, she argued forcefully for free school meals and health checks for slum children. She was a well-known public figure, and appeared at meetings up and down the country to argue for better welfare provision for young children. She was a polemicist and described heart-rending Dickensian scenes of children's lives in her pamphlets and newspaper articles, in order to stir up public concern.

Working in Deptford, London, with her sister Rachel, she developed the idea of the Open Air nursery school, which gave children an experience of space and freedom that was denied to them in their cramped and often squalid homes.

> Children want space at all ages. But from the age of one to seven, ample space is almost as much wanted as food and air. To move, to run, to find things out by new movement, to feel one's life in every limb, that is the life of early childhood . . . In the open-air Nursery Schools nine hours is a reasonable nurture day. *Not* five out of the twenty-four but nine; and this is the minimum if the work is to be really effective.
>
> (McMillan, 1930, pp. 10–11)

She elaborated her view of nursery education in a number of articles, but most explicitly and consistently in her book *The Nursery School*, first published in 1919. She argued that the first step was to design a suitable environment for children. Rich children had always had separate spaces, their own nursery room and space to play with nurses to look after them – why not poor children too? She considered that the natural end of early childhood was age 7, but was prepared to take in children of under one. She thought the various stages of early childhood should be catered for in separate groups, although the organisation of the day should allow brothers and sisters to mix, and older children to help younger ones. The buildings should have verandas, and each room should lead directly onto the garden. Children had need of health and hygiene, 'steady feeding, and regular sleep'. Each group room should have its own bathroom, plentiful toy cupboards and suitable furniture. The design of the room and the pictures should 'caress the eye'.

The garden in particular should be enticing, with trees, herbs, a kitchen garden, roses and flowers of all description: 'lilies of all kinds; even Eastern lilies that scent the garden, lilies of spring, summer and autumn' (McMillan, 1930, p. 25). She thought there should be a greenhouse: 'this may seem a luxury but that is only because we have spent so much, hitherto on things that are of little interest to children, and have not yet begun to think of school or even nursery as a natural world' (ibid., p. 27). Much as she wanted it, she drew the line at ponds and fountains for reasons of practicality; they might foul up. As well as being attractive, the garden should be a kind of gymnasium, with challenging apparatus, made as much as possible out of natural materials, stones, steps and paths, swings and slides. The garden full of children was, by her account, a draw for the entire neighbourhood.

No one passes the gate without looking in. All day there are groups near the entrance and eyes watching through the paling. They make me think always of the queues waiting to go into a theatre.

(ibid., p. 13)

Music was important too. Children appreciated and benefited from musical activities.

If as in one Nursery School some teachers learn the violin it will be a great joy. For very little children appear to have a love of stringed instruments. The flute is also a good instrument, and also the zither and the banjo.

(ibid., p. 19)

Reading and writing should come naturally from other activities; for example, blackboards on the outside as well as the inside walls if children want to draw or scribble. By five years the children should be beginning more regular school work, but should be gently introduced.

She thought her schools, for reasons of economy and sociability, for staff as well as children, should be large – 'a community of children'. She saw no objection to schools as large as 300, providing there were group rooms and bases, so that even a large school was like many small homes together. In rural areas, small local nurseries were preferable, local access being still more important than size.

She insisted that the children should attend full-time:

A short nurture day is in great measure a waste of time and money. The great process which it exists to forward is not possible in short sessions broken by long intervals.

(ibid., p. 37)

Nor did she agree with school holidays. She quotes one of her student teachers approvingly when she said 'it is a monstrous, an impossible thing, to turn children out of a nursery . . . like turning fledglings out of a nest or people out of their homes' (ibid., p. 107).

She also disliked part-time nursery classes attached to schools, and dismissed them out of hand:

Why do I oppose them? Because they are, for the poor, a substitute: and also an excuse. The phrase 'Half a loaf is better than no bread' is a particularly cruel phrase when it is used to excuse us for giving a child no dinner.

(ibid., p. 116)

She believed in a rigorous and specialised training for teachers, a three-year training with supervised practice, focused on children aged 0–7. She thought that the job of superintendent of the nursery required considerable skill and extra training. She also believed in parent education. She ran clubs and lectures for parents, and persuaded some of her political and educational colleagues to come and give lectures for the parents at her nursery. She enticed George Bernard Shaw, Walter de la Mare and R. H. Tawney to talk on such diverse subjects as political economy, social justice and internationalism: 'in short we try to remember that we are all citizens and have the responsibility of citizens'. Stanley Baldwin, Rudolph Steiner, Lady Astor and Queen Mary were amongst her visitors. She even inveigled the dry and erudite historian H. A. L. Fisher, who was then Minister of Education in Lloyd George's government, to come and open her baby camp.

Margaret McMillan was elected president of the Nursery Schools Association, the professional organisation set up to advocate the cause of nurseries and the predecessor of BAECE, the British Association for Early Childhood Education. But as Steedman (1990) points out, many of the members were genteel supporters of Froebel and the kindergarten movement, and regarded what she was doing as a form of extremism. There were several acrimonious exchanges about her views on the length of the school day, holidays, and political education for the poor. In the end she resigned. But her influence was still widespread. She, more than anyone else, influenced the Education Enquiry Committee of 1929, when they published their report, *The Case for Nursery Schools*.

In 1924, ideas about nursery education took a new turn, when a philanthropist, Geoffrey Pyke, set up Malting House School as a systematic experiment to see what nursery schooling could offer children, and to find out what pedagogic methods were most appropriate. He advertised in the *British Journal of Psychology* and the *New Statesman* for 'an Educated Young Woman with honours degree – preferably first class – or the equivalent, to conduct education of a small group of children aged 2½–7, as a piece of scientific work and research'.

The advertisement attracted **Susan Isaacs**, a philosopher with a keen interest and research experience in psychology and psychoanalysis. She was a friend and colleague of Sir Cyril Burt and was conversant with the work of psychologists like Gesell and Thorndike, and the child development movement in the USA. She was keen to use the methodologies which were being developed and refined to observe young children and to discover norms of behaviour. She was also heavily influenced by psychoanalytic conceptions of childhood.

Malting House School was unusual by anyone's standards. In the first year it took 10 boys aged 2.8 to 4.10 years. In three years the number had risen to 20, although boys still outnumbered girls by 4 to 1; by then the youngest child was 2.7 years, the oldest 8.6 years. About a third of the children were boarders and lived at the school all the time. The children were all from professional families, and many of the parents were highly distinguished.

The staff, never more than 3, took notes all the time of the children's utterances and behaviour, writing them up in the evenings. The aim at Malting House was to develop clear and logical thinking in young children; to foster in every possible way the joy of discovery; and – in the psychoanalytic tradition – to understand children's emotional development and the source of their conflicts. In order to observe and foster these understandings and to see what emerged when children were unrestrained and undirected, children were allowed an environment which imposed as few restrictions and routines as possible – which at the time attracted rumours and adverse comments from the press. According to one of her staff, it was not that Susan Isaacs was a libertarian but that she was 'trying to get more light on what the balance should be, to find a theoretical basis for future practice, to bring some order in the knockabout of disciplinarians versus libertarians' (Gardner, 1969, p. 67).

The school was open for four years, until Susan Isaacs resigned and Geoffrey Pyke closed it. Susan Isaacs wrote up her meticulous observations in a series of articles in psychoanalytic and psychological journals, and in two books, *Intellectual Growth in Young Children* (1930) and *Social Development of Young Children* (1933). These books attracted a great deal of attention and were very influential amongst nursery teachers, psychologists and psychoanalysts. She also wrote general booklets for the guidance of parents and teachers, and contributed an advice column for the magazine *Nursery World* under the pseudonym Ursula Wise. She was so well known that when she visited New Zealand in 1937, queues to hear her stretched over several blocks (Professor Anne Smith: personal communication).

She founded the Department of Child Development at the Institute of Education in London, and influenced generations of teacher trainers, but she eventually withdrew to concentrate on her psychoanalytic practice. She was a familiar figure in the psychoanalytic world; a close friend and populariser of Melanie Klein, a colleague of Winnicott and an admirer of Bowlby. In the Kleinian tradition she considered that love and hate, aggression and guilt, were fundamental and overwhelming emotions which all young children had to learn to resolve.

Above all, Susan Isaacs considered it necessary to be scientific. Science could offer certainties.

> The scientific study of the behaviour of young children has in recent years enabled us to understand the general lines of normal development from infancy to school life. Every mother and nurse and teacher has experience of her own to draw upon in trying to appreciate the needs of the children she deals with and coming to some opinion about children in general. But nowadays we are not confined to the narrow circle of our own experience. The knowledge and judgement of a great many observers has been pooled in scientific study. We have learned *how* to watch and record the behaviour of children and how to arrange and classify the facts we have gathered, so as to come to more reliable and widely applicable conclusions about their development . . . We have learned to observe large numbers of children both individually and in groups, either by giving them problems to solve under precise conditions, experiments or tests; or by watching their behaviour under ordinary conditions in their daily lives, when they play together in the home and garden, and are at work in the school.
>
> (Isaacs, 1954, p. 6)

The focus of naturalistic observations was play, for 'it is through his play that the child tells us most about his needs of growth'. The observations are insightful and sympathetic. They cover the widest possible range of behaviour and 60 years later still have resonance.

> A striking characteristic of the three year old when he is attempting to master some skill (for instance, the use of scissors) is the bringing together of his whole body into play to aid the local movement: his tongue comes out or is twisted about, his legs move with his hands and arms, and his whole body may grow rigid with the attempt to master the particular movement required. Only slowly as the general bodily poise of the child increases and manipulative movements of his hands and arms become more skilful, does he lose this rigidity of the body as a whole when attempting to perform some particular movement.
>
> (ibid., p. 11)

Her books are straightforward, clear and authoritative. The authorial voice speaks with such certainty that it is not easy to disagree or demur. She focused on 'the whole child' that is on the child's physical, intellectual, social and emotional growth – although for her the notion of emotional growth, and the resolution of primal conflicts in the Kleinian tradition, had a far greater significance than it does now.

As with Piaget, who visited her at Malting House, the 'whole child' is an individual who operates without a context; the child's family or community is only of relevance as an additional variable which affects the child's behaviour. Mothers' needs, opinions and wishes are considered only in so far as they help or hinder the optimal development of their children as perceived and defined by knowledgeable experts. Many parents needed educating about how this optimal development takes place, since they lacked expert knowledge, and they needed early tuition in case they made mistakes that teachers cannot undo.

> We still tend largely to take it as a matter of course that we know by nature . . . what is best for our children's mental health; and whenever the child behaves in a way that does not please us, we are ready to act. We do so, out of our own good or bad humour, out of acting so, out of our 'principles'; but rarely out of a full knowledge of what in the child's mind has led him to do the thing we don't like. Yet without that knowledge we cannot be sure that we are dealing with him in the way most likely to help him. Without it, we move in the dark, and may do much harm, with the best intentions in the world.
>
> (Isaacs, 1929, pp. 2–3)

Owen and McMillan considered that the nursery school was an institution, whose location, organisation, staffing, management and effects on the wider community had to be discussed. But for Susan Isaacs the focus is entirely on the children. From a child-centred point of view, the nursery school offered space 'which has in itself a calming and beneficent effect'; appropriate play material; skilled and trained help; and companionship for the children themselves.

THE INFLUENCE OF CHILD DEVELOPMENT THEORIES

The next major theorist on the scene considered nurseries far less important than ensuring that mothers had the right kind of relationship with their children. **John Bowlby**, a psychoanalytically oriented psychiatrist, was commissioned by the World Health Organisation to report on children who had been separated from their families by war. His 1952 report *Maternal Care and Mental Health* was extremely influential and suggested that the mother – child bond was so important that if it were in any way impaired or interrupted the child's emotional health would be severely threatened. This theme was widely accepted and popularised. The psychiatrist D. W. Winnicott, one of Bowlby's close colleagues, gave regular radio broadcasts offering advice to mothers, and interpreted Bowlby's views in relation to nursery education.

> The entry into a nursery school is a social experience outside the family. It creates a psychological problem for the child and an opportunity for the nursery teacher to make her first mental hygiene contribution. The entry into school may also create anxieties for the mother, who may misinterpret the child's need for the opportunities for development beyond the scope of the home, and who may feel this need arises from her own inadequacy rather than the child's natural development.
>
> These problems, which arise on the child's entry into the nursery school, exemplify the fact that throughout the whole period at the nursery school, the teacher has a dual responsibility and a dual opportunity. She has had the opportunity of assisting the mother to discover her own maternal potentialities, and of assisting the child in working through the inevitable psychological problems which face the developing human being . . . Also to a greater or lesser extent there may have been maternal failure, and the nursery school then has the chance to supplement and correct maternal failure when this is not severe. For these reasons the young teacher has to learn about mothering.
>
> (Winnicott, 1964, pp. 191, 195)

These views about separation and loss in infancy heavily influenced the 1967 Plowden Report which although recommending an extension to nursery education, did so with extreme caution. One member of the Advisory Council produced a minority report suggesting nursery education was not justified, and children should remain at home with their mother. The Plowden Report established the current pattern and concept of nursery education, when it determined that nursery education should be part-time and not begin until three, because neither children nor their mothers could – or should – cope with an earlier age or longer hours. It also regarded nursery education as, in Margaret Clark's (1988) words, 'an injection against educational failure', and the first priority in providing nursery education had to be in areas of social deprivation. In such areas children needed compensatory education which drew on the best of contemporary knowledge of children's learning to make up for their otherwise restricted and stultifying lives.

The views of Bowlby and his colleagues have been reviewed by later commentators. They are now regarded as a response to the extreme conditions of the war years, and as a reflection of Western traditions of middle class childrearing. From a Majority World perspective, the exclusive dyadic bond of mother and child is an unusual phenomenon. Children are not harmed *per se* by separations from their mother: what now is seen as important is that children are offered warm, consistent and contingent relationships in stable settings, whatever and wherever they are. Moreover parental concern and responsibility can be exercised in many different ways (for a recent review of the evidence, see McGurk *et al.*, 1993). The theoretical perspective which has had so much influence on nursery schooling in the last 30 years, that children could only cope with separation from their mother for a short period and from the age of 3, is no longer tenable. Whatever the arguments for providing nursery education on a part-time basis, the rationale that short hours are in the best interests of the child can no longer be cited as one of them.

By the time of the Plowden Report, child development had been firmly recognised as the discipline underpinning nursery education. Because of the need to provide a compensatory education, the best and most up-to-date knowledge was necessary. The initiative in developing practice no longer lay with gifted and articulate practitioners but with psychologists who focused on the behaviour and cognitive processes of young children, and who were interpreted by those responsible for training nursery teachers and nursery nurses.

The Plowden Report, as well as reflecting the ideas of Bowlby, was heavily influenced by the work of the Swiss psychologist **Jean Piaget**. He attempted to describe the stages of thinking that a child passes through. He believed that children learn through being actively involved with the world around them, testing out hunches about how things work, and revising and adapting these hunches to cope with new information. He observed children, including his own, minutely and came to the conclusion that children play an active part in reaching understanding through their manipulation of the physical environment, and that this understanding is reached essentially alone and without adult intervention. He describes a child playing with stones in a garden.

Now to count these pebbles he put them in a row and counted them one, two, three, up to ten. Then he started to count them in the other direction. Once again he found ten. He found this marvellous. So he put them in a circle and counted them that way and found ten once again . . . he discovered that the sum was independent of the order.

(Piaget, 1964, p. 179)

This theory of the child as a small empirical scientist, busy experimenting with the world around her, had a major influence on the content and layout of nursery classrooms. This 'learning by discovery' method was recommended in the Plowden Report. The job of the teacher was to provide an enriching environment and leave it as open as possible for the child to choose between carefully graded and structured activities. The skill of the teacher lay in preparing the appropriate materials and guiding the children towards them. Social interaction with adults and other children was important in so far as it offered the child additional checks and balances in coming to her conclusions about the physical world and faced her with more evidence; but essentially any discovery was her own.

A recent widely promoted approach to early learning, and one which is currently popular, is that advocated by the **High Scope** method, developed by an American, **David Weikart** (Weikart, 1989). It stems from Piagetian ideas but departs from other ideas of nursery education in that he emphasises that it is a method of learning which can be adopted in a wide range of settings, not merely in a designated nursery class. He has argued that this method of 'plan, do and say' should focus on developing self-esteem, self-worth and resilience in children. Weikart and others have argued that a key challenge of early education, wherever it takes place, is to find a method to increase a child's feeling of being in charge and in control, to help her to succeed in accomplishing and achieving self-set goals. By enhancing a child's notion of herself as a competent individual, she is better able to cope, even in adverse circumstances.

Whereas Plowden emphasised the role of nursery education as compensating for social and cultural deprivation, as does Weikart, a new perspective began to emerge stimulated by the work of **Lev Vygotsky**, a Russian psychologist working in the 1930s, whose work was slowly becoming known in translation in the 1980s. Vygotsky suggested firstly that learning was socially and culturally bound; and secondly that language and dialogue is the medium in which all early learning, even mathematical learning, takes place. He stressed that a child's learning was 'a complex dialectical process', which did not progress evenly but in fits and starts. Adults in close contact with children provide a framework for learning, a 'scaffolding' around which a child can construct her own meanings.

Studies of language and conversation patterns used by young children at home, by Tizard and Hughes (1984) and Wells (1987), have suggested that this kind of learning and meaning making is almost inevitably richer at home than in a nursery because of the continuous, shared and intimate linguistic understandings between mother (or carer) and child, which a nursery cannot easily hope to rival. This research has challenged the notion of social and cultural deprivation and the nursery as a compensatory environment which figured so prominently in Plowden.

Munn and Schaffer (1993) have argued that the most meaningful way of encouraging literacy and language development in a nursery is to facilitate its organisation so that individual conversations are possible between adults and children – 'islands of intimacy' – which replicate the kinds of conversations that children are likely to have at home with their mothers, fathers or other carers. In the view of theorists such as Tizard and Hughes, Munn and Schaffer, nurseries may offer care, opportunities for children to play, to socialise and to develop relationships within a wider group, to have physical freedom, none of which may be available at home. But the most important language learning for young children – and through that their access to a literate, numerate world – comes through the intimacy of continuous close relationships. This can only be provided in a nursery, if at all, with very careful organisation, given staffing ratios and the short periods of attendance by children. While nurseries may introduce young children to an exciting and unfamiliar world of convivial activities, essentially teachers can only complement what goes on at home, not compensate, replace or substitute for it. This view is encapsulated in the cliché 'parents are the child's first educators'.

Child development is not, as it was in its early days, a unitary body of theory, which has clear implications for practice in nursery education, as Susan Isaacs once assumed. It contains divergent and contradictory ideas to try to explain a wide range of behaviour patterns. While there are strong arguments for saying those who work with young children should have a sophisticated view about how the children they work with think, feel and learn, and that they should be familiar with some of the arguments and the kinds of debate which are taking place in child development, this is not easily translated into daily practice. These contemporary views of child development, and their application in contemporary practice in nursery education, are explored further in Chapter 6.

PUTTING NURSERY EDUCATION INTO CONTEXT

There have been many different visions of nursery education. For Robert Owen and Margaret McMillan nursery education was a radical way of addressing the terrible stresses of urban industrial life. For Friedrich Froebel it was a semi-spiritual and romantic celebration of childhood in an authoritarian era, and offered a new definition for the role of mothering. For Susan Isaacs it was the most rational and effective way of bringing up children and dealing with their primitive instincts. In the 1940s it was part of a pronatalist philosophy and seen as a way of easing a mother's traditional tasks of childrearing. For John Bowlby and David Winnicott it was a carefully graded step in extending the relationship between mother and child. For the Plowden Committee it was a way of intervening in disadvantage and providing compensatory education. For some recent advocates, it has been seen as a vital opportunity to develop children's intellectual potential in a fiercely competitive society, of enabling a child to progress to schooling more quickly and learn required subjects more effectively.

Different visions produce different concepts of nursery education, from

Margaret McMillan's full-time service for 0–7 year olds to the Plowden Report's part-time service for 3 and 4 year olds. Yet there are also some common themes. Each protagonist acknowledges that early childhood is a time of extreme vulnerability and extraordinarily rapid physical and intellectual growth. Each of them also recognises that traditional didactic methods of schooling do not work, and that a child learns through direct experience and play. All of them argue that highly trained and skilled staff are necessary to support and sustain young children in group settings.

This potted history of nursery education illustrates how much the agenda of nursery education has reflected contemporary values and concerns. Our argument is that ideas about what nursery education is for and how it should be provided have often changed, but that thinking about nursery education in the UK has stagnated since Plowden despite all the social changes and theoretical revisions that have taken place since then. Social contexts have changed dramatically since the 1960s and, we would argue, many of the assumptions commonly held about nursery education are badly dated – assumptions about access and patterns of delivery, about ways of supporting children's playfulness, development and learning, about the outcomes of the learning which takes place, about staffing, and about the roles of parents. We think it is high time for another radical transformation, to fit nursery education for our vision of a comprehensive, integrated and coherent early childhood service for children from 0–6 years. We consider next how one nursery school currently operates and how it might change and develop.

6

What Does Nursery Education Offer Children?

Lomax Nursery School is an inner city nursery school in London. It draws children from a mixed neighbourhood catchment, which includes well-to-do owner occupier housing as well as a run-down council estate. These four children are typical of the range of those who attend:

Juniper is plump, neat, clean, and very well-dressed with designer label clothes. She is an only child. Her mother is a well-known barrister, and her father a television journalist, and they live in a smart square of early Victorian houses. They also have a house in France. Juniper is very self-confident, articulate and inclined to boast of her skills. At 4, she can already read and write and she plays the violin at a Suzuki class. Her nanny usually brings her to and from nursery.

Peter is a lively, noisy, assertive and aggressive boy, whose family lives on the council estate. Peter has a younger sister, who is at home with his mother. His father is not around. The family is dependent on social security benefits. His mother looks tired and haggard, and often shouts at Peter when she brings or collects him.

Kara is a shy, thin little girl who seems reluctant to join in or touch anything at the nursery. Her family are Tamil refugees from Sri Lanka. Her father – or the man who usually brings her and collects her from nursery – speaks rudimentary English, but no one else in her family speaks English. It is not very clear who her family is; there seems to be a lot of coming and going. So far she is the only Tamil speaker in the school, but there is an older child, perhaps a cousin, in the neighbouring primary school.

Tonia is deaf. She has four brothers, all in their teens. Tonia was born prematurely when her mother was in her late forties. Her father is a plasterer, and although he is skilled, the family has recently endured bouts of unemployment. Tonia's mother has had part-time jobs in local cafés to eke out their income. Tonia is the apple of her mother's eye, and she is fussed over considerably, and not allowed to do very much for herself. Her mother was at first very reluctant to let her come to the nursery because she was afraid that Tonia would be picked on because of her disability.

In this chapter we explore the practices and procedures of contemporary nursery education. Nursery education is the most widespread service for children under 5 apart from playgroups; and as we illustrated in Chapter 5, it has been presented widely and frequently in the popular and academic press over a considerable period of time as an essential first step to statutory education. Many people, when they argue for better provision for under fives, have assumed this means more nursery education – as currently delivered.

Nursery education at its best offers a service of which we can be proud, in its understanding of how young children learn and in the range and depth of the activities it provides. But we argue this is not enough. In this chapter, we look at current trends and issues in nursery education, at the range of functions it undertakes and at the practices it follows. We raise questions about the structure and delivery of nursery education; about its content and the theory on which it is based; and about its relationship to primary education. We highlight its shortcomings and make suggestions about how they can be addressed.

While much of our critique refers to function it also refers to practice. This is because we believe that although in many ways it is outstanding, current nursery education practice has serious weaknesses. Not least this is because of the theories which inform it, and in the emphasis it has placed on child development as a central underpinning discipline for the work. Blenkin and Kelly (1987) argue that the idea of education as a process linked to child development is the unique contribution early years educators have to offer. We argue that while necessary this is not sufficient, and indeed has served to distract from other important issues.

ISSUES AFFECTING NURSERY EDUCATION

Relationship to other early years services

Although nursery education as a non-statutory service has to justify itself in relation to statutory education services, when compared with other forms of provision for children under 5 it is an élite service. Nursery schools and classes allow more space per child, and more money is spent on equipment and other resources. As we illustrate in the next chapter, compared with staff working in other early childhood services, teachers are better trained, earn considerably more and work shorter hours and a shorter working year. Many nursery teachers and early years educationalists – and the unions which represent them – argue that the only way forward in developing early childhood services is to preserve their status, conditions and training because anything less will serve to 'dilute' and lower standards of provision.

However, from the perspective of many workers in 'day care' services and those seeking to extend 'child care', nursery education needs to fundamentally change the hours for which it operates, and therefore the ways in which nursery teachers work. Otherwise, it may be by-passed in any expansion, because the service it operates is too limited and wasteful of resources to meet contemporary circumstances. One example of this is the growth of private sector day nurseries, whose claims to provide 'nursery education' are widely promoted by employers and private sector representatives and, increasingly, by local authorities themselves.

As we stress continually there are many different kinds of early childhood services besides the service currently called nursery education. At the time of writing, the government has proposed that parents of all 4 year olds should be given a voucher to spend on 'pre-school education'. We have discussed the shortcomings of a voucher system elsewhere in this book. What is pertinent here is that any providers who can demonstrate they are following a specified curriculum – defined as 'a set of desirable achievements for children's learning covering the areas of language, mathematics, art and co-operating with others' (oral statement by Secretary of State for Education to Parliament, 6 July 1995) – will be regarded by the government as offering 'pre-school education' and will be treated in the same way as nursery education. Under the new system, education for 4 year olds is seen neither as necessarily school based nor as being necessarily delivered by teachers – in short, it is not synonymous with what is currently viewed as 'nursery education'.

While the nursery education lobby acknowledge that the position of their service is being undermined, the usual solution proposed is that nursery education must be more rigorous, more self-promotional about the unique service it offers. Our view is that, rather than more of the same, nursery education as it is today must review and broaden its remit, to make it more suited to the needs of the increasingly heterogeneous communities in 1990s Britain.

Local communities and demographic change

Lomax Nursery School, which our four case study children attend, is in a cosmopolitan and socially mixed area, in inner city London. The school's catchment area reflects contemporary circumstances in a number of ways. Firstly, children come from widely differing circumstances. Their needs, the demands they make and the skills and capabilities they demonstrate are a product of diverse backgrounds and widening economic and social inequalities.

Secondly, 'conventional' families, with a wage-earning father and a mother at home with two or three children, form a decreasing minority of families. Work, marriage and reproductive patterns are no longer stable or easily predictable. Mothers are more and more likely to be employed, fathers may be absent or unemployed, employment grows more insecure and 'flexible', parents increasingly separate and re-partner, grandparents or other members of the extended family are often a long way away.

Thirdly, many young children, particularly in inner cities, do not speak English at home. For some of their families, as in Kara's case, life has been traumatic in a way that in orderly England we find it hard to imagine – fear, violent death of close relatives, painful flight and adaptation to very new circumstances and a strange language and culture, and sometimes a transition from relative affluence and respect in a community to considerable poverty and alienation.

These demographic, economic and social trends are similar in many industrialised countries. As various commentators surveying the international scene have commented, we are witnessing an irreversible social revolution (Cochran, 1993), marked by an increasing pace of demographic, economic and social change and ever more transitions to be coped with. Our four children, although so different, typify the results of this revolution. Some nursery schools and classes may have much more homogenous catchments, but all operate in the same demographic, economic and social context and experience, to a greater or lesser extent, the same consequences.

As we have seen from the history of nursery education outlined in the previous chapter, how nursery education is defined, the hours which it operates and the practices which it encapsulates reflect contemporary circumstances. In the UK, since the publication of the Plowden Report, nursery education has been provided on an overwhelmingly part-time basis because it was predicated on two assumptions. The first was that the nuclear family of wage-earning father, stay-at-home mother and two or three siblings was not only the norm, but the desired norm, and nursery education should reflect and support that norm, and attempt to compensate for it where it did not exist. This assumption was so fundamentally assimilated that it is no longer part of the explicit dialogue of administrators and politicians, and is rarely questioned – it is widely assumed that nursery education must use a part-time model, more part-time than even Plowden recommended!

The second assumption is that 'learning' is a conceptually and practically distinct activity separate from a child's other activities, and therefore that it can be delivered as a professional package in a condensed time-frame of 2 to 3 hours per day. Often the learning experience in nursery education is perceived as being so intense that a longer period in nursery might over-extend or tire a child.

Relationship to primary schooling

Nursery education has also, necessarily, been seen in relation to schooling. The transition from home to formal schooling, from domestic and intimate situations to learning prescribed subjects as part of a large age-grouped cohort of children, has been handled in different ways in different countries. In most other European countries, there is a three-year period of nursery schooling or kindergarten, either already on offer or in development, before compulsory schooling begins at 6. This nursery schooling or kindergarten is usually available for at least the equivalent of primary school hours, if not longer (EC Childcare Network, forthcoming). In Britain, by contrast, children are offered

1 or 2 years of part-time playgroup or nursery education, and often a bit of both, before a compulsory school age of 5.

It is instructive to remember, given its contemporary unquestioned status, the arbitrary way in which a compulsory school age of 5 became incorporated into the British education system:

> Until 1870, all the evidence suggested the UK would adopt what has become common practice almost everywhere else in Europe, namely a starting age of 6 (or even 7). W. E. Forster, who was the draughtsman of the Bill, seems not to have attached much importance to the issue until the Bill was before Parliament. Members were divided in their support for 5 or 6. But Disraeli (leading the opposition but supporting the Bill) persuaded the House of Commons to avoid delay with the result that the amendment in favour of 6 was withdrawn. Parliament settled on the age of 5 for the start of schooling in the context of a general expectation (confirmed by existing practice) that schooling would end at 11. The issue for the reformers was whether to provide for 6, or only 5, years of elementary education. It should not surprise us that they chose the former – and set a starting age of 5.
>
> (Ball, 1994, p. 65)

Another element in the decision was a degree of familiar Europhobia. In 1870, the Austro-Hungarian Empire had just decided that schooling would commence at age 6. 'Englishmen and English women, are Austrian children to be educated before English children?' argued the Bill's sponsor.

Over time, and especially in the post-war years, many children have been admitted even earlier to primary school, so that today there are many 4 year olds in reception class. This is partly but not entirely a response to a dearth of nursery education; admitting children to school has been easier and cheaper than providing nursery education. But it is also seen as aiding the children themselves, as if school failure could be averted by starting children on their 'education' earlier, and more formal schooling early on could improve performance and counter the alienation and failure experienced by so many children as they proceed through school. One might argue cynically that in an education system which stresses individual achievement and competitiveness, early entry to school merely introduces many children to the notion of failure sooner.

We cannot see a sound argument for admitting children to school at age 4 except that it is a cheap – although in the long term a singularly ineffective – way of providing education. Even in its own terms it has not been successful. As Dearing (1995) has pointed out, children in Britain start school earlier and engage in a curriculum sooner, yet do less well at 16, than children from other countries. Despite our earlier starting age we are outperformed by countries where children do not start compulsory school until 6 or 7.

In 1990s Britain, most nursery education is attached to primary schools and locked firmly into schooling. In 1994, in England, there were 552 nursery schools like Lomax, down from 561 in 1985, but over 5,100 nursery classes in primary schools, up from 4,100 (Department for Education, 1995, Table 1). The physical location of most nursery education reflects its common perception as a short-term introduction to the requirements of formal schooling, a status reinforced in other ways.

The training of teachers has traditionally covered the ages 3–8 or 3–11, so that the work undertaken by teachers in nursery education is paced by and has to anticipate children's subsequent attainment and abilities. The 'continuity' of approach by teachers over this age range is seen as the main strength of such a system. This professional education discourse about continuity obscures the incoherent, patchwork nature of early childhood services viewed from a 0–5 perspective and the consequent discontinuities actually experienced by young children as they move rapidly from one kind of early childhood provision to another and between 'day care' and 'early years education' (Powney et al., 1995).

Budgetary as well as curriculum pressures have also served to blur the boundaries between nursery education and formal schooling. Nursery schools are losing the staffing patterns which make them more distinctive but more expensive to run than nursery classes – for example, the supernumerary deputy headship posts are going while headteachers are expected to teach more as well as to manage. In some cases, reception classes are becoming a hybrid between nursery education and infant schooling, with the adult–child ratios being pitched somewhere between the two in these 'nursery units'. So what was once recognised as an expedient, early admission to primary school, now becomes legitimised as 'age-appropriate', without, however, asking the more fundamental question of what 4 year olds are doing in primary schooling rather, as in most of Europe, participating in the mid-phase of a 3-years nursery schooling.

The National Curriculum

Whilst Piagetian methods were popular and in vogue, infant and junior schools adopted and extended some of the theory and methodology on exploration and free play advocated by nursery teachers. But now the process is being reversed. As schooling in Britain has become more competitive, and teacher training has become subject based, the pressures to show how nursery education anticipates the National Curriculum have become more urgent. Many contemporary texts (e.g. Early Years Curriculum Group, 1992) now include substantial sections on how this might be done as early as possible while attempting to preserve a child-centred approach.

Although the National Curriculum does not contain requirements for children under five, its influence has nevertheless percolated downwards, and many nursery classes and schools now frame their planning in terms of the nine areas of the curriculum. This concern with the curriculum extends beyond nursery education to other forms of provision for children under five. A number of early years lobby groups agree that some kind of consensus about the curriculum is necessary, although fully trained nursery teachers should remain the specialists

– however consulted – in delivering it (Hurst, Lally and Whitehead, 1993). The most explicit National Curriculum for early childhood is the Chinese curriculum, which runs to 18 volumes and prescribes the course of individual lessons, down to suggestions about the vocabulary teachers should use; it was designed precisely to unify a diverse system (Huang Cen, 1989). It is not envisaged that we go to this extreme, but there are considerable pressures to systematise what children learn before compulsory school in all settings.

Nursery education, like schooling, is increasingly explained and justified in terms of the curriculum. The curriculum is the range of subject matter and activities with which children are expected to become familiar at school. Many early years practitioners have argued that it is as important to know how children learn as what they learn – hence the emphasis on child development which it is claimed provides essential information for understanding the processes of learning. While we think encouraging a zest for learning is a vital function of early years services, it is not the only function, and cannot be achieved in isolation from those other functions.

The format of nursery education

These assumptions about the nature of family life and young children's place within it, and about schooling, curriculum and cognitive development, have been given physical expression in the format of contemporary nursery education – in hours of opening, in the age range catered for (starting at the earliest at 3 and ending at the latest at 5), ratios of adults to children, the training, pay and conditions of service of the various levels of staff employed, and in the physical environment provided. But as we have stressed in Chapter 5, nursery education was not always provided in this way. Other objectives for example, physical development and fitness – fresh air and exercise and a healthy diet – companionship, socialisation, care while parents were at work, had equal or greater priority. Methods of teaching have been both more and less directive than they are now. Nursery schools have in the past routinely accepted younger children, and opened for longer hours.

The relationship between nursery education and primary schooling and between nursery education and other forms of services for children under five, and the format assumed by nursery education are peculiar to 1990s Britain. But times change and no service can afford to remain static. This has been recognised by a number of local authorities who have attempted to broaden the nursery education they offer, and are trying to integrate 'day care' and 'early years education'; we present examples of such projects in Chapter 8. In our view, there needs to be a fundamental shift in the way in which nursery education is conceived and delivered, moving it towards a more holistic approach to the needs of all young children and their parents. As such it can transform itself to become an important part of the comprehensive, integrated and coherent early childhood service that we envision. Indeed, this service could come to bear the honourable title of 'nursery education' which would then cover a range of high quality provision committed to meeting the needs of children from 0 to 6 and their parents for care, socialisation, health and support, as well as opportunities for learning.

LOMAX NURSERY SCHOOL

Organisation

Nursery education, however much it is seen as part of schooling, still retains a distinctive and more child focused approach. Lomax, the Nursery School we have used for our example, typifies this approach. It argues that it offers children a qualitatively different experience from that of a reception class.

It is a school with a very good reputation. The headteacher is well-known in the profession as a dedicated innovator. The school, which is used for teaching practice by the local university education department, has attracted many students and visitors.

Lomax has 52 children in the morning, closes at lunchtime, then another 52 in the afternoon. It takes children of three and four years, but because the catchment crosses the boundaries of two education authorities with different school admissions policies, some children go on to primary school as soon as they are four, while others stay until they are nearly five. The children's parents apply directly to the school to have their name put on the waiting list. There are some afternoon vacancies, but there is more pressure for morning places, and not everyone gets a place.

For example, the headteacher was reluctant to take Tonia, one of the children whose cases we have cited, and has in fact turned down several requests from social workers and the educational psychologist to take other children with special needs. She feels they would be better off somewhere else. She believes in integration of children with special needs in principle, but equally believes it should only be done with proper facilities and properly trained staff. She is worried Tonia is not getting the special attention she needs.

The nursery was built in 1972 and is a light and airy building, with French windows leading onto a small paved area, beyond which is a grassed space. The building was designed to be used flexibly, and although the original plan was to have two separate group rooms, each with its own set of toilets, the headteacher has decided that she can make better use of the resources and provide a richer environment if the space is used freely and is not subdivided. Children can go where they want although each group of children has a base, and a teacher who is responsible for the activities in that particular base. As well as the group rooms, there is an office for the headteacher, a smaller office for the secretary, a staff room, a medical room, and two walk-in store-rooms. There is also a kitchen, although this has never been used because the school has always closed during the midday break.

Before children are admitted to nursery, the headteacher interviews the parents, and also tries to arrange home visits. She sends out a letter with acceptance of a place, explaining that it is important to bridge the gap between home and school, and that she or one of the teachers would like to visit the home. Of our four case study children, only Tonia's mother replied. Tonia's mother has had long experience of dealing with different professionals and answering questions about her daughter and explaining what Tonia can do. However, Tonia's mother said she would prefer to come to the school to talk it over, because two of her sons were at home and out of work, and she was worried that there would not be enough space to have a quiet discussion. In the case of Juniper, the headteacher decided that probably a visit was not necessary, and in any case her staff might be slightly in awe of Juniper's parents. For Kara, also, she decided not to pursue the matter – she was not sure who to get in touch with to follow it up nor how to make the request understood. For Peter, she thought it would be worth trying to follow it up and made several attempts to broach the subject with his mother, all unsuccessful.

The organising principle of Lomax is the perceived need to support and enhance children's learning. The headteacher sees the curriculum as the vehicle for doing this, as a means of analysing, clarifying the relevance, coding and describing the many activities she and her staff provide for children. She has read – and purchased out of school funds – a number of recent books on nursery education. She fully endorses the view, outlined in an Open University text (Faulkner, 1990), that a teacher's job is

> to guide the child towards tasks where he will be able objectively to do well, but not too easily, not without putting forth some effort, not without difficulties to be mastered, errors to be overcome, creative solutions to be found. This means assessing his skills with sensitivity and accuracy, understanding the levels of his confidence and energy, and responding to his errors in helpful ways

(p. 3)

She agrees with the recent report of the RSA, *Start Right: the Importance of Early Learning*, that in providing this kind of environment and being alert to each child's capabilities and skills, she will enable children to develop 'emotional self-reliance, to build up their success and self-esteem'. (Ball, 1994, p. 15).

In her regular planning sessions with the teachers and nursery nurses, held every Monday lunchtime, the headteacher reviews each week one of the eight areas of the early years curriculum outlined in the report of the Rumbold Committee of Enquiry, *Starting with Quality* (Department of Education and Science, 1990): aesthetic and creative; human and social; language and literacy; mathematics; physical; science; spiritual and moral; and technology. For each of these broad areas, there are many resources: wooden blocks of many sizes; all kinds of small intriguing objects to count and sort like the tray of shells and the box of buttons; story books galore, some with taped readings and detachable pictures and finger puppets of the characters; many painting and drawing materials exploiting different media, and even some raw pigments to grind for colours; various modelling materials including clay and soft wood which can be filed as well as cut on the woodwork bench; a cookery corner with herbs and spices as well as jars of rice and pasta. There are dressing up clothes, and one corner has been made into a hat and wig shop.

Most of these materials are always carefully labelled and kept within reach, although a few, like the pigments, are only brought out for particular work stations at special times. Many of the materials which are provided are home-made or assembled and provided by the teachers themselves. The children's work is carefully named, mounted and displayed on the walls, sometimes with little comments written by the teacher to connect various groups of drawings or paintings – 'we looked through a magnifying glass and saw the ants' heads' or 'we made pizzas, mushroom, sweetcorn and pepperoni'.

The outside space is also carefully monitored. There is a minimum of big equipment, only a new and complicated climbing frame. But there is sand, water, tyres swinging from the two big trees, many kinds of balls and bats, some trikes and scooters, gardening implements and a little gardening plot where the children grow some vegetables and herbs.

There are many representations of children and adults of Afro-Caribbean descent, from the Indian continent, and from Chinese and South Asian backgrounds in wall pictures, photographs, book scripts and toys. The nursery has an equal opportunities policy, and attempts to celebrate multi-cultural events such as the Chinese New Year or the Jewish festival of Chanukah.

When the staff discuss curricular themes at the staff meeting, they do it in a number of ways. In the discussion about mathematics, they look at mathematical activities which are going on as an integral part of a series of other activities, and how specific children have utilised mathematical concepts, for instance in making pizzas. They also focus on a specific mathematical activity, such as a new matching game, and discuss whether or not it may be too difficult for some of the children. Throughout the week the teachers have been keeping notes and making observations, and they talk them through with each other and the nursery nurses.

The headteacher and the staff feel that, through hard work, discussion and review, they are creating an environment in which each child's intellectual, social, emotional and physical needs are being taken seriously. They have succeeded in establishing links between the principles and practice of early years education and the intentions of the National Curriculum. They have scrutinised the document published by the Early Years Curriculum Group (1992), and feel that they are meeting the principles outlined:

- the starting points are the individual children and their environment;
- children develop through making meaningful choices and sharing responsibility in relation to their learning;
- children learn from first-hand experience;
- a cross curricular approach should be encouraged;
- children should be given time to produce work of quality and depth (ibid., p. 21).

They also believe that parents are the first educators, and that information and insights shared and produced collaboratively between parents and staff will help to build a more complete picture of the child at home and at school. They have folders for collecting the work of each child. The children can take these folders home, and parents are encouraged to comment on them. The school issues a termly report on each child, couched in terms of the National Curriculum. In the concluding section on 'attitudes to learning', for example, the teacher has written tactfully about Peter that he 'prefers the activities which do not involve writing or drawing'. Juniper has earned a more positive commendation: 'Juniper is always gainfully occupied. She moves from one activity to the next always finishing her task before she tackles another.'

The headteacher and the staff feel that they are making a real and long-lasting contribution to the lives of the children who attend, which will not only stand them in good stead when they start school, but will endure into adulthood. They cite as evidence some of the longitudinal studies from the American Head Start programme, which suggests that children are less likely to need remedial treatment or become delinquent if they have had a good early start (Schweinhardt, Weikart and Larner, 1986). They feel it is important to stress these long-term benefits to children, as well as their own expertise and understanding of child development because they consider nursery education to be undervalued, and they wish to show the rigour and application that are the hallmarks of good nursery education. Indeed, they echo claims that British nursery education is amongst the best in the world, with a unique heritage, an impressive repertoire of activities and highly skilled staff who have parity of pay and conditions of service with primary and secondary teachers.

The children and the school

How do our four children fare in this good nursery school? For Juniper, the nursery is in some ways a home from home. Her house, and particularly her bedroom, are full of toys, and she expects to have lots of things to play with and choose from. However, she is sometimes a little bored at nursery. Her nanny, and also her mother and father, have been teaching her to read and write; she enjoys this and wants to spend more time writing out words and deciphering books. She likes poetry and can recite Blake's *Tyger Tyger Burning Bright*, accurately and with some relish. She is familiar with a number of the Greek myths, which have been told to her in story form, and sometimes asks her teacher about characters like Zeus and Athene. She knows some French words, and has begun to understand from her stays in France that language is more than words and sounds, and that words cannot always be literally translated. She can use the computer at home for basic word processing. She enjoys simple sums. She is musical, and can already play simple classical pieces on her violin.

Her parents know she is precocious and have very high expectations of her. They feel the nursery school is a bit laissez-faire, probably a bit of a waste of time for her intellectually and does not extend her enough, although it is a friendly and safe environment. At school Juniper is always polite and well-mannered, but is not particularly playful; she prefers to get on with tasks or have conversations with the teacher about her preoccupations. The staff feel she is being pressured and needs more time to play, but in fact she is a rather relaxed child and gives no sign of being tense.

Peter comes to the afternoon session, because the headteacher believes that it will be easier for him if there are less children. He seems to regard Lomax as a kind of toy supermarket where he can pick and choose all kind of goodies previously denied him. He finds it very hard to believe he can just lift things off the shelf and play with them. He tests this out to the limit, taking a great many things all at once, cannot remember where they came from, discards and loses them. He is also overwhelmed by the physical space, and spends a great deal of time running up and down, inside and out.

He is a child that finds it hard to settle. Within the open-plan setting of the nursery school, where children are free to move from one space to another, inside and outside, he roams about, knocks or throws small toys on the floor. He challenges other children frequently, and seems often on the verge of fighting. He has to be physically restrained from hitting other children. He does not seem to hear what the teacher or nursery nurse tells him or understand when he has to come to the group base. Peter displays great energy, but sometimes seems wan and tired and sits by himself sucking his thumb.

The headteacher has attempted to discuss his behaviour with his mother, but she is reluctant to stop and talk. She always has the younger child in tow, and seems herself to be suspicious and exhausted. Although the staff try to avoid it, Peter is labelled as a difficult child. Despite his desperate attempts to use and understand the environment, he has learnt above all that his behaviour is unacceptable; he is not shouted at but he cannot fail to notice the carefully voiced disapproval.

Kara is still more of a problem. She looks and probably is terrified. She hides herself in a corner, and will not even touch the soft toys she is given to hold. She flinches when adults come near her. The man who brings her seems quite stern and although the headteacher tries to talk to him about Kara, he does not understand when she tries to explain what the children do at nursery school, that Kara can bring toys or comfort objects from home with her and that he can take some toys or books home for Kara. The headteacher hoped that Kara would settle down, but increasingly often now she is absent.

Tonia paradoxically is the child who finds it easiest to settle, despite her disability. She is an amiable and sociable child. Although her hearing loss is quite severe, she wears a hearing aid. Tonia's mother has taught herself sign language, and signs to her daughter. Tonia shows some fluency in signing, but none of the staff can understand it. Unfortunately Tonia's speech is unclear and it is not easy to discern what she is saying. However, Tonia is an undemanding child. She watches adults and other children with minute attention, and usually anticipates what is required of her.

The nursery school, like many nursery schools and classes, is extremely good at what it sets out to do, which is to provide children with an enriching curriculum to foster their learning. It offers carefully planned, exciting and wide-ranging activities designed to anticipate the demands of the National Curriculum. In one sense the teachers are skilled artisans, shaping and extending their ideas and practices with children. The teaching staff, at least those who were trained in early years, can also draw on their understanding of child development. They are familiar with ideas about how young children learn, and how children's schema of learning are transformed as they mature. Borrowing a phrase from the American literature, they have a view of the developmentally appropriate curriculum, and what activities children of different ages can do and profit from.

Yet excellent as it is, it is not enough for these four children. Juniper, who is a gifted child, is not encouraged to do what is most highly regarded in her home, to read, write, speak another language, explore more sophisticated mathematical concepts, or practise her violin. On the other hand, Peter cannot cope with all the choice and freedom and, indeed, the cornucopia of the nursery school, and Kara is terrified by it. The language of the nursery school is incomprehensible to Kara, and the tone of it may also confuse Peter. Tonia is benefiting but she needs to learn strategies for communication which the teachers feel they cannot adequately provide. Yet it would benefit still more if her disability were more widely understood and accepted as part of the normal range of ability, something to be accepted rather than, as in a medical model, a special condition which requires special treatment.

But for whatever the reason these four children do not settle, it does not seem resolvable through more acute child observations or by extending curricular choices. The curriculum does not appear to be an adequate framework for analysing their difficulties. Nor would more understanding of child development theory and closer observations of the children make the difference that some practitioners claim. We believe the solutions lie outside the current range of practice at Lomax.

CHILD DEVELOPMENT

The powerful influence of Piaget

Early years practitioners consider that a knowledge of how children learn is as important as what they learn – and indeed this is a valuable perspective. Unfortunately even in nursery education many of the staff lack such a perspective. It has not been included in their training (Blenkin *et al.*, 1995). But our argument is that it is not a sufficient basis on which to develop practice; nor do we believe that it should be as prominent as some advocates would wish.

Like many other nursery education practitioners since the 1970s, Lomax has drawn heavily on the theoretical view of Piaget that the young child is above all a learner, and cognitive development is best enhanced by giving young children an opportunity for independent exploration and play in a richly equipped environment. Moreover, although benefiting from social interaction and challenges from peers, the child is seen as essentially egocentric and both physically and intellectually unable to cope with the demands of group education and learning before the age of three; here Piagetian theory is fused with Bowlby's ideas about attachment.

Piaget outlines the cognitive stages of development which all children pass through, and posits that young children learn through systematic experimentation and manipulation of their environment. He views learning as essentially an individual and isolated process, and co-operation between children as a source of potential and possibly enriching intellectual conflict – children have to come to terms with ideas and modes of thought and action that are different from their own and modify their own position as a result. Although concept learning can be confirmed, clarified and enhanced through the language and comments of sympathetic adults, the cognitive initiative and the developmental progress is always at the pace of the child. Translated into nursery education practice, it means that teachers should provide an environment and daily programme which offers maximum choice to individual children in terms of access to equipment and space, use of time, and opportunities for collaboration with others. A teacher's job is to provide a well-conceived, well-organised resource-based environment which offers opportunity for discovery across all curriculum areas, in a way which encourages the personal autonomy of each child (Early Years Curriculum Group 1989, p. 2).

Barbara Tizard (1985) has expressed doubts about this kind of analysis:

> Today the nursery school world is given over mainly to play. The physical environment largely consists of a great variety of play materials and the staff interactions with children generally occur within the context of play . . .
>
> The epitome of this pedagogy can be found in 'open plan' nursery schools . . . Here up to a hundred children instead of being cared for in separate classrooms, are encouraged to wander through the whole building and shared playground, sampling a vast array of toys and play materials made possible by this arrangement. The theoretical basis for this kind of educational practice is Piagetian. It rests on the doctrine that the child's active perceptual and motor exploration is an essential precursor to abstract learning . . . Equally important in nursery school practice is the stress on learning from other children. Both the theory and practice of this branch of pedagogy are weak. Exactly what children learn from each other as opposed to what they learn from adults is rarely defined, nor is there agreement on what the adult's role should be.
>
> (p. 117)

There is now an increasing body of literature which, while acknowledging the contribution of Piagetian theory and the sequences of development he outlined, suggests that it may be missing the point about how young children learn. Stemming partly from the work of the Russian psychologist Vygotsky, this suggests that all learning is essentially social and culturally weighted; that young children learn from other people, rather than from manipulation of objects, about what is important; that adults, or other children, cue, shape, guide and structure what is learnt, through language and conversation.

> The more complex the action demanded by the situation, and the less direct its solution, the greater the importance played by speech in the operation as a whole . . . children solve practical tasks with the help of their speech, as well as their eyes and hands.
>
> (Vygotsky, 1978, p. 24)

Without this 'scaffolding', that is without the opportunity to cue into social and cultural expectations and to explore and construct theories around them, children cannot learn – learning is never a solitary affair.

> Human learning presupposes a specific social nature and a process by which children grow into the intellectual life of those around them.
>
> (ibid., p. 88)

Vygotsky uses the concept 'zone of proximal development' to describe how learners learn what comes next. The zone of proximal development is set out for them – deliberately or inadvertently – by the adults or teachers with whom they spend their time. As we indicated in Chapter 5, many psychologists now believe that much if not most of this early learning is informal and linguistic and takes place at home; and teachers dealing with large groups of young children for a short time cannot easily hope to exert a powerful influence on their learning.

Child development, which protagonists for nursery education argue is the key underpinning discipline for work with young children, is now a diverse and complex body of knowledge, and some of the more recent findings cast doubt on what is taking place in nursery education. There are three relatively recent areas of research in child development which particularly illustrate our point about the complexities and diversities of child development: research into young children's relationships and peer groups; research into language development; and cross-cultural research.

Young children's relationships

Attachment theory, which influenced the Plowden report, stressed the importance of the dyadic relationship between mother and child as the prototype of and basis for all other social learning. But a great deal of subsequent research has illustrated the multi-faceted nature of children's relationships with parents and other relatives and carers, with siblings and with friends. Judy Dunn (1993) has summarised much of this research, as well as describing her own longitudinal studies in the UK and USA. As she points out, young children's relationships are complex, rich and varied, and differences between children are so marked and poignant that the subtlety and variety of these relationships deserve more attention. The evidence is overwhelming that young children, far from being egocentric, are highly responsive to emotional and social cues.

> Most children recognise and respond to the feeling of others and behave prac-
> tically to improve or worsen other people's emotional state. They understand
> the connections between others' beliefs and desires, and their behaviour. They
> have some grasp of what is appropriate moral behaviour for different rela-
> tionships. Such sophistication means that even young children can be
> supportive, concerned, intimate and humorous with others – or they can be
> manipulative, devious and teasing and deliberately upset others.
>
> (Dunn, 1993, p. 109)

She goes on to argue that the concept of the competent child is misleading; children, like adults, behave differently in different situations.

> We should move away from a simple notion of the 'competent' or
> 'incompetent' child and towards a differentiated view of relationships in
> early childhood. Socio-cognitive capacities are used differently in different
> relationships, even by the same individual, depending on the quality of these
> relationships.
>
> (ibid.)

Relationships between children and adults, or between children and children, can also be viewed as friendships, with similar criteria to those used to describe successful friendship between adults – humour, self-disclosure and connectedness, a shared history of events and a shared unravelling of them.

Dunn focused on children's networks of relationships at home rather than at school. A classic study of relationships between children at nursery is that of Corsaro (1985). He used participant-observer methods to demonstrate that children create their own cultural meanings and shared jokes to form a sub-culture in the adult-dominated world of the nursery. He suggested that children are active in creating and maintaining their relationships with one another, and that their friendships are consistent and matter to one another a great deal. Howes, Hamilton and Matheson (1994) also show that children's relationships with one another in a nursery environment are enduring, and not casual or temporary.

A number of studies suggest that what mothers value in nursery education is this opportunity for their children to create and develop their friendships. As we described in Chapter 2, the national survey of parents conducted in 1990 shows clearly that socialisation, the chance to play with others, was the first and foremost need that parents looked to services to meet (Meltzer, 1994); while in a study in progress by one of us (Helen Penn), which examines the views of mothers and carers about the curriculum being offered by a nursery school, all but one of the 30 respondents ranked the opportunity for their children to socialise and make friends as the most important function that the nursery school had to offer; Hughes, Wikely and Nash (1994) also suggest that this finding is common.

Parents have at heart their children's happiness, and happiness, to use a hackneyed cliché, depends on other people. Or put another way, the socialisation function of nursery education has been underestimated by many experts. It can be a place for friendships between children, and more unusually between adults and children, a place to enlarge horizons and develop relationships which are necessarily constricted at home – but in order to do so it requires a continuity and regularity which are often not possible in part-time provision.

Language acquisition

A second area where research has indicated that young children's development proceeds through, and is shaped and directed by, those with whom a child has the closest relationships and reciprocal friendships is that of language acquisition. The studies of Tizard and Hughes (1984) and Wells (1987) are by now well-known. Young children struggle through language to make sense of and interpret the gist of the situation they are in. This may relate to the properties of objects such as, in an example given by Tizard and Hughes, the tiling of a roof; or it may, more significantly, relate to the nature of the relationships between people with whom the child is in contact. People's relationships to one another are an endless source of speculation for small children as well as for adults. Wells uses the phrase 'the meaning makers' to describe young children's' endless puzzling over the words addressed to them.

As well as a vehicle for exploration and questioning, language is expressive. Bloom (1993) has studied the acquisition of language of 14 children from mixed social backgrounds between the ages of 9 months and 24 months. She and her colleagues used an extremely sophisticated methodology, involving analysis of video and audio tapes made at home and in a university playroom, as well as mothers' diaries and standardised tests of infants' performance. Extending Vygotskian ideas she concludes that young children are intentional creatures, having beliefs, desires and feelings about something, and language is a means of sharing these mental states:

> Taking the internal, personal, private meanings of individuals and making them external and public, so that other people can know and share them . . . children achieve the power of expression by learning the public, conventional meanings of a language for expressing and articulating the private, personal meanings they have in mind. This happens because of a child's social connectedness with other persons who need or want to know what the child has in mind, and developments in cognition and affect are integrated with one another in the endeavour.

> (Bloom, 1993, p. 19)

Bloom puts forward three principles of early language acquisition: relevance, discrepancy and elaboration. Young children try to find words about what is relevant to them, to express what they feel and believe; they notice discrepancies when what they believe is not shared by others and they have to express and explain themselves; and they elaborate their language to provide increasingly more sophisticated expression and description. This process is fragile and tentative, and children gain their understanding of language through a fusion of word and context. Bloom quotes St Augustine to illustrate her point about the cues which children use to develop language:

> It was not that my elders taught me words . . . in any set method . . . When they named anything and as they spoke turned towards it, I saw and remembered that they called what they would point out by the name they uttered. And that they meant this thing and no other, was plain from the motion of their body, the natural language, as it were, of all nations, expressed by countenance, glances of eye, gestures of limbs, and tones of voice, indicating the affections of mind, as it pursues, possesses, rejects or shuns.
>
> (ibid., p. 84)

In contrast to the rather neutral emotional tone of the school, where the teacher inevitably has limited knowledge of the child, and the child is more wary about speaking up, there is a continuity and intensity at home which makes learning much more immediate and relevant. As Tizard (1985, p. 127) remarked, 'it is true that the emotional intensity of the parent–child relationship may sometimes interfere with the child's learning, but on balance, it leads to a great potential educational advantage for the home.'

Again this research suggests that it is the intimacies and continuities in talk and discussion which are important to young children. These are not easily pursued in large open-plan nursery classes where children attend part-time for nine months.

Cross-cultural research

A third area of research which sheds a different light on Piagetian ideas of cognitive development is cross-cultural research. Some of this research acknowledges a debt to Urie Bronfenbrenner (1983), and his ecological model of different levels which influence young children's lives – from the intimate personal relationships children experience up to the broader social and cultural expectations of the society in which they live. Whiting and Whiting (1975) carried out a psycho-cultural analysis of children in six cultures, and concluded that 'none of the traditional theories alone can account for the social behaviour of children' (1975, p. 7). Super and Harkness (1986) in a much quoted paper have developed the idea of the ecological niche. They argue that the range of behaviour a child shows is determined by the physical and social setting in which the child lives; by the customs of childcare and childrearing, and by the psychology of the child's caretakers, and that behaviour and expectations vary significantly between different cultures and subcultures. Weisner (1989) draws on anthropological research to define 14 cross-cultural conditions which contribute to the social ecology of childhood, varying from characteristics of the parents' and caregivers' working life and gendered division of labour to child chores and children's peer groupings. He concludes that 'in a democratic society, the nurturance and understanding of diversity rather than the production of conformity should remain a fundamental social value' (p. 75).

Rogoff (1990) has studied cognitive development in a sociocultural context and similarly argues that what may appear as developmentally appropriate in one context, may be inappropriate in another.

> Cognitive activities occur in socially structured situations that involve values about the interpretation and management of social relationships. Individuals' attempts to solve problems are intrinsically related to social and societal values and goals, tools and institutions in the definition of problems and the practice of their solutions.
>
> (p. 61)

There are several major cross-cultural studies of centre-based early years services, all of which emphasise the cultural specificity of the nursery environment and the needs which it sets out to meet (cf. Olmsted and Weikart, 1989; Cochran, 1993). Lamb (1992) concludes that 'development is a complex multi-faceted process, so we are only likely to understand it if we look, not simply at patterns of non-parental care, but at the patterns of care in the context of other experiences, ideologies and practices' (p. 9). Other studies look more closely at parenting from a cross-cultural perspective and examine the way in which parents' perceptions are understood (or not) and enlarged upon in nurseries and schools (Brice-Heath, 1983; Belle, 1989; Goodnow and Collins, 1990; Bornstein, 1991).

A Majority World early years expert could legitimately conclude that young children in the West are bizarrely treated, as isolated individuals without social responsibilities or obligations. As Lamb (1992) comments, 'some view assertiveness as a desirable characteristic, whereas others view it as one manifestation of undesirable aggression. Everywhere debate persists over the relative value of individualism and co-operation' (p. 9). It is not of course possible to act independently of cultural and societal norms; they permeate our behaviour and expectations. But such comparisons serve to remind us, as indeed a number of writers have pointed out, that in Britain, as in the United States, we do place a high value, possibly too high, on individualism and competitiveness, and this is reflected in the way that we bring up our children. Moreover, they suggest, we are foolish to ignore wider societal pressures and demands. As Lamb (1992) stated firmly, 'we know of no society or country in which the basic demand for non-maternal childcare has not been driven by economic forces' (p. 25).

These findings argue for scepticism about 'developmentally appropriate' practice in nursery education and elsewhere. Pence (1995) uses an environmental analogy to describe childrearing: that the variety of childrearing practices which currently exist in different cultures and subcultures are like endangered species which must be preserved, since they contain the genes for new and challenging ways of thinking, learning and being which we may one day need as conventional Western ideas fail us. He has developed this notion into a model of the 'generative curriculum' in which standard professional Euro-western ideas about learning processes are matched against specific local conditions and ideas and discussed and developed in as open and inclusive a way as possible with parents, workers and other stakeholders in early childhood services – a far cry from Susan Isaacs' scientific certainties.

Apart from the complexities of methods, scope and findings within child development, there is a view that it is intrinsically ahistorical and asocial as a discipline, and therefore *cannot* offer a comprehensive view on the upbringing and education of children. For instance, Zelitzer (1985) in her classic book *Pricing the Priceless Child* gives a convincing account of the change over time about our views of young children as contributors to and participants in the economic life of the family. Summarising this evidence, Williamson and Butler (1995) maintain that 'childhood is socially constructed and politically and culturally determined, often – in Western societies – with quite dramatic redefinitions of childhood taking place in each succeeding generation' (p. 294). They go on to voice the familiar argument that

> there has been a contention in developmental psychology that the achievement of adulthood is the culmination and consummation of a sequential process of mastery (sic) and control – thus conveying a *de facto* 'deficit model' of childhood. The child is but an inferior and less developed version of the adult.
>
> (p. 295)

It is certainly the case that the School Curriculum and Assessment Authority (1995) in presenting the case for developmental outcomes for 4 years olds, views them essentially as inferior entrants to the national curriculum.

Those who rely on child development as a discipline might argue that it does indeed show children think in conceptually different ways from adults and that their processes of thought are qualitatively different. Nevertheless emphasising stages of development posits the inevitability and invariability of change, and makes it more difficult to accept and listen to children in the here and now, or to acknowledge the importance of cultural and historical context. These comments about child development are not to deny its contribution and value, but to recognise its limitations.

CAN NURSERY EDUCATION CHANGE?

A broader perspective

Where does this exploration of child development leave us in terms of nursery education? Or, more specifically, in terms of Lomax Nursery School and the four children we have described? It suggests that what, how, why and when children learn is highly complex, minutely cadenced, and situational, and there is no easy translation from the research literature to daily practice. It suggests that some of the claims made for nursery education in the UK are simplistic and rooted in professional insularity. As Martin Woodhead (1988) has noted, in relation to claims based on American longitudinal data from the Head Start programmes that nursery education has long-term effects lasting into adulthood, there are dangers in perpetuating simplistic models and exaggerating the effects of a particular model of early schooling.

> On the one hand that view places unrealistic emphasis on the early years for effecting permanent individual change through educational and social programmes. On the other hand it distracts attention from other concurrent and subsequent processes in community and school that interact with experiences in the early years to determine long-term patterns of development. Accordingly, a first responsibility of social science advocacy is to avoid perpetuating and indeed to actively seek to counteract the tendency in public debate to adopt simple deterministic views of the scope for intervention in human development.
>
> (Woodhead, 1988, p. 452)

We have argued that child development is a narrow basis on which to train those working in early years. It risks a kind of tunnel vision, most of it highly Eurocentric or westernised, focusing exclusively on the child (Konner, 1991). While it is an understandable perspective given the general disregard of childhood and the focus in statutory education on what is learnt rather than on how learning takes place, it is not enough. Indeed, it distracts from a more rounded or holistic view of what nursery education might achieve. As we have stressed, this view has been expressed by many commentators, most notably by Bronfenbrenner when proposing his 'ecological' model of understanding childhood which requires looking at macro societal issues as well as micro learning issues.

Using this kind of model suggests other components of training for working with young children. For instance, an introduction to social policy would give a clearer understanding of the ways in which political, social, fiscal and legal decisions affect the way in which people are grouped together and live their lives. Social anthropology offers various methodologies for understanding the point of view of people whose cultural expectations are dissimilar. Community development literature gives insights into assessing the needs and reflecting the concerns of local communities (Nelson and Wright, 1995).

To acknowledge and study the complexities of providing a holistic early childhood service does not mean ignoring the richness of a proper study of children, or undermine the need for a full consideration of how children spend their time in nursery school or other early childhood services. As Bronfennbrenner himself recently commented, a critical and rigorous approach about what goes on in a nursery – what is provided and how children make use of it – is vital.

> Recently I had occasion to examine what current textbooks and their counterparts in the nation's bookstalls have to say about the conditions and processes that foster, or undermine, children's development. Once one gets beyond the new demographics of family forms, two-wage households, gender roles, childcare, poverty and minorities – important as those are – the discussion of what goes on (or should go on) *within* any of these settings is mostly a rather sparse, dull and curious mix of facts and ideas from the 1960s and 1970s. It is still 'ages and stages' with occasional doses of behaviour modification. Nothing important that needs to be done takes longer than just a few minutes – Sesame Street style. The processes mentioned are always one way, with no turns allowed. There is more talk of parental discipline than of joint activities of parents with their children. Genetics only happens to twins and they produce effects all by themselves. Objects and symbols are things used in tests. And the only time children develop are when they are with somebody else.
>
> (quoted in Mallory and New, 1994, p. 108)

Nursery education in Britain has in this respect a solid tradition and an extensive repertoire. Nursery teachers, by virtue of their training, are usually highly skilled in providing a generous and challenging range of activities for children. No doubt like any such repertoire this can be extended, and like some of the Danish or Spanish nurseries described in later chapters, development of the creative arts, such as painting and appreciation of paintings, mime and drama, storytelling and narration, music and dance, would make for a lively and pleasurable day for children. But in this sense the best of British nursery education has a lot to offer. We do not wish to deny this – indeed we are proud of it. But we do wish to broaden ideas about how and when and to whom it is offered.

Daily practice, in the last resort, depends on values and beliefs. To state this is not to denigrate what currently exists, but to suggest how it might be used as a basis for development. We have suggested that, given the fundamental changes in social context and the direction of recent theoretical perspectives, it would be sensible to rethink nursery education – in terms of who it is for and how long it is available; the prominence given to curricular initiatives and children's learning and the wish to see child development as its main theoretical underpinning. Nursery education is one of the main services we have for young children, and it has many good and enduring features. How can we now transform it to meet contemporary needs and to respond to new theoretical perspectives?

Learning is not the only goal

In the current climate, with the financial, administrative and legal restrictions which exist, it is hard for any individual nursery school or class to make changes. But change is not impossible either as some nursery schools have already shown. Lomax could adopt broader and more holistic aims and objectives – for instance, the enjoyment, comfort and health of the children and their mutual supportiveness – and conceive of other ways of organising the nursery school in the light of these revised objectives. It could recognise their family circumstances and needs, and direct support for them. It could prioritise group and co-operative activities within the nursery, and identify and support children's friendships by limiting group size or by subdividing the rooms again, although with plenty of opportunities for children to expend their physical energy or to rest; and by making one member of staff responsible for and counsellor to a particular group of children. It could discuss the teaching and behaviour strategies of staff, the nature of relationships they have with children as well as the activities they provide for them.

Lomax could broaden its functions: take fewer children, but offer access for longer hours to children of different ages, for children under three, and for children over five out of school, particularly if they have brothers or sisters at the nursery school. Parents would not only be viewed in relation to their children. They would also be gendered and viewed in their own right as men and women with hopes and aspirations of their own who could contribute to, influence and themselves benefit from the opportunities that Lomax has to offer – although to view them not as adjuncts of their children, but as fellow citizens, may well be a difficult step for professionals. Lomax could develop more of a community perspective and make links with the local community and local organisations. It could share its valuable resources with the community – who in turn might support it in many ways.

Respecting parents' needs

Juniper's parents would like her to stay all day – they have difficulties with employing a live-in nanny and would much prefer to spend the money on some kind of collective care. Juniper could contribute more to the other children in the nursery; she is an exceptional child and could be given some useful tasks, for instance, helping her to befriend or mentor Kara. Peter's mother would welcome a crèche for the baby, and a break for herself. She would like to take advantage of literacy tuition – her poor literacy skills are one of the reasons why she feels so inadequate in dealing with the school and responds so poorly. Peter might feel more grounded if his younger sister was there and he could, carefully supervised, help look after her. Kara's older sibling or cousin at primary school could visit the nursery or come to an out-of-school club at Lomax.

Peter and Kara are not well fed and good food, well cooked, may make a real difference to them. Margaret McMillan began her career as an agitator for nursery education by arguing for free school meals. While we do not like to admit, as a prosperous society, that some children are very hungry, we do admit that many children have a poor and unsatisfactory diet of highly processed, fatty and sugar-laden foods, and that consumption of such foods might seriously affect their health, in the long term if not the short term. Eating food is also a highly social occasion which can be very pleasurable and very tempting. Offering lunch to children and parents, as well as occasional evening or weekend meals as special social events, could be a boon, and educative, for both, as well as providing opportunities for parents to contribute dishes from their own repertoire.

A longer school day would be a boon also for Tonia's mother. She works intermittently at a café, which is local and suits her because she knows that she needs to be on hand for Tonia's visits to specialists of one kind and another. She would work regular lunchtimes, if Tonia could stay at school. She also wishes that the other children knew sign language – perhaps the nursery school teacher could learn it. Perhaps one of her out-of-work teenage sons, who has also learnt sign language, could teach the teacher and Tonia's friends.

Developing a community perspective

None of the teachers live in the area, so their contacts with parents other than in a school setting are non-existent; they are unaware of the parents' circumstances or networks except what they can glean at school. But if more priority were put on developing and maintaining community links, they could get in touch with the Tamil refugee community, and work out strategies for helping Kara and her family. They could maybe utilise the talents of some local unemployed or retired people as storytellers or for other tasks around the nursery school or as governors or for secretarial help. Peter's mother, for instance, might be interested in developing a food co-op on her estate, with some back-up from Lomax, which could in turn involve some of the children in food shopping and educative discussions about various kinds of produce and how they can be obtained and prepared.

A pleasurable and convivial day

In taking on this broader role, the 'curriculum', in the sense of a stimulating and coherent range of activities, would not be diminished, although staff would adhere less closely to the National Curriculum; they would treat it for what it is, a system for organising subject knowledge which is less relevant – if not irrelevant – for young children who cannot even read and write and whose conceptual frameworks are constantly changing and developing. Instead, there would be more emphasis on the quality of life in the here and now, conviviality, pleasurable and creative activities, fun and exercise, painting and puppetry, dance and drama, singing and music, cooking and eating, digging and building – in short what Robert Owen called 'merriment'.

Since many of the children would attend Lomax full time, there would be more opportunity for outings and for participation in the life of the local community, to shop and visit local places. Lomax would be less hidebound by age and gender segregation. It would be able to consider innovative ways of working across age groups, including in its everyday life older children who came back to the nursery school at the end of the primary school day and in school holidays.

This broader role for the nursery school and transformation of nursery education may seem challenging but none of it is impossible. In fact **all of this has been done already** somewhere in Britain, by enthusiastic and committed staff working innovatively in existing services. The descriptions of the children have been disguised for confidentiality, but they are real children, just as the examples of a more holistic approach are real examples. Many nursery teachers acknowledge the need for change and development in nursery education and would welcome support in developing their ideas away from the aridities of a narrow curriculum and child development focus. In subsequent chapters we describe how such changes might be encouraged and supported.

IMPLICATIONS FOR PRIMARY EDUCATION

Earlier in this chapter, we described nursery education as a stage between home and school. We have focused more on the links and overlap between home and nursery education, than between nursery education and primary schooling. We realise that the ideas and research we have discussed also have implications for later schooling. The social contexts of children's lives are as relevant when they get to primary school as when they were in nursery education. Issues such as extreme differences in material circumstances, reconciling parental employment with caring for children, and the needs of multi-ethnic communities still have to be addressed.

Like many educationalists we have considerable reservations about recent directions in primary education. But we feel the changes which have taken place are hard to reverse, nor are we competent to judge how this might be done. However, we suggest that our vision of a transformed 'nursery education', providing a comprehensive, integrated and coherent early childhood service for young children and their families has implications for later schooling. Instead of asking only how early childhood services should change to meet the needs of primary schooling, there needs to be a two-way dialogue and review which asks how primary schooling might change to ensure continuity with a transformed nursery education.

We are, however, clear about one implication of our vision for primary schooling. As we have made clear already, we think a child of four years is too young to be in primary school, and that taking children into school at that age has had a distorting effect on the development of early childhood services, making it increasingly subservient to the interests of this stage of formal schooling. We consider that 'early childhood' or 'nursery education' should be regarded as a separate and distinct stage in the education system, with its own imperatives and identity, important in its own right and covering the first six years of a child's life (although leaving it to parents to decide when their children should start).

At present, those children who get nursery education (and they are only a minority of 3 and 4 year olds) receive, on average, about 500 hours each – equivalent to just over 1 per cent of their first five years. This is all that is on offer from the government's new initiative, which offers 3 terms of part-time nursery education to 4 year olds assuming such provision is locally available. This does not seem much to offer children. We would like to see a much more radical transformation of nursery education.

7

What About the Workers?

Teaching young children is one of the most important and most difficult of educational jobs. Early years practitioners have to deal with complexities that include: the social, emotional and intellectual needs of developing children; a curriculum which has been designed for over-fives with little attention to the way children acquire skills and understanding; a multiplicity of potentially conflicting relationships with parents; and learning contexts which need to embrace the routine and stability required by young learners. Above all, early years specialists provide the groundwork from which children learn how to learn and become useful and valued adults. They do this and still keep the experience fun!

(Professor of Education)

There are contradictions. I believe that teachers should be trained. I don't want untrained teachers. Teaching is a lot more than a mums' army, more than nice women looking after children. But I also want to take account of outside experience and skills. I think there are a lot of under-employed people who could contribute to the service. I would like to see a cross-fertilisation between care and education. I would like to see a multi-disciplinary team, but I know there are all sorts of unresolved issues about pay, conditions of service and hours and weeks worked between teachers and non-teachers. I think working in a nursery is as intellectually demanding as, say, teaching maths in a secondary school, partly because nursery teachers pay such close attention to individual children. Yet I don't think I want to see an all-graduate profession.

Perhaps we could think of teachers as a resource, not working on the same basis as the rest of the staff, but offering training and expertise within a nursery to others. But I would not necessarily want the person in charge of a nursery to be a teacher. I think we should have 'the best person for the job' whether that is a teacher or someone from some other background. I suppose there are contradictions that we have not worked through.

(Ex-teacher, now chairwoman of a local authority under fives committee)

I came into it by a fluke. I used to work in a shipyard as an engineer and I got made redundant. I was a volunteer at the local school, and they got me to sign the form for the NNEB course. At first I thought it would be hard. There was no way I wanted that sort of job. I like working with young children but to me working in a nursery was a woman's job being poorly paid. My first impression on the course was that it was going to be sitting with a room full of young girls and having to do cookery, knitting, sewing, all that sort of thing that it wasn't a man's job to do. I only agreed to try the course for three months. I stuck it out, although it was a year before I could admit it to the family and friends. Then it slipped out and I even got praised for it. 'Go for it lad' they said.

When I got qualified nine years ago I worked in a centre running a mother and toddler club. More husbands and wives came together because I was there. Since then I have worked in various positions until I got my present job.

Parents sometimes ask if I am gay but then they say even if I was it doesn't matter. Some people ask if I have had a police check, but I would feel the same need to ask if I was the parent. I know there have been problems about men in nurseries, and I am very careful about the things I do and say on the job.

You adapt to working in a female environment but it is easier if there is another male there too. I run a male support group, three of us and a male cook meet up about once a month – it's a great help.

I get a lot of job satisfaction and I've been promoted so the money isn't so bad now. I think pre-school is more about conversation; if you can relate to the children they can relate to you. It's surprising how many of them call me dad. I say, I am not your daddy but I am a daddy. In one of the nurseries they call the male worker 'nursery daddy'. I think that's a nice explanation.

I enjoy meeting people and working with children. I'm sure there are other men out there who would like to do it if they knew that there was such a lot of job satisfaction. It's very rewarding, and the pay is not as bad as you think.

(Deputy Officer in Charge, social services day nursery)

I came to this country from India when I was 18. I speak several languages but my English is not always perfect and people do not have a very high opinion of you when you make mistakes. I have three children and my husband works at a restaurant. It is very hard to find the time, and we must plan carefully. I get up very early to get the children up and make their packed lunch, then I come to work and my husband takes the children to school. He also picks them up after school. When they were little I was a childminder. It was difficult because we did not have much room. I wished I could send the children to a nice private nursery like this, it is what every parent wants, the best education. There are only white children here because no one else can afford to come. I stayed at home. Then I worked in a playgroup, and I took a playgroup certificate, but it was not a real job, just

*two mornings and I did not earn enough money. Then I came to work here.
I think I am not qualified for this job and I am paid on the lowest rate. I am
trying to get better qualifications. The owner says I should take the NVQ
but I would prefer to get a proper training like an NNEB because I need to
learn more about how to work with children.*

(Nursery assistant, private day nursery)

A fundamental principle in our vision of an early childhood service is that
children's zest for learning is of the utmost importance and should be enhanced
and encouraged in theory and in practice in every way possible. But we have
also argued that while this early childhood stage, from 0 to 6 years, should be
part of the education system, it should also be seen as a separate and distinct
stage from compulsory schooling, with its own pedagogic imperatives. It is not
merely a form of preliminary tuition or induction to enable children to perform
– and behave – better at primary school.

We have also stressed that our vision of a comprehensive, integrated and
coherent early childhood service is not exclusively about learning. Care,
socialisation, health and support for children and their families is crucial in the
early years, and services that are responsive to their local communities may
also be able to provide other functions. A distinguishing feature of the multi-
functional service we envision is that parents should be able to negotiate much
more flexibly about their use of the service – it should not be a 'take it or leave
it' service. It will be far removed from current nursery education, which largely
offers an inflexible package of 5 mornings or afternoons, 12–15 hours per
week, term-time only, and then only for 3 or 4 year olds.

But if we are arguing that we need to rethink and transform the model of
nursery education we provide from a restricted and part-time service into a
comprehensive and flexible service which seeks to meet the needs of all children
and families, then we also need to address issues of staffing and training. For it
is more or less impossible to have an integrated and coherent early childhood
service without fundamentally revising the training, pay and conditions of the
workforce. What might have been appropriate for today's limited nursery
education service will not be appropriate for a multi-functional and flexible
service for children from 0 to 6 years. Nor can we continue to have, as today,
enormous disparities in the training, pay and conditions of workers.

The staff in the early childhood service we propose should be able to
promote children's zest for learning, and meet their families' need for care and
support. This means providing a child-centred environment which children
enjoy attending; where parents who are in work or training can leave their
children safely, knowing they are happy and occupied; and where children or
their parents who need support, because they have a disability or for some
other reason, will be able to obtain it. But the present-day reality is that there is
no professional training or set of pay and conditions which meets the
requirements of our multi-functional early years service. How we might make
this good is explored in this chapter.

Table 3. Staff working in early childhood services

	Teacher	Nursery nurse education	Nursery nurse social services	Playgroup worker	Childminder	Private day nursery
Approx. no. employed	7,000 (exc. reception)	7,000	7,500	40,000	100,000	25,000
Generally acceptable qualifications	BEd or degree/PCGE minimum 4 years post 18	certificate/diploma in nursery nursing (NNEB/BTEC) 2 years post 16	certificate/diploma in nursery nurse (NNEB/BTEC) 2 years post 16	no legal requirement: local playgroup foundation course/playgroup practice diploma/NVQ	no legal requirement: local childminding course approx. 6–10 weeks, 1 session per week. NVQ	no legal requirement; usually senior staff NNEB/NVQ*
Age-range	3–8, 3–11	3–5	0–5	2–5	0–8	0–5, 0–8
Adult/child ratio	1:13	1:13	1:3(0–2), 1:5(2–3), 1:8(3–5)	1:5 (2–3); 1:8 (3–5)	1:3	1:3(0–2), 1:5(2–3), 1:8(3–5)
Contracted weekly hours	1,265 hrs/195 days per year	35 inc. breaks	37–39 without breaks	average 5–15 hrs per week	average 50 hrs, no breaks	37–40 without breaks
Contact hours with children	average 25–30 hrs per week	average 25–30 hrs per week	37–39 hrs per week	5–15 hrs per week	50–60 hrs per week	37–40 hrs per week
Shifts/working hours	9.00–3.30/4.00, no shifts	9.00–3.30/4.00, no shifts	8.00 a.m.–6.00 p.m., 2/3 shifts	average 9.00–11.30, no shifts	8.00 a.m.–6.00 p.m. continuous	8.00 a.m.–6.00 p.m., 2/3 shifts
Overtime pay if extra hours	no	yes	yes	no	maybe	usually
Holidays	12 weeks	12 weeks	3–6 weeks	12 weeks (unpaid)	3 weeks (half-pay)	3–4 weeks
Sick pay/pension	LA conditions	LA conditions	LA conditions	none	none	unusual
Career prospects	promoted posts	no promoted posts	9 grades promoted posts	none	none	no national scale
Parity with other groups	with teachers	none	none	none	none	none
Basic pay scale	£11,800/£13,500–£18,000	£9,300–£10,797	£8,226–£21,357	hourly rates, approx. £2/3	hourly rates, approx. £2/3	£6,000–£18,000
Recognised union	NUT/NASWT	Unison/T&G/GMB	Unison/T&G/GMB	none	none	none
Line manager	only teacher	only teacher	NNEB/social worker	none/mgmt committee	none	private employer
Staff facilities, staffroom etc.	yes	yes	yes	no	no	maybe
Supply cover arrangements	yes	yes	yes	no	no	maybe

* The Children Act which regulates private and voluntary provision does not contain a specific training requirement but leaves it open to local authorities to impose their own requirements. In the case of playgroups and private day nurseries these are likely to vary throughout the UK. Similarly pay and conditions vary considerably, and in the absence of reliable information we can only make a guestimate based on extrapolations from existing data.

PRESENT TRAINING

Table 3 summarises some of the main details of six groups of workers in today's services for children under 5; the main omission is nannies. We discuss the training of these workers in more detail in this section.

Teacher training is a graduate level four-year post-18 training, covering primary teaching and nursery teaching together. It is subject based, although sometimes (but by no means always) it includes theory about child development and early learning. There may be some theory included about the learning of children under three, but practice experience with such an age group would be very unlikely. The training might include a section on theory and practice of working with children with learning disabilities, but only exceptionally would it include a theoretical or practical consideration of the management of physical disability, or dealing with children and families under emotional stress. Teachers therefore are only likely to have come across children aged 3-4 in a typical part-time nursery education setting, although they will be familiar with the routines and practices of teaching children in primary school.

Teachers working in nursery education are in a paradoxical position. They work to the same pay scale and conditions of service as teachers in primary and secondary education, although their hours are slightly more favourable, and the ratios of adults to children are considerably more generous. Yet because nursery education is a non-statutory service, usually provided in a class in a primary school, they are frequently regarded as junior colleagues within a school setting; if they seek promotion they must either do so within mainstream school, or hope for a relatively scarce career position in a nursery school. On the other hand, their pay and conditions are much more attractive than for anyone else working in early childhood services, and their status is usually much higher. But although they are well educated, they may lack the breadth and length of experience of many other workers in early childhood services.

We do not include social workers in Table 3 because they are not likely to be found working directly with young children. Nevertheless they may manage and/or inspect non-educational services, and the perspective they bring has heavily influenced practice. Social workers like teachers also have a graduate level four-year training (although with more access routes) which is both theoretical and practical. It is focused on supporting vulnerable families and protecting vulnerable children, and there is considerable sophisticated attention paid to social policy and legislative frameworks. It covers the span of life from babies to the elderly. However, the specific theory of child development and learning is scanty, and social workers are highly unlikely to have any direct experience in nursery or primary education or to be familiar with educational practices, except in so far as they themselves are parents.

Nursery nurses have had a two-year post-16 training, and have been awarded an NNEB (National Nursery Examination Board) certificate. This training has had an academic transferability of between GCSE and an A level certificate, and its theoretical underpinning, although covering the range of child development and learning from 0 to 7 years, is cursory by conventional academic standards. Students will have had a range of practice, including local authority and private day nurseries, nursery schools and classes and nannying in private households. There are variations on this college-based course.

The BTEC in nursery nursing is rated slightly more highly than the NNEB, and can serve as an entrance qualification to teacher training or social work. Some colleges also offer an HND in childcare, covering a similar range but to a higher academic level than BTEC, intermediate between a basic qualification and a degree.

There are also a considerable number of short (i.e. 6–12 weeks) *ad hoc* locally based courses which carry little if any academic transferability and which have been designed to meet an immediate local need to systematise and regulate specific local practices. These include childminding and playgroup courses.

More recently, a national vocational qualification (NVQ) in 'childcare and education' has been introduced. Like other national vocational qualifications, it is a competency based assessment of skills acquired in the workplace. It includes several modules or areas of competency, the assessment covering underpinning knowledge as well as task performance. The assessment is carried out by an accredited assessor, usually someone in the workplace of the person who is seeking to gain the NVQ qualification; or in the case of family day carers, someone experienced in childcare and education. The assessors are attached to an assessment centre, a base which trains them and validates their assessments. Some assessment centres are 'a box under the bed; others are more sophisticated affairs managed and funded by consortiums of local private and voluntary childcare organisations.

The NNEB has recently reconstituted itself as the CACHE (Council for Children's Care and Education). As well as retaining the NNEB qualification, but at two levels (certificate and diploma), CACHE is one of several national awarding bodies for the NVQ in childcare. Others include City and Guilds and BTEC. The awarding bodies produce guidelines about the competencies required, and validate assessment centres and assessors.

Those undertaking the NVQ are not eligible for education grants, and the employer and/or the applicant must pay the costs. The estimated costs for background documentation and assessor time amount to about £500–£600 per applicant, more if the applicant also needs to take some kind of training course to meet the underpinning knowledge requirements. In some cases the local TEC (Training and Enterprise Council) pays the costs. Since most childcare workers are low paid, relatively few people have completed an NVQ in childcare – around 4,000 have so far been awarded by the various awarding bodies out of a possible 200,000 early years workers in the private and voluntary sector.

The NVQ in childcare is the subject of much debate. On the one hand it has an extraordinary radical potential. Women (or much more rarely men) can be formally accredited for the skills they have built up over many years of work, paid or unpaid, with children. On the other hand, the level at which they are being assessed, 2 or sometimes 3, is still a basic level. It nowhere near approaches, nor is intended to, the rigour of training that is required for teacher training or social work training. Yet such is the low status and low expectation for work in early years, that for those who have obtained an NVQ qualification, it is a qualification which is a source of considerable pride and regarded as the end of the road rather than the beginning.

From one perspective, the NVQ in childcare can be regarded as a liberating form of training, and the assessors as workplace mentors who enable applicants to develop self-reflective and critical practice in early years through discussion about the requirements of the various modules. From another perspective, however, it is a very basic performance rating with no particular implications for training or practice, merely enabling those who have completed the assessment to progress either to more detailed and rigorous assessment or to enter formal training in education or social work. An additional problem is that it is not routinely accepted as a recognised qualification by employers.

OTHER MODELS OF TRAINING

None of these qualifications would be sufficient for work in our early childhood service. However, it is not only in our visionary world that these existing qualifications are inadequate and inappropriate. Even in the present fragmented system of services, there is wide acknowledgement that there is inadequate training for nursery education, or for work in social services day nurseries where intensive family support is necessary, and that the present low levels of training for the majority of early years workers is unsatisfactory.

Some early years professionals argue that the various aspects of work with young children and their families are so diverse and specialised – teaching, care, social work, even health – that no one form of training, and no one type of worker, can hope to encompass them all: what is needed is multi-professional teams rather than a multi-professional training. Our view is that multi-professional teams do not address the damaging disparity of pay and conditions; but in any case they are something of a chimera. The term 'multi-professional team' is often used to gloss over the old divide between nursery teachers and nursery nurses as a way of avoiding more basic issues about the demands of working with young children in early childhood services. More to the point, multi-professional teams are inappropriate in an early childhood service attempting to develop a holistic approach to the needs of young children and their families. Of course there must be a role for external specialists like social workers, health visitors, psychotherapists and educational psychologists – and for that matter, sculptors, musicians, gymnasts and other creative artists. But the staff working in early childhood services should enjoy a common training and profession.

There are other models of training elsewhere which are more appropriately designed to meet the needs of the service we envision. In a series of papers, Haydn Davies Jones (1993, 1994) discusses 'social pedagogy' as a unifying concept for work across a spectrum of childhood services. This is a model adopted in Germany and Scandinavia, and increasingly in France.

Social pedagogy is defined as 'all the processes of nurturing and upbringing of children outside of the family' (personal communication). It encompasses therapeutic, caring and educational work with a wide range of ages, not just young children, and it is not specific to a particular situation or institution. A social pedagogue could work with very young children or with youths, in a nursery or in a children's home. Social pedagogy can be characterised as versatile, working within the 'life-space' of clients, gaining status through direct practice, taking a developmental and integrationist stance and being community based. The training is rigorous, generally lasts three and a half years at post-18 level and is both theoretical and practical.

While the concept of social pedagogy has widespread currency in parts of Europe, and is the standard qualification for many workers in early childhood services, it is completely unfamiliar in Britain. It has also gained currency as an early childhood qualification in countries with little or no tradition of providing services for young children in the education system. On both counts, it would prove difficult to introduce as the new basic early childhood qualification in Britain.

More relevant to the British situation, with its substantial existing educational presence in services for young children, is what might be called the Spanish model. The reform of early childhood services in Spain is discussed in more detail in Chapter 9. The relevant part for this chapter is that the basic early childhood qualification in Spain is now an 'early childhood teacher', trained to work with children aged 0 to 6 years across the range of early childhood services, either in schools or in separate centres, providing both care and education. The training is a three-year post-18 university course, comparable in duration and level to training as a primary school teacher, and is akin to what was previously a teachers certificate in the UK. It is a theoretical and practical training and encompasses a variety of psychological, sociological and subject-based topics.

TOWARDS A NEW APPROACH TO TRAINING

How do we get from where we are now to a coherent and integrated model of training? To staff our vision of a comprehensive, integrated and coherent early childhood service, we need to resolve a number of issues:

- What level of training should we accept? Do we want a degree led profession?
- What kind of training do we want? Specialist or general?
- What topics should the training encompass?

- On what basis should workers in services be remunerated?
- What conditions of service are appropriate?
- Who should represent the interests of early years workers?
- How can early childhood services become less gendered?

We do not pretend to have pat answers to these questions, and we think that a new system of training must evolve slowly. For some time to come, we imagine the old system of teacher training and nursery nurses will remain in place. But as new, holistic early childhood services begin to develop and expand, then we suggest the following changes might take place.

We would like to see a new standard qualification – 'early childhood teacher'. This would involve the equivalent of four years post-18 training to degree level, within an education framework. Training courses would offer theory and supervised practice for work with children aged 0 to 6 years, with a strong educational or pedagogic focus. As well as being specifically geared to the learning needs of the 0–6 age group, the training would also cover other functions of the early childhood service, for example placing emphasis on working with parents and providing support. What we are advocating, therefore, is a workforce of generalists rather than a variety of highly specialised but narrow professionals. Highly specialised professionals such as educational psychologists or social workers could be consulted and involved in various capacities, but we think that the core of the workforce should be 'early childhood teachers' and the basis of their training should be theory and practice for a range of work with children under six and their families.

Training would be modular and accessible. It could be taken as a single continuous full-time or part-time course; or it could be taken in parts spread over several blocks of time, at the pace and to the level that was desired. The existing NVQ in childcare and education, at levels 2 and 3, could form part of the modular approach. These levels could be an end in themselves for some workers, or be steps to obtaining higher level qualifications, in particular the 'early childhood teacher' qualification.

There are various early childhood degree courses being developed at the time of writing, in Manchester, Suffolk and Bristol, which provide a good starting point for the development of the new qualification of 'early childhood teacher'. These courses span a variety of fields, and draw in modules from other courses such as health and social work. As yet, because of teacher training regulations, there are problems about supervised practice, but these could be overcome if the regulations were changed. Much more development work needs to be done about relevant course content; for instance, about the inclusion of topics such as social policy and social anthropology as well as more practical arts and aesthetic subjects. Before any system was introduced, there would have to be a series of carefully monitored pilots, with feedback from the field, as well as from academic boards.

The aim would be to build up to 60 per cent of all workers in publicly funded centre-based services qualified as 'early childhood teachers', with most of this target attained within a 10-year transition period (the concept of the 10-year transition period for establishing a comprehensive, integrated and coherent early childhood service is developed in Chapter 11). To achieve this target would depend on a large-scale upgrading and retraining programme for existing workers in early childhood services; they have a critical role to play in the success of the radical reform we are proposing. During the transition period there would be a special training programme enabling existing workers (teachers, nursery nurses, playgroup staff, family day carers) to take training schemes to convert to the new 'early childhood teacher' qualification. These special training schemes would accredit existing qualifications and experience. They would also allow existing workers to take some training modules if they did not wish to pursue the full 'early childhood teacher' qualification.

Those who are teacher-trained for work with children between 3 and 8 could work in early childhood services as an early childhood teacher, at least initially, but would have to take an additional qualifying training if they were to seek promotion within what would be a hugely expanded field. After a time, however, this training would no longer be recognised in the early childhood service; primary teachers wanting to become early childhood teachers would need first to take the additional specialist training. Career prospects for early childhood workers would be much better than at present; not only would there be more services offering a range of jobs, but there would also be new support, advisory, monitoring and management roles within the early childhood service. Those early childhood trained staff wanting to progress their careers would not have to switch to primary education – although if they wished to go into primary school work, they could take a 'top up' education qualification, rather like the present PGCE.

We envisage too that there will be various post-graduate courses offering masters degrees in early childhood, as is already the case in some countries such as France. These courses would train people for research and investigation in the field, and for managerial posts – rather like the current MEd degree.

As well as initial or qualifying training, we regard regular in-service or continuous training as vital and integral to the new early childhood service. This would enable all workers, whether qualified or unqualified, to seek new or higher qualifications if desired, and the opportunity for everyone to review and evaluate practice.

More difficult to resolve is the question of pay and conditions. As Table 3 illustrates, there are dramatic differences in pay and conditions between the different groups who work in early childhood services. Job satisfaction may be an important factor, and many people genuinely enjoy the company of young children – their liveliness, their changeability and their charm, and the extraordinarily rapid rate at which they learn. But team-work, leadership and all the other motivating forces which managers lay claim to cannot iron out the gross discrepancies in pay and conditions, and the fact that for everyone except teachers and nursery nurses in education, the job of looking after young children entails low pay and long hours, and for an overwhelming majority of workers, insecure conditions, minimal benefits and lack of representation.

As the saying goes, 'if you pay peanuts you get monkeys'. We consider that highly trained early childhood teachers should be paid at a level equivalent to other teachers. The pay of other, less qualified workers should be reviewed and related, according to their level of training and experience, to that of early childhood teachers, which would mean lower than teachers but, in most cases, substantially higher than current earnings.

However, the working hours of early childhood teachers would not be equivalent to other teachers; we are assuming that the working day and working year for all staff in the early childhood service would be longer than the current teaching day and year, although not so long as the hours currently worked in many 'day care' services, i.e. 35 hours a week with 6 weeks holiday a year (plus public holidays). This is necessary both on economic grounds, to keep costs within bounds, but also for the good working of a comprehensive and coherent service. It is central to the type of multi-functional service we have in mind that it must be open on a full-day and all-year basis, and not just for school hours and in term-time. It would be difficult, if not impossible, to operate on this basis if half the staff or more worked traditional school hours, leaving the remaining and less qualified staff to work different and longer hours.

This change in hours would be attractive for many non-teachers – but not to teachers. However, to offset their longer working hours, early childhood teachers would enjoy a number of advantages over teachers working with older children: at least 10 per cent of the working week for early childhood teachers (and other staff) would be non-contact time, available for training, preparation and work with parents; there would be more opportunities for promotion, because early childhood services would be organised in more but smaller scale units than primary and secondary schools and there would be an extensive infrastructure offering a wide range of jobs; there would be better adult:child ratios; and there would be none of the pressures and constraints that arise from attempting to meet nationally determined requirements such as the National Curriculum and SATs. Indeed one of the attractions of the job would be its diversity, in a service which is multi-functional and community-based, and the encouragement of innovation and creativity.

Alongside the development of a new training and new early childhood worker, we would want to see a less gendered workforce. At present, there are strong gender expectations about working with young children. The effect is compounded by other factors to produce very low levels of male employment in early childhood services. Recent child abuse cases have led to an insistence on extreme caution in employing men to work with young children; some organisations claim that men should not be employed at all in direct work with young children because they are too much of a liability. Even if this caution about child abuse was recognised as over-reaction, work in early years is generally unattractive to men because of its cultural image as a female profession, its low pay and lack of career prospects.

We believe that it is important to have more male early childhood workers, and suggest a target of 20 per cent male workers within 10 years would be achievable. We think that this change would be in the interests of children, who should have a right to expect a mixed gender staff group; and of parents, for if centres are to involve fathers and mothers then they need to include male workers as part of a general strategy to become more 'father friendly'. To achieve the target, there will need to be a deliberate strategy, covering training and recruitment, to encourage and support increased male employment (what this strategy might involve is discussed further in Jensen, forthcoming). Certainly part of the strategy would be to recognise and seriously address anxieties about child abuse, and among some women – both workers and parents – at the prospect of men taking up more employment in early childhood services. We expect that increasing the number of men at a time of general expansion of services will ensure that employment opportunities for women workers, at all levels, are not reduced.

Finally, although it is beyond our remit to suggest how it might be accomplished, we would argue for unitary trade union representation to provide a vigorous and united voice on behalf of all those working in the new early childhood service. Today, membership of unions in Britain is as fragmented as the service itself. Nursery nurses are represented by a variety of manual and clerical workers unions, where they get relatively little attention or priority. Those in the voluntary and private sector may have some professional representation through the Pre-school Learning Alliance and the National Childminding Association but this carries no bargaining rights or legal status. Teachers' unions at present protect the interests and position of teachers in relation to other staff. Moreover, after many years of right wing government, unions themselves are in disarray and often disregarded as legally constituted representatives of the workforce; competitive tendering, local management of schools, and the growth of the private sector have undermined the power of the unions to act as the voice of the workforce.

We think this situation is unsatisfactory both for the workforce and for the early childhood service we envision. If one trade union were to take on all staff working in early childhood services, as happened, for example, with the teachers' union in New Zealand which took the initiative to enrol all early childhood workers in a special division, this would present a substantial increase in membership; from being a very small sector within the union, early childhood would become a very large one. However, there have been no signs so far that this might be possible in Britain – we wait and hope to be proved wrong.

We have put forward a model of a trained workforce to match our vision of a comprehensive, integrated and coherent early childhood service and appropriate to the important and demanding nature of working with young children and their families. We have presented a very general picture, which we recognise would need considerable fine tuning if it were to be implemented. In a nutshell, we would replace nursery teachers and many other workers by early childhood teachers trained to graduate level to be able to work in a multi-functional and flexible service; they would be supported by less trained workers, able, however, to acquire extra qualifications, as and when they chose, including early childhood teacher status.

Our proposal means abandoning some long and dearly held assumptions about who should work in early years services, how they can be trained, how much they should be paid, and how many hours they should work; in particular, it means breaking the link with primary teaching and embedding work with the 3–6 age group in an early childhood stage of the education system. We are gradualists: but we do not see how anything less than a radical solution can truly address the present incoherence and inequalities that afflict the early years workforce and remove the low expectations and standards that pervade so much of the training and employment standards in this vital field. But once such reforms have been carried out, they will provide a sure foundation for a transformed nursery education.

8

Can It Be Done in Britain?

Gumboots is a community nursery in south London, taking 30 children from 0 to 5. It is open from 8.00 a.m. to 6.00 p.m. throughout the year and has an out-of-school club attached. It is a pleasant architect-designed brick building, in its own spacious grounds. It is run by a management committee of parents and people from the local community; these include a retired bus driver, a local councillor from the education committee, a local housing officer, a teacher from the neighbouring school and the fathers and mothers of some of the children attending. Madge, an indefatigable woman in her early seventies, is the treasurer, managing the entire budget and doing all the accounts. She is a founder member, and at various times has been the secretary and treasurer, and as she describes herself 'head-cook and bottlewasher'. The nursery is her pride and joy and she comes daily.

The nursery began with a grant from the Greater London Council. Madge drew up all the proposals and costing. She was helped by a local trade union official and various local women. They lobbied systematically for the money from the GLC childcare fund. Gumboots got a capital grant for the building and for running costs, in total £250,000. When the GLC was abolished, Madge and her colleagues and the parents lobbied the local council, and secured a replacement grant towards running costs. The grant has been whittled away, and the management committee has reluctantly had to raise the fees to £55 per week, although parents who cannot afford the fees are treated with sympathy and there are informal concessions.

The nursery serves a multi-racial community in a mixed district of owner-occupier and local authority housing. The children who attend are drawn from all backgrounds. The staff are multi-racial, and the officer in charge is black. The multi-racial nature of the nursery is emphasised in its curriculum. On the wall as you go in is a map of the world, with a name and a passport sized photo of each child placed to show the origins of her family, and a postcard telling how grandparents or parents reached England and what they thought about coming. The staff are also included on the map.

There is a wide range of resources available in the large central room, and children choose their activities. But the day is planned so that after lunch the youngest children sleep, the middle group use the playroom, and the eldest group of children are withdrawn to another room for literacy and numeracy games. Madge is trying to persuade various specialists to come in – a dance teacher, for example.

The local authority, Southwark Council, has integrated the administration of all its early years services under the education department (although nursery classes remain within the governance of primary schools) and the local teachers' centre puts on all kinds of early years training and seminars, which all staff from the borough, whatever their background, are entitled to attend. The nursery staff have been to many of these courses. The council is also able to provide back up and support resources to the nursery and help them with interviewing and cover arrangements. The annual inspection of the nursery is carried out by officers from the education department using carefully devised criteria which are drawn from both educational and social work frames of reference. Gumboots has a separate training grant from the council which it uses to sponsor staff who want to obtain further qualifications.

Hillend Nursery *is on a large council housing estate on a windy bluff above an estuary. It takes 40 children. 15 of these are aged 0–5, of whom 5 are profoundly disabled and non-ambulant, and a further 10 have some kind of disability ranging from blindness to Down's syndrome. Twenty-five children, mainly aged 3–5, come from the immediate locality. It is open for 52 weeks (excluding public holidays) from 9.00 a.m. to 4.00 p.m., and also on one Saturday per month and evenings. As the nursery points out in its introductory booklet: 'a normal day at Hillend does not exist. The structure of the day is flexible which is essential when working within family and community life.' It is in relatively new and purpose-built accommodation which includes a parents' room with a one-way screen giving onto the room with the most disabled children, two playrooms and various group rooms. It has a landscaped garden.*

A number of specialists visit and support the nursery, including educational psychologists and physiotherapists. The nursery was an amalgamation of an assessment centre for children with profound disabilities, and a playgroup funded by social services, and was originally bitterly opposed by both groups and the local community. However, that was over ten years ago, and the nursery is now very successfully integrated. As one of the few communal buildings on the estate, it plays an important part in its local community: it is the base for a branch of the local credit union and for adult education classes, and opens for various Saturday activities such as horse rides for children from the nursery and their brothers and sisters and friends. The children, both with and without disabilities, frequently go on outings in the locality, from short visits to shops to excursions to the airport and harbour. It is striking in the way that not only the children but also the parents help and support each other, and accept disability as a perfectly normal situation and caring for each other as a normal way to behave. Although the nursery is maintained by the local authority, it has its own management committee and all parents have a voice in management decisions, a responsibility which is treated very seriously by all parties.

Hillend is maintained by Strathclyde Region (Inverclyde Council after May 1996) which has an integrated early years service within the education department. The Region has developed a curriculum guide for children aged 0–5, which provides a frame of reference for all nurseries and other providers. The Council has integrated training for all its care and education staff, and the staff of Hillend, who have a range of qualifications, take part in regular training and discussion about the service they provide with other staff, teaching and non-teaching, from across the region. Maureen, the charismatic head, has been seconded to work on specific disability projects within the Region, and has also undertaken a sponsored MEd degree at the university in order to extend, develop and record her work.

This nursery is also inspected according to education criteria devised by the Quality Inspectorate in Strathclyde, which is a scheme of inspection that encompasses provision for children aged 0–5 in a wide variety of settings.

Margaret McMillan Nursery School opened officially in March 1991 with the amalgamation of Highgate Nursery School and Hornsey Rise Children's Day Centre. As part of Islington's plans to extend and integrate services for young children and their families, the school offers nursery education to around 200 children. These include a percentage of children with special needs. This percentage varies according to the severity of the need, a non-ambulant child requiring more space for a wheelchair and equipment than an ambulant child, but in general places are offered to 12–14 children. It is open 8.00 a.m. to 6.00 p.m. and throughout the year for those that need it, but is routinely open during school terms.

By providing places for children under three years, in baby and toddler rooms, and by offering a flexible programme outside traditional school hours and terms, Margaret McMillan aims to extend traditional nursery education to meet a wide variety of family needs. The school serves a socially and ethnically mixed community. More than 15 languages are spoken by the families using the school.

Over the years a package of nursery provision has evolved from the constant search for resources and activities which match the children's learning needs. Each day at the nursery school children can express and extend themselves through Home Play, drama and outdoor work. They can explore materials, shape and space as they use bricks, construction toys, sand, water, clay and so on. Children learn to use arts, crafts and science workshop areas, gain skills from a wide range of drawing and painting materials and become familiar with books, stories and music. The garden provides direct contact with the natural world in all its richness offering realistic challenges and endless opportunities to explore materials, the seasons and growing things.

Margaret McMillan has a governing body and is funded by the London Borough of Islington, which has also integrated all early years services in the *education department. Although originally intended as a pilot model for integrated nursery education, the authority has subsequently focused its efforts on integration on its former day nurseries. They have been redesignated as Under Fives Centres, and a qualified teacher has been put in charge of each of them – although not on teaching conditions of service.*

In this chapter we explore how these innovative nurseries have been able to cope with the issues we have been raising about providing a comprehensive, multi-functional service which takes a holistic approach to the needs of children and families. None of them provide the fully comprehensive service we would like to see, but in different ways they come close to it. Each, in a different way, has moved beyond the narrow and conventional concept of nursery education as a part-term service for children aged 3 and 4, exclusively concerned with providing early learning experiences.

Gumboots provides a service for children aged 0 to 5 whose parents work. But it is also a non-profit self-managed service which reflects the make-up of its local community in the families who use it, and in the way it is managed and run. It does not merely involve but is dependent on men and women such as Madge who, despite her age and ill-health, has an extraordinary amount to contribute, and in turn derives much pleasure from the nursery and in helping the children and families who come to it.

Hillend has admitted children who would normally be excluded from nursery schooling because of the severity of their disabilities, and in admitting them has deliberately and successfully challenged ideas about young children's capacities. It bases its philosophy on the idea that young children can sympathise and empathise, and are willing to help and co-operate and offer support and friendship to children more vulnerable than themselves. Hillend is also rooted in its local community, and the parents who use the nursery, and their friends and neighbours, see the nursery as some kind of focus for their communal life.

The third centre, Margaret McMillan, is explicitly a nursery school offering nursery education, and offers a widely admired curriculum along the lines advocated in the Rumbold Report. However, it is also open to cover working hours, and provides for children from 0 to 5 years. It integrates children with minor and more severe disabilities; for instance wheelchair-bound children. Although it is a nursery school, parents pay scaled fees for the service over and above a core time – two and a half hours for 3 year olds and a school day for 4 year olds. Not all parents are employed, and some opt for part-time nursery education, others for a full day in term time but not in the holidays. The time the children attend is negotiable. Nursery education workers and support workers look after the children under 3 in separate group rooms, and also care for those children who come before and stay on after school hours in a separate space from the main teaching areas. A number of local women work in the project as support workers. Their work is closely integrated with that of other staff, and the nursery offers them NVQ training.

We consider now some of the issues which these innovative services have had to face.

THE PROCESS OF CHANGE

For all of them, getting to where they are today has been a long and sometimes painful and dispiriting process, although all would claim that in the long run it has been worthwhile and even exhilarating. It is remarkably difficult to break the cordons of tradition. It took Madge five years from 1980 to 1985 to secure the grant for Gumboots. Hillend went through rounds of angry meetings and long negotiations. Margaret McMillan was an amalgamation of an existing day nursery and a nursery school, and the changes were steered through by an external consultant; day nursery staff felt very undermined by the decision to make the amalgamated centre education-orientated, and the majority of the daycare staff at that point chose to leave.

All three nurseries were dependent on the support and commitment of local councillors. Without their support it is unlikely that the nurseries would have got off the ground. Conversely, the kind of issues the nurseries raised were in turn a spur to each local authority to integrate its own services and provide a more coherent approach.

Each of these nurseries has had to grapple with the problems we outlined in Chapter 3, and to do so independently, without benefit of national policy or guidelines on key issues. They have had to articulate their values and philosophies to explain and justify what they are doing. They have made decisions about what kind of staff to employ and how much to pay them. They have had to decide, within the terms of inappropriate legislation, what ratios to adopt for what age children. They had to decide about hours of opening – they are all open throughout the year and parents can negotiate the hours their children attend. They all offer, in theory at least, open access, on a first come first served basis, but they all have long waiting lists and face severe pressure for places. They have all had to juggle with finances and decide what, if anything, to charge parents.

STAFF TRAINING AND CONDITIONS OF SERVICE

Standard teachers' conditions are no longer appropriate in any of these nurseries, because the hours of nursery education are too short and its age range too narrow. Teachers also cost more than other types of staff, and if paid on a pro-rata basis would be even more expensive. In the case of Gumboots and Hillend this money was not available; in the case of Margaret McMillan it was available only because of economies of scale – more than 200 children attend each week – and because of the innovative use of nursery education workers and support workers.

A current teacher's qualification, even where it includes an early years element, is not enough for the work in these nurseries. No one would deny that children need sympathetic and knowledgeable adults to encourage and enhance their zest for learning, but the staff these nurseries employ do not fit neatly into existing categories, in terms of either their qualifications or their pay and conditions of work. Each centre has arrived at a different staffing solution.

In Gumboots and Hillend there is a core of trained workers, with a variety of qualifications, and some staff with no formal training. There are no teachers in Gumboots. Madge, as an ex-administrator, is a competent manager, secretary and financial administrator – although she receives no remuneration for this work. Maureen, at Hillend, is a qualified teacher who has also specialised in community work, although most of the staff are nursery nurses. The staff in both nurseries work longer hours and on average are paid less than teachers; but the hierarchical division of nursery teacher and nursery nurse does not exist. Both nurseries would welcome an opportunity to develop their curricular input, and to widen the range of activities they provide, and they have each received some help in this from the education authority which helps maintain them. But they do not undervalue the richness or the stability of what they are already offering. Given the way they work, it simply would not be possible or welcome to introduce a teacher, on teacher's pay and conditions and with a conventional agenda about early learning, into their more informal and holistic way of working.

Margaret McMillan has opted for a different solution. It has upgraded its nursery nurse staff to become nursery education workers, so that their conditions are closer to those of teachers, and it has also been prepared to take on unqualified workers. The head and deputy head work shifts, although their pay and conditions are preserved. The nursery school prioritises learning and curriculum and there is an extraordinary rich range of resources.

But as pioneers, all three nurseries are dependent on the goodwill and commitment of their staff. They have all – with the assistance of their local authority – compensated for the lack of appropriate training with substantial in-service and post-qualifying training programmes.

RATIOS

Because Gumboots is classified as offering 'day care', it has reluctantly accepted the Children Act ratios, even though the nursery considers them unnecessary for the older children, and an additional expense it can ill afford. Hillend had to invent its own ratios because of its unusual circumstances, but relies on very willing volunteers to augment the staffing. Margaret McMillan classifies itself as a nursery school, and as such is not subject to regulation under the Children Act. It has adopted nursery education ratios for the core day for the older children, while its ratios for the younger children approximate much more to the Children Act.

AGE INTEGRATION AND INTEGRATION OF DISABILITY

Gumboots and Margaret McMillan take children from 0 to 5, and have devised arrangements where the babies are separate but can mix together with other children – for brothers and sisters in particular. Gumboots also has an out-of-school club for children who have left the nursery to go to school, but still need before and after school and holiday care. Hillend takes children from 2 to 5, but mothers – and fathers – can bring their younger children with them to the nursery.

The medical model of disability, that is of a specific deficit which requires early diagnosis and specialist intervention, is still a current one. It is reinforced by ideas of developmental appropriateness, which lay stress on the capacities of the average child and on unvarying patterns of development rather than on the capacity of the teacher to respond to individual and unforeseen needs (Solity, 1995). However, there are also strong arguments for integration. This has been described as a viewpoint which stresses

> that all children should receive whatever support their families want for them, right from the start, irrespective of how long it might be needed, and that services should reflect an acceptance of the ordinariness of disability which is often neither preventable nor curable. This view rejects the medical model of prevention and cure in favour of a view which is more positive about children as they are.
>
> (Potts, Petrie and Statham, 1992)

This is certainly the view which Hillend and Margaret McMillan have chosen to adopt, and both nurseries lay stress on the importance to non-disabled children of learning to accept and help those different from themselves.

EMPLOYING MEN

Both Margaret McMillan and Hillend employ men. At the time of writing, a male part-time supply teacher is on the staff at Margaret McMillan, and the deputy officer in charge at Hillend is a man. Gumboots would like to, but as a voluntary organisation it cannot offer competitive enough rates. All three nurseries consider that a gender balance is important, in terms of role models showing that men can and do manage to take on a nurturant and caring role; and in terms of enlarging the experience of those children who, because they come from single parent families headed by a woman, do not often come into contact with adult men. They have weighed the balance about the risk of child abuse, and consider that their staff selection procedures and staff support and training processes have minimised any such risk.

THE SUPPORT OF THE LOCAL AUTHORITY

We have chosen these three examples – and there are many other examples of innovation to choose from, not all of which are centre-based – because each of these three nurseries is located in a local authority which has combined its 'day care' and 'early years education' services. The problems the nurseries face are far better understood than in most local authorities, and there is some help available in facing them. In each authority this has involved the administrative reorganisation of all services to young children within the education department, where an education officer at a relatively senior level has a brief to manage them. The education department is now responsible for maintaining a variety of early childhood services besides nursery education, and has taken over responsibility from the social services department for regulating voluntary and private services – childminders, playgroups and day nurseries.

In Southwark, there was a consensus at chief officer level that integration of early years services in the education department was a sensible step. Both the Director of Social Services and the Chief Executive of the Council actively welcomed and supported the decision of the members to transfer day nurseries from social services to education, although anomalies remain; the management of family centres and referral procedures to day nurseries are still controlled by social work. However, the policy of the officers and the council has been to proceed very cautiously. There have been no amalgamations of services, no changes to nursery education; but a great deal of emphasis has been placed on bringing various education, social services and voluntary groups together in a number of forums, and on developing a solid in-service training strategy. In current financial circumstances, the council is unwilling to experiment with more radical solutions in the services it provides directly, although it supports a number of community nurseries like Gumboots.

In Strathclyde the decision to transfer all social work services, both provider and regulatory functions, to education was bitterly disputed, as much by education and teacher union representatives as by social work interests. Nor in the beginning was there consensus amongst members; the original decision to integrate services was steered through by two powerful councillors. This process has been described elsewhere (Penn, 1992; 1995a).

Strathclyde has attempted more radical solutions; for example, converting some existing services into its own version of 'community nurseries' where staff have been redesignated, whether or not they were previously teaching or nursery nurse staff, and offering a service for children aged 0–5 to cover the working day and the working year. As yet these changes apply to a small percentage of the services provided, but the changes have been very carefully documented and researched (Munn & Schaffer, 1993; Wilkinson, 1994). It has been the intention that they will form the basis of development and expansion when further monies become available – although local government reorganisation may undermine this intention.

As well as experimenting with new kinds of provision, Strathclyde has put a great deal of effort into curriculum development across the range of ages and types of services, and into in-service training. The quality assurance and inspection procedures of the Region have assumed a broader perspective, and take account of the diversity of aims and objectives of the services they cover, rather than adhering to solely educational criteria.

In Islington, the decision to integrate services was also member led. Margaret McMillan was intended as a pilot scheme, but the furore was such that members backed off similar schemes, and chose instead to revamp the authority's day nurseries by putting a teacher in charge of each of them, although not on teacher's pay or conditions of service. This has been a problematic resolution of the staffing problems that dog every attempt to integrate services. But the decision to integrate services, as elsewhere, has led to a more coherent overview of the full range of services for young children, and more coherent in-service training arrangements.

Our examples illustrate what can be done when the local authority is in a position to back up local innovation. But for all three nurseries it was hard going, and depended on the determination and commitment of outstanding individuals to see change through; and then on the vision of the local authority and the resources at its disposal to back the initiative. The local authorities we have cited would willingly undertake a great deal more development and create and support imaginative new services if only they had the resources to do so. As it is, it has been a struggle to preserve the funding for non-statutory services and in all three authorities some valuable services have been reduced rather than expanded.

THE LACK OF A FRAMEWORK

To make change happen, and to develop a more coherent early years service which reflects contemporary social needs, action has to take place at a variety of levels: at the level of service innovation, in nurseries like Gumboots, Hillend and Margaret McMillan; at a local authority level – like Southwark, Strathclyde and Islington – where imaginative and committed local authority officers and members are prepared to push through change; and at a national level, where a policy, legal and financial framework has to be put in place. These levels of intervention should feed into, reflect and support one another.

In Britain, this partnership falls down at national level. There is no national framework to support the development of a comprehensive, integrated and coherent early childhood service at local level. Local initiatives manage as best they can, in spite of, rather than because of, government policy, grappling with the complexities of legislation, funding and staffing, all of which require national solutions. The vision which infuses and enthuses Gumboots, Hillend, Margaret McMillan, and their local authorities, finds no counter-part with central government, whose only vision is to distribute vouchers to ensure 'pre-school education' for all 4 year olds.

In the next chapter we look at examples from two countries where a partnership, including national government, exists to develop a comprehensive, integrated and coherent early childhood service, while in Chapter 11 we look at the kind of initiatives which are necessary at a national level if Britain is to develop such a service.

9

It Has Been Done Abroad

We have seen how some British local authorities are working to develop a new, more comprehensive, integrated and coherent approach to early childhood services. Similar initiatives have been taken by some local and regional authorities in Northern and Central Italy. Here many nurseries, which are exclusively for children under 3, are the responsibility of local education departments; although originally developed to provide care for young children while their parents were at work, these nurseries have developed a strong and explicit educational role. In many areas in recent years there have also been moves to diversify services available to children under 3 and their families, to offer opportunities for socialisation, support and learning for children not using nurseries and for non-employed parents and other carers, as well as part-time care for parents who do not want their young children in a full-day nursery place. Nearly all children from 3 to 6 attend full-time nursery school, many of which recognise in their opening hours the care needs of children with employed parents.

Italian local and regional authorities working to develop new approaches to early childhood services, like their British counterparts, are not supported by national policies and structures, although unlike Britain there has been considerable regional autonomy. What they do, they do despite of rather than because of the national system. In this chapter therefore we focus on European countries seeking comprehensive, integrated and coherent early childhood services at all levels.

THE DANISH EXPERIENCE

A comprehensive early childhood service

Most people are aware that the Nordic countries – Denmark, Finland, Norway, Sweden – have a high level of parental employment and a high level of provision for young children. But equally important features of the services are less widely understood. For example, all four countries offer paid parental leave over at least the first year of a child's life, in consequence of which there are now few children under that age attending nurseries or other services. No countries better illustrate the potentially close connections between leave policies and early childhood services and the need in a modern society to consider both of these measures, and others, as part of a broad strategy to help parents reconcile employment and family responsibilities.

But most important to the subject of this book, early childhood services in these four countries are based on an approach that is comprehensive, integrated and coherent. The country that best illustrates this approach is Denmark, which has the most developed early childhood services in Europe, and probably the world – a remarkable achievement given that major development of services only began in the mid-1960s.

Like the rest of Scandinavia, Denmark has very high levels of parental employment. Three-quarters of mothers and nearly 90 per cent of fathers are employed, and it was the growth of maternal employment, which began to occur strongly in the 1960s, which stimulated the development of early childhood services. Legislation in 1964 extended public funding to early childhood services for all children, whereas previously it had been restricted to services taking children from low income families; ensuring general provision of services became a public responsibility. The way was open for a genuinely comprehensive service and a major expansion of services followed.

Since then, the growth rate in services has fluctuated; for example, with a slowing down after the economic crisis in 1974. In recent years, however, there has been further rapid growth in publicly funded services. The number of children attending early childhood services and services providing care and recreation for school-age children rose by 39 per cent between 1989 and 1995, an increase of over 110,000 children (equivalent to more than a million children in Britain, which has ten times the population of Denmark).

In 1993, the Danish Prime Minister announced that all parents would be guaranteed a publicly funded place for children aged 1–6 years by 1996. This commitment was combined with a new system of parental leave, introduced in 1994, and supplementing existing rights to maternity and paternity leave and to 10 weeks parental leave to be shared between parents as they choose. The new parental leave scheme, after some early revisions, now gives each parent the possibility to take up to 12 months of leave per child, at some point during the child's first eight years, paid at approximately £900 a month (each parent has an absolute entitlement to 3 months leave, or 6 months if they begin to take leave before their child is 12 months; the remaining period of 6–9 months is subject to the employer's agreement).

The assumption behind the Prime Minister's guarantee of a place for children over 12 months was that before that age most children would be cared for by parents on leave. This assumption has proved correct in practice, with the new leave arrangements proving enormously popular (OECD, 1995). Consequently, there has been little growth in services for very young children; recent growth has mainly been in services providing care and recreation for school-age children, with some increase also in services for children over 2 years.

Although only a recommendation to local authorities, and not backed by legislation, the government's statement guaranteeing places for children over 12 months has been taken seriously by local authorities. Currently (1995), two-thirds of local authorities offer some sort of guarantee and waiting lists have fallen from 35,000 in 1992 to 12,500 in 1995. It is unlikely, however, that the guarantee will be fully achieved by the target date of 1996, not least because the child population is increasing as birth rates have risen in recent years (it has been calculated that an extra 60,000 new places in services will be needed by the year 2000 simply to meet the need arising from increasing births).

Despite only partial success in meeting the government guarantee, the level of coverage of services is impressive, putting Britain to shame. In 1995, nearly 50 per cent of children under 3 attended publicly funded services (this proportion needs to be seen in the light of low attendance among children under 12 months, implying that around three-quarters of 1 and 2 year olds attend services) and 79 per cent of 3 to 5 year olds. Children do not begin compulsory schooling until 7. But nearly all 6 year olds go to part-time 'kindergarten classes' which are part of primary schools, while many also attend publicly funded services providing care and recreation for school-age children.

This level of service has been achieved through long-term political commitment, which has permitted a sustained development of services and provided the resources to support this development. In 1994, public expenditure on services for children under 6, excluding capital costs and infrastructure costs such as staff training, was DKK10.9 billion, or about 1.2 per cent of GDP (at 1994 exchange rates, this is equivalent to about £1.12 billion for a population a tenth the size of Britain's). In addition, there is substantial public expenditure on parental leave.

A multi-functional early childhood service

The early childhood service is therefore increasingly comprehensive in terms of coverage. It is also comprehensive in the needs it seeks to meet. In a society where nearly all parents are economically active, the provision of safe and secure care for children while parents are at work or studying is a fundamental function of services. Although the principle is that services are available for all children, in the case of a shortfall in places one of the priorities is for children with employed parents.

Services also provide opportunities for learning and socialisation. A 1990 Circular from the national Ministry of Social Affairs puts forward five broad principles on which the social and pedagogical objectives of services should be based, the first of which is:

Children's development, well-being and self-reliance must be promoted; services must provide a secure and challenging everyday life, with an emphasis on close contact between children and adults and children developing on their own terms through free play and their own space. There should also be planned and shared activities, together with adults, in which children can become involved in creative and practical tasks, cultural activities and other shared experiences; these will support children's development and their ability to co-operate with other people.

Finally, services have a clearly defined support function. Children with special needs have priority admission and the integration of children with disabilities into ordinary services is considered an important objective. Another principle in the Ministry Circular says that 'services are a resource in preventative work . . . which should include providing the special support which some families need'.

An integrated early childhood service

As well as being comprehensive, services for young children are integrated. The Ministry of Social Affairs has overall responsibility at national level, with local authority social welfare departments responsible locally (with the exception of kindergarten classes for 6 year olds, which are provided by education authorities). Services, as in all Nordic countries, are therefore integrated within the welfare system. However, as already seen, they are universal in nature and have a strong pedagogical orientation. This has the effect of social welfare departments providing generally used services, rather than limiting their remit to a minority of stressed and distressed families.

A coherent early childhood service

This integration, in turn, leads to coherence across services in the early childhood services system. There is a common legal and administrative framework. The principles outlined in the Ministry's Circular apply to all services. Although levels of provision for children under 3 are lower than for children over 3, the difference is far less than in any other non-Nordic country. All services are funded in a similar way, with public funds covering about 80 per cent of total costs and the rest coming from parent contributions. These contributions are based on common principles; national regulations lay down that no parents should pay more than 30 per cent of costs, with reductions for lower income families, for families with more than one child attending and for children with special needs. All services, whether for children under or over 3, have similar opening hours, throughout the year (with no school holiday closure) and for a full day of 9 or 10 hours – although most Danish parents try to arrange their working hours so that their children only attend 6 or 7 hours a day.

Coherence also applies to staffing. There is a common basic training – a three and a half year post-18 course, covering work with all children from 0 to 6 years and including two six-month salaried placements. The curriculum consists of psychology, educational studies, social studies, health education and a subject known as 'communication, organisation and management'. There is a strong emphasis on creative subjects, such as drama, music, movement, environmental studies, art and crafts and Danish; together, these account for 40 per cent of the course. About two-thirds of workers in centres have this training; many of the other, untrained staff go on to take the basic training, often in their twenties, after gaining initial experience. Common levels of pay and other employment conditions apply across the system. This coherent approach to staffing ensures that work with children under 3 is valued equally with work with older children.

One consequence of an integrated and coherent system has been the increasing importance within the early childhood service system of 'age-integrated centres', which take children from 0 to 6 years, sometimes also providing care and recreation for school-age children. Between 1989 and 1995 the number of children attending this type of service increased by 80 per cent, compared to falling numbers in nurseries which only take children under 3 and a modest 16 per cent increase in kindergartens for 3 to 6 year olds. Jytte Jensen (1993), a Danish expert, has written about the advantages of age integration:

> Growing up in a setting where there are children of different ages is important for development, because the child in this situation experiences many different kinds of social relations. In mixed age groups of children there are opportunities for playing various roles and taking different positions. There are also opportunities for acquiring forms of social competence that are qualitatively different from those acquired in groups of children with a narrow range of ages . . . Living in a typical Danish family of today, with its two children born soon after each other, means that the average child does not live with other children of a completely different age with whom he/she can identify. It is important that childcare centres compensate for this situation . . .
>
> As one of the greatest advantages of mixed age centres, staff emphasise the fact that the children can avoid having to change their surroundings. The greater number of years that the children can remain at the same centre gives continuity for the individual child, especially when the staff also work in the institution for many years which they actually do. It also gives continuity to the children's group which contributes to good group cohesion . . . The broad age span in the age-integrated centres provides the possibility for siblings to be in the same centre for a longer period of time. Parents seem to be very pleased about the age integration. Parents and staff get to know each other well when the children attend the same centre for many years.
>
> (pp. 35–8)

Diversity and choice

This integrated and coherent system also permits some diversity. The Danish system is not a monolithic regime of state-run nurseries, but highly decentralised to local authorities and individual centres, a point to which we return. Although local authorities provide most services themselves, a substantial minority are run by private, non-profit organisations (there is virtually no for-profit provision in Denmark, apart from a relatively small number of private childminders). As well as day nurseries, kindergartens and age-integrated centres, there is an extensive system of 'organised family day care' with family day carers recruited, paid and supported by local authorities. This form of provision accounts for nearly two-thirds of children under 3 using publicly funded services.

In recent years there have been other new developments. 'Pool scheme centres' have been opened, established by parent or other groups who receive a lump sum grant from the local authority to run the centre. Another recent innovation has been 'forest kindergartens', provided for 3 to 6 year olds, with children and staff spending every day (winter or summer) in the countryside, with a small building for really bad weather but most of the time being outdoors. There are now between two and three hundred of these kindergartens (equivalent to over 2,000 in a country the size of Britain), and they have proved extremely popular among everyone concerned, children, parents and staff.

Parents therefore may have some choice about the service their children attend, although the amount varies according to where you live and other considerations; some communes (local authorities), for instance, only provide 'organised family day care' for children under 3. But choice is not considered the dominant value. Too much choice, Danish officials argue, undermines social cohesion and might place some families with extra needs at a disadvantage in a situation where parents were encouraged to shop around and centres could decide who they admitted.

Diversity, however, is encouraged in other ways, especially through the high level of autonomy given to individual centres. Most staff are highly trained, and expect to take a high level of responsibility for their centres. There is also a long tradition of close but informal co-operation between parents and staff. Since 1992, this relationship has become more formal; all centres and organised family day care schemes run by local authorities must have a management board with a parent majority and which has wide responsibilities for activities, finance and staffing.

Increasing attention is also paid to children and to treating them as active members of services rather than passive objects. The second principle in the 1990 Ministry Circular makes this perspective explicit:

Children must be listened to. It must be emphasised that children, according to their age and maturity, be involved in the planning and execution of activities in child care facilities, and that in this way they are able to gain experience of the connection between influence and responsibility on a personal and social level.

This official statement reflects the growing influence of a children's culture in

Denmark, which places high value on listening to children and involving them in all aspects of society, including the services they attend. Another example of this process is a 'Children as Citizens' Project, set up by an inter-ministerial working party concerned with children, and which has examined many different ways of giving children more influence, including children in early childhood services. The aims of the Project give the flavour of what a children's culture means in practice:

> To focus on children's everyday life and their possibilities for participation in decision-making; to strengthen children's right and opportunities to say things that will be heard and to which importance will be attached; to give children information that makes real participation in decision-making possible; to develop working methods where children can exert their influence; and to make adult practices and attitudes to children the subject of debate.

The overall effect on the system of these interlocking factors – a well-trained staff and increasing inclusion of parents and children – has been described by Claus Jensen (1994), an official with the trade union for trained workers:

> The Danish system is characterised by great variety. The system encourages variety instead of homogeneity, with a view to meeting everyone's needs . . . Related to this, the system also encourages experimentation and the evolution of new types of centre . . . Individual centres in Denmark are now allowed a good deal of self-determination. The state and communes only lay down a few general guidelines and targets, leaving the rest up to the centre concerned . . . And no problems have arisen as a result. On the contrary: decentralisation has lead to great activity in and around individual centres, and children, staff and parents all feel that they can contribute to an active democratic process in which changes are allowed and even approved of. This means that children, parents and staff at centres can be given the chance to be the leading figures in their own centre, as opposed to being the pawn in someone else's game. They have great influence on daily routines, the way groups are made up, the activities and rules of the centre and so on . . . Quality in services in Denmark is very much discussed, implemented and reviewed at the level of the individual centre and includes children, parents and staff. The system permits and encourages diversity and change.

(pp. 153–5)

The emphasis here is placed on achieving diversity through centres responding to their community of key 'stakeholders' – children, parents, staff – rather than seeking diversity through a plethora of competing services. The emphasis is on social cohesion, inclusion and democracy rather than competition and markets.

THE SPANISH EXPERIENCE

Denmark, like the other Nordic countries, has a well-established early childhood service, that not only is integrated and coherent, but is also increasingly comprehensive. However, these countries have gone down a very particular road: integrating services within the welfare system. Although early childhood services have a clear pedagogical role, they are not part of the education system and indeed see themselves as a separate entity, with their own purposes and identity. This distinctiveness, and the 'edge' it creates between the two systems, is described by Claus Jensen:

> One of the main aims of schools is to prepare pupils for a life as adults and grades are given for achievement . . . This has always been the role of schools, and preparing pupils for adulthood will probably continue to be the dominant task. By contrast, child care centres focus on the here and now, on fellowship, enthusiasm and self-determination. No grades are given for achievement. So far, Danish child care centres have developed and maintained an independent philosophy of caring which can survive without the support of its big sister, educational theory.
>
> (Jensen, 1994, p. 153)

While this view raises important issues about early childhood services, issues which have received too little attention in Britain's impoverished debate, the reality of early childhood services in Britain and a number of other European countries is that the education system is already strongly represented in provision for children below compulsory school age. Countries such as Belgium, France, Italy and Spain already provide, or intend to provide, 3 years of nursery education for children between 3 and 6. It would be impractical to integrate all services, including a strong education sector, into a welfare system which would have to re-orient itself to provide general services. Integration and coherence therefore must be sought in the education system.

This is the basis for the reform of early childhood services in Spain. In 1990, a major new education law (*Ley de Ordenación General del Sistema Educativo* – LOGSE for short) was passed. This law covers the whole education system, but of particular relevance to this book, it recognised 0 to 6 years as the first stage of the education system – the 'early childhood education' stage, preceding primary and secondary education stages. Responsibility for all services for children from 0 to 6 years passed to national and regional education authorities.

Teacher training has become the basic training for workers in early childhood services. Students can choose to specialise in work with this age group, the training for which is at the same level as primary school teaching. Teachers who specialise in working with children aged 0 to 6 are also able to work in primary school, but not vice versa. A 'special plan' for training during the transition to the new system gave less qualified workers the chance to train as specialised teachers through in-service courses.

However, while early childhood services in Spain are now clearly located in the education system, with teaching as the main qualification, the 'early childhood education' stage is considered important in its own right. It is not viewed just as a preparation for the next primary stage. It is considered, instead, to be a separate and self-contained stage in education, with its own characteristics and intrinsic value (Balaguer, 1994).

A sophisticated outline for infant education has been set out by the Ministry of Education and Science (Ministerio de Educatión y Ciencia, 1989). It includes such aspects as identity and personal autonomy and physical and bodily expressiveness, as well as more conventional learning areas. It explains the pedagogic principles on which each curricular block is based, gives practice examples and makes suggestions about methods of evaluation.

Within this broad general framework, the emphasis is on local responsiveness. At each level – regional, commune or city – and at the level of the nursery itself and of group rooms within each nursery there is scope for initiatives. The safeguard is that any initiative must be explained in the documentation produced and systematically evaluated; all nurseries are required to produce such documentation and show evidence of evaluation. This local autonomy means that allowances can be made for language and culture. For instance, in the Catalan speaking areas of Spain, Catalan rather than Spanish is the medium of instruction, or else nurseries are bilingual, and Catalan culture is featured within the curriculum – its artists, writers and musicians. Most nursery age children in Barcelona, for example, would be familiar with the work of the painter Miro, and the Miro Foundation art museum puts on special events and arranges special admissions for these young children. Similarly, regional cooking is featured in the food children eat at nursery, and the cuisine itself is a matter of discussion in the curriculum.

Early childhood education is not compulsory, but, like education for older children, it is viewed as a social right, and the law places a duty on government to meet this right. Article 7 of the LOGSE states that while 'infant education shall be voluntary . . . public authorities shall guarantee the existence of a sufficient number of places to assure the schooling of those who request it'. Priority has been given to assuring a place for all children aged 3 to 6 years, and it may take time to ensure places for all children whose parents want them to attend: but the principle of a comprehensive service is part of the law.

The significance of these reforms has been described by Irene Balaguer (1994), a Spanish expert and leading reformer:

The reality of services for children under the age of 3 in Spain is rather complex. Not so long ago these services came under the auspices of various Ministries – Labour, Interior, Health or Culture – depending on the purpose of the service. Conceptually the services were aimed at assisting working women or underprivileged children. In some cases, this history is still influential. But starting in 1990, with the passing of LOGSE, a substantial change has occurred in how services for children under 3 are conceptualised. The education of very young children and their right to enjoy high quality service are new basic concepts . . . In almost all cases, this policy has meant an important transformation and a qualitative improvement in the existing services.

(p. 58)

Spain is at the early stages of a process of implementation. There are many problems, not least regional differences in implementation, inadequate funding, and priority given to services for children over 3 when provision for children under 3 is under-developed in many areas.

Yet despite these difficulties, the Spanish reforms are enormously important. A framework has been created within which a comprehensive, integrated and coherent early childhood service can emerge: the basics are there, if Spain is able and willing to build on them. The reform is based not only on the education system, but also on an education principle, that all children are capable of learning and can benefit from opportunities for learning. But if education is the main underlying concept, the reform is also based on the recognition of other needs and the inseparability of care and learning for young children. Fully implemented, the Spanish reform will entail a transformation of 'nursery education' away from a service for children over 3 to become a comprehensive service available to all children under and over 3, taking account, for example, of other needs such as care and support.

Finally, the Spanish reform is an example of vision put into practice. There was a strong movement for reform from the 1970s, which in turn drew inspiration from debates and policy initiatives earlier in the century, in particular just before the outbreak of the Civil War (which effectively blocked any developments for over thirty years). The whole education reform was the conclusion of five years of public discussion and experimentation, including government-supported experimental projects for those parts of the education system for which changes were proposed, including early childhood education. The spirit in which reform was approached is summed up in this introduction to the English translation of LOGSE:

Reform (was) proclaimed to be necessary, (but other reasons encouraged it to) be undertaken in a mature, serene and reflective way. Experience with more advanced countries has shown us that relevant changes require long periods of maturity and consensus from the educational community and society as a whole. This is even more the case when it is not a question of ephemeral, but indeed basic structures that must be firmly sustained for many decades . . . The conviction that a reform of this type, and the desire to organise the Spanish educational system until well into the next century could not lead to success unless support were gained from a large majority, gave rise to the widest possible debate on the subject, an essential and lasting agreement about basic objectives being its aim. This led, firstly, to embarking upon rigorous experimentation which would then make it possible for the educational community and society as a whole to discuss the matter at length.

(Ministerio de Educación y Ciencia, 1991, p. 10)

A clearer contrast to the approach to early childhood services by British government would be hard to imagine.

IN CONCLUSION

These examples are not put forward to be copied in detail. Systems cannot be simply transposed from one society to another; they are too firmly embedded in their own home soil. Like early childhood services everywhere, the systems in Denmark and Spain do not stand in splendid isolation, but are products of and meshed with a wide range of other historical, cultural, social and political features unique to their own societies.

But nor can they be ignored. They show that a comprehensive, integrated and coherent early childhood service can be turned from vision into practice, given sufficient commitment and will. They illustrate that there are different ways of putting vision into practice – there is no one right solution. Finally, they make clear the critical importance of sustained, reflective and inclusive debate about ends and means, values and principles, structures and relationships.

10

Footing the Bill

It is when it comes to money that visions most often meet the charge of being unrealistic. That's all very well, comes the sceptical cry, but who will pay? In this chapter we confront the issue. We consider what a comprehensive, integrated and coherent early childhood service for children aged 0–6 might cost – but also what its off-setting benefits might be. We discuss how the costs might be distributed – in short, who would pay. Finally, as the last stage in the exercise, we consider the mechanisms for distributing the public funding element.

We hope to convince that the sort of service we advocate is a good investment in social, educational and economic terms, bringing returns to children, families, employers, the government and society as a whole. But we also recognise that ultimately the whole issue hinges on political considerations: what importance is attached to the upbringing of young children and supporting their families? What priority is given to different values, for example choice as opposed to social cohesion? What should be the balance between private consumption and public expenditure, between personal tax cuts and public investment?

WHAT WOULD OUR SERVICE COST?

Two recent exercises have attempted to cost an improved and expanded system of early childhood services. Based on 1989/90 costs, Bronwen Cohen and Neil Fraser (1991) estimate that a major development of early childhood services would have running costs ranging from £3.15 billion to £7.2 billion per annum. In addition, they estimate that to expand the existing system would require additional capital costs ranging from £1.23 billion to £2.84 billion and training costs, for the many extra staff needed, between £1.1 billion and £2.9 billion. More recently, using 1995 prices, Sally Holtermann (1995) concludes that expenditure to provide a good quality early childhood service that met parental demand would cost between £4.3 and £4.4 billion, in addition to current expenditure on education for 3 and 4 year olds.

The devil of course is in the detail. Costings for hypothetical services depend on a combination of inputs: the concept of the service (who is it for? what is it for?), what items are covered in the cost calculations (as well as running costs, do the figures include capital costs and training and other infrastructure costs?) and the nature of various assumptions, not least about demand. Our concept of an early childhood service is based on the age range of 0–6. Holtermann and Cohen and Fraser assume that 5 will continue to be the compulsory school starting age, and the figures given above from the two reports are for services for children under 5 (although both reports also give separate and additional costings for providing 'outside school hours care' for children aged 5–11 years). Other costing exercises, not dealt with here, confine themselves to 'pre-school education for 3 and 4 year olds' (National Commission on Education, 1993; Ball, 1994). Like us (see Chapter 11) Cohen and Fraser assume paid parental leave; unlike us, they assume a low flat-rate payment and a relatively short period of 3 or 6 months. Holtermann makes assumptions about overall demand, and preference between different types of service, based on local surveys of parental preferences and a 1990 national survey (Meltzer, 1994). By contrast, Cohen and Fraser make three estimates of cost based on three different assumptions of coverage. Cohen and Fraser have separate costings for training and capital costs; Holtermann includes an element for capital costs and for the support and development of private sector services, but nothing specifically on training.

Finally, while the cost estimates of both Holtermann and Cohen and Fraser are based on providing care and education, both assume a continuing degree of division between 'day care' and 'education' services; they work within the existing system. This is most apparent in their staffing cost estimates, which are based on existing patterns of staffing, with teachers working with 3 and 4 year olds in school and less qualified workers (e.g. nursery nurses) mainly or wholly working with other children (although Holtermann bases her cost estimates on improved levels of pay for existing workers). We assume for our early childhood service a restructured workforce, with most workers having a new early childhood teacher qualification.

Another approach to costs is to consider the experience of another country with a service similar in concept and meeting a high proportion of demand. A good example is Denmark, which we have already described. To recap, Denmark has an integrated and coherent early childhood service, including an integrated staffing system with most staff having a level of training similar to what we are advocating. Provision is made for about half of all children under 3 and for nearly 80 per cent of children aged 3–6, and although there is still some unmet demand (expressed in waiting lists), at present this has fallen to a low level.

Denmark is the only country in Europe which can supply up-to-date and comprehensive data on running costs for services for children aged 0–6 years. In 1994, these costs were DKK10.93 billion. At 1994 exchange rates this comes to about £1.12 billion for a country whose population is only 10 per cent of Britain's (in other words, Danish expenditure is equivalent to over £10 billion in the UK) (EC Childcare Network, 1995).

Fluctuating exchange rates and different price levels make such direct comparisons of limited value. An alternative approach is to look at costs as a proportion of GDP. On this basis, Danish expenditure comes to about 1.2 per cent of gross domestic product. Applied to the UK, this would come to about £8 billion. There are, however, details that need to be taken into account.

The figures for Denmark, and the £8 billion figure for the UK, do not include capital costs or infrastructure costs, in particular training. Both of these costs would be relatively higher during a period of expansion, when building up from a low base. Both of these costs also depend on standards, so that the basic 3.5-year post-18 training in Denmark will be considerably more expensive than the 2-year post-16 nursery nurse training in the UK (the basis, for example, of a large part of Cohen and Fraser's training cost estimates).

The Danish figure also does not include an element for the cost of parental leave benefits. This will have increased substantially in Denmark in 1994, with the improvement in their leave scheme introduced in that year which is paid at a substantially higher level than the payment assumed by Cohen and Fraser in their estimate of parental leave costs. It is also too soon to know whether this new scheme has produced any off-setting savings on services for children under 3 or whether places 'released' by fewer children under 12 months attending services have simply been used to provide higher coverage for older children.

Denmark provides some other relevant cost lessons. The Danish system, and its costs, are the product of 30 years of service development, including not only more provision but major improvements over time in the levels of staff training and pay. They are also the product of changing demand, not least as maternal employment has increased; in the early 1960s, when the system began to expand, it is unlikely that there would have been demand for 50 per cent of children under 3.

Any British early childhood service would develop over time, as would the costs. Even with all the cash and commitment in the world, it is inconceivable that a good system could be in place next year or even in five years. Moreover, as the system was developing, there is likely to be continuing change in demand, as more mothers join fathers in the labour market, as other circumstances vary (for example, birth rates and levels of unemployment) and also because parents' expectations of services would change as more became available. In short, we need to consider costs in the context of a dynamic and evolutionary system and changing family circumstances, needs and preferences.

Where does this leave us in relation to the cost of our early childhood service? We have avoided making an estimate of the final cost of a fully implemented system; as we have suggested, this may be of limited use because estimates must be based on assumptions which may well prove unfounded. Instead, we think it is more useful to put forward a medium-term target for expenditure on early childhood services for children aged 0–6, to be reached within ten years of beginning the development of a comprehensive, integrated and coherent early childhood service. In the longer term, the expenditure level might well be higher, so this ten-year target figure should be regarded as an interim figure, but sufficient to ensure the achievement of substantial progress.

Considering the British cost estimates and the experience of Denmark, we think that this target might be around 1.2 per cent of GDP, or about £8 billion per annum (GDP at current prices in 1994 was £669 billion (Central Statistical Office, 1995b, Table 2.1)); this would include an element for capital costs and infrastructure costs, including training, but excludes the cost of payments to parents on parental leave which would be separately funded.

WHAT RETURNS WOULD THERE BE?

As well as costing exercises, there have been various attempts to quantify the benefits to be derived from early childhood services. These have taken two forms. British exercises have focused on the various economic benefits derived from the effect of 'childcare services' on women's labour market participation. The argument has been that more services would enable more employment among women with children (but also more employment generally among women due to increased employment opportunities in early childhood services themselves), which would increase income for families and for the Exchequer. At least two studies have concluded that public expenditure on services would be exceeded, in the long term, by increased public revenue, so that public investment in services would more than pay for itself (Cohen and Fraser, 1991; Holtermann, 1992); but a more recent study concludes that the employment effect, and therefore the return to the Exchequer, will be smaller than expected and not cover public expenditure on services (Duncan *et al.*, 1995).

A lot of research has documented the developmental and educational benefits for children of early childhood education. The results of this work led the National Commission on Education (1993) to conclude that 'high quality provision [of early years care and education] was of long-term value both for individuals and society in general'; this conclusion has been echoed in a report from the Royal Society of Arts: 'good pre-school education leads to immediate and lasting social and educational benefits – especially for those from disadvantaged backgrounds' (Ball, 1994, p. 6). One famous US study has looked very specifically at the long-term economic returns, concluding that over the lifetimes of the participants in the study, the pre-school programme returned to the public an estimated $7.16 for every dollar invested (Schweinhart and Weikart, 1993).

These studies seeking to quantify benefits in economic terms generate their own particular debates. The benefits from increased employment depend on a wide range of assumptions, most of which can be questioned. Controversy arises around the so-called 'deadweight' effect, where extra public expenditure does not create new employment but simply reduces the costs of already employed parents; in other words, it is counter-argued that extra public expenditure produces fewer economic gains from increased employment, but simply substitutes for private expenditure on services by already employed parents. The generalisability of results from a study of disadvantaged children in the USA has also been queried (Woodhead, 1988).

Over and above this, studies of the economic returns from early childhood services take a narrow perspective. Typically, they focus on one or two potential benefits, usually concerning employment and income. At best they may recognise other benefits, but do not incorporate them into the detailed cost-benefit equation. The study by Cohen and Fraser is more wide-ranging than most, yet it has to admit its limitations in a section headed 'benefits for children':

> We have already discussed the prospects that more childcare can reduce poverty amongst children through the effect on household incomes of improving chances for mothers to take paid employment. But there are other potential gains via educational (human capital) effects. These benefits are among the most difficult aspects of pre-school childcare to quantify for a cost-benefit analysis. In the case of disadvantaged children US research has shown considerable benefits from investment in pre-school provision, including substantial savings in the cost of remedial provision, unemployment benefit and prisons. However, this research related to a particular educational and family context and we have not attempted to undertake a similar analysis here.
>
> (Cohen and Fraser, 1991, p. 121)

A more recent study which offers an 'economic analysis of alternative strategies for subsidising childcare in the UK', recognises in passing that 'pre-school education' may have benefits for children. But because its focus is 'the labour market behaviour of women with pre-school children', methods of subsidy are assessed in terms of their consequences for women's labour market activity (Duncan, Giles and Webb, 1995).

To say that cost-benefit studies are often narrow is not to be critical of those who do them. The particular interest of a researcher may legitimately be a particular area of potential benefit. Economists are not alone in taking a narrow and fragmented view of early childhood services, focusing on one function (e.g. care or education) for particular groups of children (e.g. children with employed parents, 3 and 4 year olds). Even if a researcher wants to take a broader view of economic benefits, this ambition may be constrained by the limitations of the available data; quantifying benefits becomes more problematic for this reason when moving beyond labour supply and income issues. Such limitations can be appreciated and the results can be useful – if the wider picture, and other potential benefits, are recognised.

The danger comes, however, when limited studies focusing on one area of benefit reinforce a narrow and fragmented approach to early childhood services; and if what is more readily quantifiable gives undue prominence to just one of many potential benefits, distracting attention from a more rounded view of the role and potential benefits of early childhood services.

We argued in Chapter 1 that our concept of a comprehensive, integrated and coherent early childhood service can provide multiple benefits to a wide range of groups. Good services can benefit children's development and, more broadly, their quality of life. Good services can not only enable more mothers to enter or remain in employment, but can also offer them more choice in employment – and it is important to remember that a strategy adopted by many employed mothers with young children at present is to work short part-time hours, often at weekends, evenings or nights, to fit their work around limited informal care arrangements. Good services can also produce another employment-related benefit; together with other measures (e.g. leave arrangements and workplace 'family friendly' policies) they can benefit employed parents (fathers and mothers) and children by helping parents to reconcile employment with the upbringing of children. This support function of services for employed parents is, in our view, critical and overlooked in economic studies which simply focus on the effect of services on labour market participation.

Good services can benefit families where there are parents who are not employed. They can enable non-employed parents to train and improve their employment prospects. They can provide support, in a variety of ways, both for families in general and in a more specialised way for those families which are particularly stressed and distressed. Last but not least, the benefits of good services can go beyond children, parents and families – to local communities, to employers and to society as a whole.

A wide-ranging approach to the potential benefits of early childhood services was taken by the Working Party on Early Childhood Care and Education set up by the New Zealand Government in 1989 as part of the process of radical reform of early childhood services undertaken in the late 1980s and early 1990s (another example of a country which has worked to put a vision of a comprehensive, integrated and coherent early childhood service into practice). 'Early childhood care and education', the Working Group's remit, was defined as including 'all formal state and independent arrangements for the care and education of infants up to the age of six'. Their report, *Education to be More*, played a critical role in shaping subsequent reforms, and remains one of the most important reports on early childhood services ever written (Working Party on Early Childhood Care and Education, 1988).

Among its tasks, the Working Group had to make recommendations on 'the costs and benefits of early childhood care and education services to children, parents, providers, employers and society'. Adopting the concept of an integrated early childhood service for children aged 0–6, the Working Group set out the benefits of such a service to different groups. We reproduce their summary of this exercise here in Fig. 2; in our view, it provides a model approach to approaching the issue of benefits.

One of the strengths of the New Zealand Working Group report is the clear appreciation that the potential benefits of early childhood services go beyond children, parents and families.

We believe that the overall benefits to society are considerable from early

Benefits to society

- Improvements to the social fabric: children start their schooling on a sound foundation; parents get to play a fuller role; families are supported; employers get regular attendance.
- The creation of networks within the social structure which helps bind communities together in times of crisis.

Benefits to children

- Children have time out from intensive one-to-one relationships with parents.
- Children can make friends with peers and other adults.
- Children can be nurtured by other social 'parents' and so build up an 'assurance policy' for times of crisis.
- Children can find out that parent substitutes have other values and ways of expressing authority.
- Children can fulfil themselves in different ways and so enhance their self-esteem.
- Children learn a wider repertoire of social skills.
- Children in child-centred settings are given the chance to be children – and to play, have fun and learn.
- Children construct more ideas through working at play.
- Children can get more opportunities to develop their physical motor skills.
- Children can get different/additional opportunities for learning tikanga Maori.
- The benefits to children of mothers who are not overburdened should not be overlooked . . .

Benefits to parents

- Women (the primary caregivers) get the choice to join the labour force . . . or to control their lives in other ways.
- Time out from child-rearing; to give to other family members; to have rest and recreation; to do community work; to support friends and wider family . . .
- Knowledge gained from contact with staff and other parents on: parenting; management of children, adults and resources; learning and teaching of young children (and adults); community work.
- Formation of a support network . . .
- Sense of empowerment and confidence . . .
- Opportunity for developing/maintaining Maori and Pacific Island languages and cultures.

Benefits for the family

- A liveable income for families who use childcare for employment purposes as well as for their children's care and education.
- Parenting skills shared amongst parents.
- The siblings 'catch' some of the developmental benefits of care and education . . .
- More confident, relaxed and/or fulfilled parents who then have fewer angry interactions.
- Community networks for parents.

Benefits for providers

- A profit (but only to a very few commercial centres).
- The satisfaction of contributing to a publicly valued service.
- The learning of management skills . . .
- Increased knowledge of child development.
- Access to government grants.

Benefits for employers

- Continuity of work from employees who return after parental leave.
- Regular work-attendance habits by parents who have their children in reliable early childhood services.

Figure 2. Benefits of early childhood care and education services

Source: Appendix 2 of the Report of the New Zealand Early Childhood Care and Education Working Group (1988)

childhood care and education. Many of the gains just mentioned are enjoyed by people outside the immediate circle of the child and family, and both the economic and social benefits can enrich the community. At a basic level, a major benefit from early care and education is the preservation and passing on of our culture . . . good early childhood care and education improves the efficiency and effectiveness of this process.

Without an enriching and empowering environment for our children and their parents . . . society is impoverished and we all suffer. Early childhood care and education is education to be more: for children, families . . . and society to be more than they are now.

(p.13)

Like the New Zealand Working Group, we believe that the potential benefits of early childhood services are wide-ranging and pervasive for young children and their parents – but also for others. These potential benefits will only be fully realised in a comprehensive, integrated and coherent early childhood service that recognises its broad purpose and its many stakeholders and can be genuinely multi-functional and flexible. Whether or not these benefits can ever be fully quantified seems to us unlikely, although a wider assessment of benefits than we currently have must surely be feasible. In the meantime, there is a strong prima facie case that, for a multitude of reasons, early childhood services represent good value for money.

WHO PAYS THE BILL?

Elsewhere in Europe

So far we have discussed expenditure on services and considered who benefits from them and in what way. We have concluded that the benefits are numerous and widespread, though difficult to quantify comprehensively; and that the cost of a good comprehensive, integrated and coherent early childhood service will be substantial. This brings us inevitably to the crux of the issue: who pays for the service?

First, though, it may be useful to consider how other European countries allocate the costs of their services for children aged 0 to 6. What follows is a brief overview of a complex subject. It draws on a recent report in which fuller information can be found (EC Childcare Network, 1995).

Publicly funded services for children under 6 in Europe are found in two service systems – welfare and education. The funding of services differs between these systems. Services in the education system (mainly nursery schooling, but in the Netherlands, Ireland and the UK, early admission to primary school) are entirely publicly funded through education budgets; parents pay nothing (except for additional services like school meals). As most mainland European countries with nursery education systems are moving towards, or have already achieved, universal full-time nursery education provision for 3–6 year olds, this is a significant item of provision within total national expenditure on early childhood services.

Some countries have services divided between the education and welfare systems. Others (notably the Nordic countries and Germany) have all services for children under 6 within the welfare system; in these cases, widespread provision is made for children aged 3 to 6, but within kindergartens or similar non-school services. Publicly funded kindergartens and other welfare system services (e.g. day nurseries, organised childminding) receive most of their funding from public sources; but, unlike the education system, it is usual for parents to make a contribution. Parental contributions vary according to family income and other circumstances (for example, number of children); they range from 12 per cent (Italy) to 28 per cent (France) of total service costs, with 15–25 per cent being most common. To take the example of Denmark, national regulations specify that parental contributions should never come to more than 30 per cent of total costs; but when account is taken of various reductions (for example, for low income families or families with more than one child in a service), the overall contribution of parents reduces to 21 per cent of total costs.

The situation needs to be qualified in two ways. First, in most countries (essentially the non-Nordic states), many parents do not have access to publicly funded services for children under 3 and out-of-school services for times when children are not at nursery school or kindergarten. In these cases, parents must pay for private, unsubsidised services, either formal or informal. Second, in a number of countries, parents' outgoings may be subsidised through tax relief or some other form of public allowance; these subsidies paid to parents (rather than services) cover less than half the costs.

Overall, therefore, the cost of services is very largely divided between parents and public sources, the balance varying between countries and between services. In every country, there will also be some individual employers who provide some form of subsidy for the service costs incurred by their employees. This subsidy can take a variety of forms – provision of a subsidised service, sponsoring places in community-based services, vouchers or some other form of direct cash subsidy, assistance in finding services. In only two countries, however, do employers pay a substantial proportion of costs.

In France, all employers make a compulsory payment into regional family allowance funds. These funds are used to pay cash benefits to families with children and to provide subsidies to early childhood services within the welfare system; in 1993, for example, they contributed 24 per cent towards the costs of services for children under 3, compared to 34 per cent from local authorities, 12 per cent from regional authorities and 28 per cent from parents. Employers' contributions are not earmarked for services for their own employees or even for services exclusively for employed parents. Services subsidised by family allowance funds are used by non-employed parents; employers' payments, therefore, are essentially a contribution to the general public expenditure on early childhood services.

The Netherlands has recently introduced a policy which encourages individual employers to fund places for members of their own workforce; unlike France, employer contributions are voluntary and earmarked to subsidise their own employees. Under the Stimulative Programme on Childcare, introduced in 1990, places in newly created services receive a central government grant covering less than half the cost. The remaining costs are split between parents and either local authorities or individual employers. It is government policy to encourage a large proportion of the new places to be 'bought' by employers, and by the end of 1992 employers subsidised over half of the new places created within the Stimulative Programme.

A proposal for a British early childhood service

Having set this European context, how would we allocate the costs of the comprehensive, integrated and coherent early childhood service that we envision? We would divide them between society (through public funding) and parents (through parental contributions). A portion of attendance time by children under and over 3 would be free of charge to parents and therefore entirely publicly funded. This free attendance time might eventually be equivalent to full-time school hours (about 1,200 hours a year), but could be less initially as the system was built up. This would ensure coherence in funding and cost to parents *throughout* the early childhood system and *between* the early childhood system and compulsory schooling; it would replace the present lack of coherence arising from some under-fives getting free schooling in the education system and the parents of other young children having to pay for part or all of the services they use in the welfare system.

For children attending for longer hours, funding for the additional hours would come from a mixture of public funding and parent contributions adjusted to take account of family income, family size and other relevant circumstances. No family would pay more than a specified proportion of total household income. This arrangement would ensure affordability, by recognising income and other differences in families' ability to pay. The needs of families with a non-employed parent would be recognised, with services available to young children and their non-employed parents: but the free attendance time should mean that these families do not have to pay for using the service. The means-tested contribution would be targeted to maximise contributions from high income families with two full-time employed parents, who would probably use the service for the longest hours: but there would still be some subsidy, recognising the entitlement of each child to services in her own right, independent of parental resources, and some element of horizontal redistribution even for higher income parents (the same principle that applies to the funding of compulsory education).

Overall, we would expect parental contributions to cover, as in the rest of Europe, less than 30 per cent of the total costs, perhaps, as in Denmark, around 20 per cent. The final figure and the precise details of parental contributions, however, should not be decided in a vacuum. They should be determined within the context of broader decisions concerning support for childhood and parenthood – what share of national resources should be allocated to investment in early childhood, how far society should subsidise the direct and indirect costs of parenthood and the degree of horizontal redistribution of resources between men and women bringing up children and those who are not.

Public expenditure

This funding formula, and the affordable and accessible services it will assure, requires substantial public funding. This is an inevitable conclusion. No country has developed extensive, accessible and good quality early childhood services, with a well-trained and properly paid workforce, without substantial public investment. Public funding is a necessary condition for equal access to good quality services. Ensuring access to good quality services cannot be left to the private market and parents' ability to pay, any more than access to schools or health services – not least in a society where, as already noted, nearly two-thirds of people live in households where income is less than the average, where one in three children now live in poverty and where inequalities in income have been growing in recent years rather than diminishing.

Public funding is not only a necessity for access. It is a public recognition of the rights of children, as citizens, to a share of national resources, and the social importance of parenting. A publicly funded early childhood service does not deny the primary responsibility and interest of parents in children and their upbringing. It does, however, acknowledge that there is also a substantial public interest in children and their upbringing, and consequently some public responsibility. A publicly funded early childhood service is not a 'takeover' from parents, but a practical and effective way of supporting parents in bringing up children and sharing both the costs and the care involved in this essential work. It represents an investment in a vital part of the economic and social infrastructure of a modern society, which will bring benefits not only to children and parents, but also to employers, local communities and society as a whole.

From where would this public funding come? We think that it should be a call on the education budget. This follows from placing responsibility for early childhood services with national and local education authorities. We have suggested total expenditure at the end of ten years running at about 1.2 per cent of current GDP; if parental contributions to running costs accounted for about 20 per cent of this expenditure, then total public expenditure would come to just under 1 per cent of GDP, or around £6.5 billion at current prices.

This sum for public expenditure needs to be put into perspective. Total current expenditure on all levels of the education system, from nursery education through to tertiary education, was 5.3 per cent of GDP in 1991 (OECD, 1994, Table P1). So, 1 per cent of GDP represents less than a fifth of public expenditure on education for an age range, 0–6 years, covering a third of childhood. In arguing that expenditure should come from the education budget, we assume that this budget will increase to take account of the expanding service, so that funding an early childhood service will not be at the expense of other parts of the education system.

Nor would it all be new money. Some public money is already spent on services for children aged 0–6. For example, English and Welsh local authorities calculated the costs of education services for children under 5 running to £1.2 billion in 1993/94 (Audit Commission, 1995). Current public expenditure for the schooling of 5 year olds is probably around £1 billion (current expenditure on all primary schooling was £5.3 billion in England in 1993/94). Within the welfare system, some public money is spent on providing 'day care' for a small proportion of children aged 0–5. Unfortunately, there is no official figure for total public spending on all early childhood services throughout the UK for children aged 0–6, but on the basis of the figures given above the sum is likely to be around £2–2.5 billion. So, we are looking at building on some existing foundations, not starting from scratch.

We are also talking about building up expenditure to our target figure over a ten-year period, not overnight. Even in the shorter term, the capacity to support increased public expenditure on early childhood services is considerable. Assuming a 2.5 per cent growth rate, a public borrowing level that keeps the national debt at its current proportional level and no tax cuts in the 1995 or subsequent budgets, by 1997/98 the Government could have 312 billion extra for spending, while 'the following year it would have a good £18 billion – and thereafter, the OECD projects, the numbers get even larger' (Hutton, 1995b).

Of course, early childhood services are not the only part of our economic and social infrastructure that need more investment. But over a ten-year period, there should be room for the type of investment we are calling for, as well as investment in other important areas. The issue is not that we cannot afford decent early childhood services. The issue is choices about how we spend money – between consumption or investment, and between tax cuts or spending on services and other policies to support young children and their families.

Employers

We would not expect employers, individually or collectively, to fund the service directly, although they will do so indirectly through the existing system of corporate taxation. An early childhood service will provide care for children while parents are at work, and so help ensure an adequate labour supply to the benefit of employers. But to expect all employers to make a special payment, through some earmarked levy, towards the cost of the early childhood service on this count would only be justifiable if they were also expected to make special payments towards the costs of the many other services that contribute towards ensuring labour supply – public transport, roads, schools, day care centres for elderly people and so on. In practice these services, like services for young children, meet a range of needs, of which labour supply is only one. Expecting employers to make special contributions for each one would be not only cumbersome, but open up many other difficult questions: in particular, what proportion of costs should employers pay for a service used by many parents who are not employed and providing not only care but a wide range of other functions? Making employers pay an additional and earmarked levy for early childhood services also runs contrary to the trend to reduce 'non-wage labour costs', in order to improve competitiveness, since in effect it would shift the funding of public services away from the general tax base and onto the production costs of goods and services.

The alternative to compulsory employer contributions is to leave funding decisions to individual employers. This seems to us to be an even more unsatisfactory basis for funding an early childhood service than compulsory employer funding (for a fuller discussion of the case against employer funding of early childhood services, see Moss, 1992). Indeed, it would only be justified if the sole function of early childhood services was regarded as ensuring an adequate labour supply; in that case, it might be possible to argue that each employer should decide whether to subsidise costs according to labour force needs. But everything we have argued for in this book rejects such a narrow concept of early childhood services; they should be multi-functional and concerned to meet the needs of many groups, not just employers. A system in which a child's access to good services can depend on the value to an employer of her parent and the situation in the local labour market must be totally unacceptable, and makes a nonsense of any aspiration to equal access.

This is not a criticism of the employers who have become involved with early childhood services in recent years, but a criticism, once again, of a failure of national policy. Few people, we believe, think that individual employer funding is defensible in principle. The fact that it has been justifiable in practice, on the grounds that it is better than doing nothing, is an indictment of society and government, not concerned employers.

Allocating public funds

The question of how public funding will be allocated comes, we believe, logically at the end of a long chain of discussion and decisions – after defining the concept of service to be funded, after deciding how it will be delivered, and after deciding on allocation of costs. Crudely, there are two options for public funding: to subsidise services directly or to subsidise parents. Subsidising parents can be done in various ways including tax relief, disregarding costs in determining welfare benefits and vouchers, as proposed by the government for provision of services for 4 year olds.

There are two apparent advantages of subsidising parents directly. First, it removes an element of inequality in current funding, whereby some parents get access to publicly funded services (for example, if they live in an area with nursery education provision) while others do not (for example, if they have to rely on a fee-charging playgroup). However, the element of inequality should reduce under a system of service subsidy as more subsidised services become available; the inequality case is therefore, at best, a transitional one.

Second, subsidising parents may increase choice in that parents can decide where to use the subsidy (subject to any conditions placed on use, for example that the service used should be approved by some regulatory authority or that there should be an invoice to show expenditure incurred). Underlying the parent subsidy approach is the view that it supports the development of a free market in services and empowers parents to participate fully in that market. For its proponents, this is one of the main attractions of vouchers.

Different types of objections are put forward to vouchers. If the voucher is set at too low a price, it may undermine services which are more costly because they have better staffing or other standards. Similarly, if set too low, then lower income families will remain constrained in the services they can use, because they will be less able to afford to 'top up' the public subsidy from their own resources; inequalities will remain and choice be undermined. Another argument of opponents of vouchers (or similar subsidies) is that, by themselves, they provide no new places.

Our opposition to vouchers (and other forms of direct parent subsidies) is different and more fundamental. While recognising that choice is an important value, we do not regard it as the only, or indeed the pre-eminent, value to be considered in the development of early childhood services. For example, we would place a high value on social cohesion and equality of access to services. Social cohesion implies creating services that are flexible enough to satisfy the needs of local communities and which encourage and support the development of local networks, of children and adults; in short, rather than having many different services, each offering to meet a limited range of needs for particular groups of families, we would want to see fewer but more flexible, multi-functional services providing for a wide cross-section of children and parents – children with and without disabilities, 1 year olds and 4 year olds, employed parents and non-employed parents and so on. Social cohesion also means that all services are open to and accept all children and parents; too great an emphasis on choice risks some services, in high demand, choosing who they take. In this situation, it is easy to end up perpetuating the current situation of separate stigmatised services for children and families deemed to be 'in need'.

We also question the model of a free market in services. We believe that there is a need for a degree of local planning of services to encourage services that are community-based, multi-functional and flexible, and so are able to respond to local needs, support local communities and promote social cohesion: left to its own devices, the market will not necessarily create such services, indeed may produce services that have quite the opposite effect. We also want a system that fosters co-operation between services, rather than competition. Finally, the concept of markets is more problematic when it comes to services for children, especially very young children, who are unable to be active consumers; they lack the resources, information or influence to choose what is best for themselves. No one has come up with, or is likely to come up with, a better alternative than parents assuming the main responsibility for making choices for their children. But should matters be left entirely to parents? We would argue that society has some right to insist on certain requirements in the child's best interest – that, after all, is why the government has introduced a National Curriculum into the school system and why there is a long tradition of requiring schools to have a well-trained workforce.

We want to give parents balanced choice, by which we mean some choice *between* different services and some choice *within* the individual service they and their children use, through the responsiveness and flexibility of that service. We are also seeking some balance between choice and other values and needs. We believe that both types of balance are best achieved through a funding system attached to services, which makes funding conditional on certain requirements being met by those services, requirements that are likely to be more demanding than regulatory conditions attached to vouchers. Our concept of a comprehensive, integrated and coherent early childhood service, flexible, multi-functional and guaranteeing equal access to good quality services for all children and parents can best be assured through a system of subsidising services which uses the subsidy mechanism to shape individual services and the overall service system to the required ends. A voucher system is similarly manipulative – but shapes services to other ends.

11

From Vision to Reality

In our first chapter, we set out a vision of a comprehensive, integrated and coherent early childhood service. We have seen examples of how some countries, and some local authorities and individual services in Britain, have already begun to work on putting this vision into practice. In the last chapter we discussed the parameters of costing. How should we proceed to make the vision a reality for the whole of our country? In this chapter, we put forward ten specific proposals, for how we might proceed.

Four points should be made by way of introduction. First, any process of implementation is bound to take time. We suggest below a ten-year implementation or transition period, but this period could probably be reduced or lengthened by two or three years. As we indicated in the last chapter, this is partly a matter of resources. A substantial increase in public funding is required and this increase cannot be found overnight; it will need to be built up gradually. But even if the extra funds were immediately available, it would take time to implement change. New training courses will need to be developed. Additional staff will need to be recruited and trained. New administrative and infrastructure arrangements must be put in place. New buildings will be required and many existing buildings renovated.

Second, the process of implementation is a total package. Change in one area is likely to be ineffective if undertaken in isolation. Each of the steps proposed supports and depends on the others. Each is a necessary but not sufficient condition.

Third, the reform is fundamental and sweeping. Regular monitoring and review are therefore critical. Problems need to be identified and rectified. It is also important to ensure that the new early childhood service is responding to changing needs and circumstances, in families, employment and local communities.

The same approach, of regular monitoring and review, is needed at the level of individual services. There is a role here for external scrutiny and input, but monitoring and review should be an integral part of the work of each service itself. We want to see services which have a high degree of autonomy, enable the active participation of all stakeholders and accept a high level of responsibility for defining, developing and reviewing the quality of their own work. This means a well-educated, well-supported and self-confident workforce, with the ability and time to be reflective about their work; the empowerment of parents to play a major role in the life and management of services; opening out services to their local communities, not least through each service emphasising public documentation of practice; and, last but not least, recognising the right of children to be listened to and to play a part in decisions that affect them.

Finally, the reform and its implementation, and the developing early childhood service, should be complemented by public discussion about early childhood services and childhood. That discussion needs to be continuous; to take place nationally and locally; and to involve a wide cross-section of society, from politicians to ordinary citizens. In particular, it needs to include and to be informed by children themselves and knowledge of their everyday lives and experiences.

The need for public discussion and how it might be achieved have been considered by Gunilla Dahlberg and Gunnar Åsén (1994), two Swedish researchers, particularly as a means to define quality:

How quality in early childhood education and care is defined and evaluated will be a concern not only for politicians, experts, administrators and professionals, but will also be a matter for the broader citizenry . . . It becomes important to create forums or arenas for discussion and reflection where people can engage as citizens with devotion and visions . . . Within these arenas a lively dialogue can take place in which early childhood education and care are placed within a larger societal context and where questions concerning children's position are made vivid . . . The creation of forums for a locally-based public discussion, with the participation of different groups, is vital to this process. Examples of the development of reflexive discourse in early childhood and other services are the growth in recent years in Sweden of numerous arenas or 'plazas'. In these plazas politicians, administrators, teachers and other representatives come together to discuss different aspects of early childhood education. Some plazas focus on the pedagogical work being done at the level of local services, while others focus on questions and problems related to the responsibilities of the community, regional or national level. The purpose is to establish a dialogue, characterised by debate, confrontation and exchange of experience. The plaza should not be seen primarily as the place for traders, but as the place for a dialogue between independent citizens. It is the symbol of a vibrant democracy.

(pp. 166–7)

Britain needs to evolve its own ways of stimulating debate, drawing on its own conditions, traditions and institutions. But however it is done, that concept of a lively, democratic, reflective debate is critical. It will provide a basis for making good decisions, it will stimulate a wider discourse about childhood and the needs of children, it will place early childhood services within a wider context and, by encouraging widespread participation and increased awareness and understanding, it will increase societal legitimacy for early childhood services.

TEN STEPS TO A COMPREHENSIVE, INTEGRATED AND COHERENT EARLY CHILDHOOD SERVICE

1. An early childhood services policy

The government will prepare a White Paper, containing a policy statement on early childhood services. The statement will specify the scope, objectives and overall concept of the new service and set out the principles governing its development and operation. This will include: defining the early childhood service as the first stage of the education system, for children from 0 to 6 years, with responsibility for providing not only opportunities for learning, but also care, socialisation, health and support; and establishing that the service will be comprehensive, integrated, coherent and accessible to all children and parents who wish to use it.

The White Paper will also include a programme for implementation of the policy over a specified transitional period. As well as establishing priorities and setting targets, the programme will set out a framework for implementation, covering the following items.

2. Legislation

There will be new education legislation – the Early Childhood Services Act. This legislation will:

- define the 'early childhood service' as the first and separate stage of the education system;
- specify its objectives in terms of age group and functions;
- amend the compulsory school starting age to 6 years;
- place a duty on local authorities to provide access to this service for all parents wanting it (although the implementation of this duty will not be immediate, but subject to a timetable set by the Secretary of State for Education and her counterparts in the Northern Ireland, Scottish and Welsh Offices);
- require the Secretary of State to establish common guidelines for parents' contributions to the cost of services;
- place a duty on local authorities to prepare early childhood services plans;
- place a duty on local authorities and central government to review every 3 years all provision in the early childhood service and progress made in implementing the early childhood services plan;
- place a duty on local authorities and central government to establish a

comprehensive, integrated and coherent system for regular monitoring of the supply, use, staffing and costs of services and a common system of standards and regulation for all services;

• require all individual publicly funded early childhood services to establish a management committee consisting of stakeholder representation (i.e. parents, staff, local community), with responsibility for budgets, staffing and quality in their service;

• identify a single locus of responsibility for the early childhood service at local and national level.

This legislation will replace the Section 19 review duty (which applies only to local authorities and 'day care' services) and Part X of the Children Act. The duty in Part III of the Children Act for local authorities to provide 'day care' services for children 'in need' will be amended to place a duty on local authorities to provide 'appropriate early childhood services'. This will guarantee continued priority access to services for this group of children, with the added advantages that the duty will extend beyond 'day care' services to the whole range of 'early childhood services', and provision will have to be 'appropriate'; for example, ensuring services used have adequate support, staffing, training and other resources.

3. Administrative responsibility

Responsibility for the early childhood service at national level will be transferred to the Department for Education in England, and to the Education Divisions of the Scottish, Welsh and Northern Ireland Offices.

Because the early childhood service will be the first stage of the education system, local responsibility will be transferred to the local education authority, unless an individual local authority wishes to make a case for an alternative arrangement and can demonstrate to the Secretary of State that the responsibilities of the early childhood service can be adequately met under the alternative arrangement.

For the ten-year transition period, a separate 'early childhood service unit' will be established in the Department for Education in England, the Education Divisions of the Scottish, Welsh and Northern Ireland Offices and local education authorities, to plan, support and review service development; this task will include allocation of public funds.

4. Training and employment conditions

Over the 10-year transition period, there will be a major reform of staffing. A new qualification of 'early childhood teacher', to the same level as other forms of teacher training, will be introduced during this period. The training will qualify 'early childhood teachers' to work across the early childhood service, i.e. from 0 to 6 years. Early childhood teachers will not be qualified to work in other stages of the education system (and vice versa), but conversion courses will be readily available.

During the transition period, particular attention will be paid to enabling existing workers (teachers, nursery nurses, playgroup staff, family day carers) to take special training schemes to convert to the new qualification. These special training schemes will accredit existing qualifications and experience. They will also allow existing workers to take some training modules if they do not wish to pursue the full 'early childhood teacher' qualification.

The objective will be that 60 per cent of paid workers in publicly-funded centre-based services have this new 'early childhood teacher' qualification, although the level reached by the end of the transition period may be rather lower. It will be necessary to determine a target for qualification levels among family day carers, who will provide an important part of the early childhood service especially for younger children. We suggest this target might be 60 per cent of publicly funded family day carers having a qualification at NVQ level 3 or higher (including the new 'early childhood teacher' qualification), although again the level achieved by the end of the transition period might be somewhat lower. To reach the target, it will be necessary to ensure not only that training is readily available (for example, it should be free of charge, and arrangements should be made to give family day carers 10 per cent non-contact time during their working week), but also that there is a low turnover rate among family day carers. The early childhood service will need to create conditions that encourage men and women to enter and remain in family day care for a substantial part of their working lives, sufficient to acquire training and then apply the benefits of that training in their work.

The modular and common training scheme will allow centre-based workers to move into family day care for a period, and family day carers to move into other areas of work in the early childhood service. Training and experience in any part of the service will be equally valid and transferable. The aim will be that family day care is thoroughly integrated into the early childhood service, rather than being a separate and lower status outpost: training is central to realising this aim.

Great emphasis will be placed on continuous training. At least 10 per cent of the working week (3-4 hours) will be non-contact time, available for training, preparation and work with parents. One of the main roles of the infrastructure (see Step 6) will be to ensure the availability of training programmes suited to the needs of individual services and staff. Staff will also be encouraged, as part of their continuous training, to visit and work in services in other European countries, with financial support from local authorities and the European Partnership Fund (see Step 10).

Pay for 'early childhood teachers' will be on the same scale as teachers working with older children. However, working hours will be different: they will be the same as for other centre-based workers in the early childhood service, 35 hours a week with 6 weeks holiday a year plus public holidays (family day carers will have the same paid holidays, leave entitlements and pension arrangements as other workers in the early childhood service but because of the nature of their job, providing individual care in their own homes, they will work longer hours for which they will receive additional pay). A comprehensive, integrated and coherent system offering multi-functional services can only operate effectively if all staff working together have common hours of work.

Finally, a target will be set of 20 per cent male workers in the new service by the end of the transition period.

5. Responsibility for individual services

Services in the developing early childhood service will have to meet conditions to receive public funding. One of these will be to give priority to families from their catchment area. There will be a range of services, including organised family day care schemes; free-standing centres; and school-based provision.

Every individual service within the new early childhood service will work with the early childhood service unit in each local education authority and be accountable during the transition period for the use of its public funds to that unit; it will also have its own management committee. This means that existing school-based provision for 3–6 year olds will no longer be accountable to primary school headteachers and boards of governors of primary schools. Instead, each will be accountable to a head of early childhood services for an individual school site together with a board of management. During the transition period, school-based services in the early childhood service will be encouraged to expand, to provide a full range of services (i.e. care and support, as well as learning and socialisation) either for children from 3 to 6 or from 0 to 6 and their parents.

While many schools will have early childhood services, not all will do so. Whether they do or not, and the contribution of school-based services to the overall supply of early childhood services in any area, will depend on a range of factors, including: the potential of individual school sites for providing an appropriate indoor and outdoor environment for a multi-functional early childhood service; the need to provide some diversity in services in each area; and the availability of other services in the area. These factors will need to be taken account of in the planning process for developing the early childhood service in each area.

6. Infrastructure

The responsible departments at national and local level will be required to set in place arrangements to ensure an effective infrastructure for the development of the early childhood service. The functions of this infrastructure will include: planning; monitoring; regulation and quality assurance; review; support and continuous training programmes; and research and development. Some of these functions will be performed directly by the local authority; others may be contracted out. By the end of the transition period, at least 5 per cent of the total budget for early childhood services will be allocated for this infrastructure.

Particularly important tasks that must be ensured through the infrastructure arrangements will be the preparation of early childhood service plans and the regular review of these plans and the early childhood service.

7. Funding

The Secretary of State for Education, in England, and her Scottish, Welsh and Northern Ireland counterparts will be responsible for ensuring adequate public funding is made available during the transitional period for the development of the early childhood service, and for developing a mechanism for allocating this public funding to local authorities.

The Secretary of State and her counterparts will also prepare guidance on the contribution to be made by parents to the cost of services, to ensure coherence across services and affordability for all families.

8. Quality

The Secretary of State, and her counterparts, will prepare proposals, for widespread consultation and Parliamentary approval, setting out 'core' standards to be applied across all services. For services that are not publicly funded, these will consist of clear minimum standards, which regular inspections will ensure are met. For services receiving a public funding, 'core' standards will be higher because public subsidy will enable the standards to be met without placing the cost of the service beyond the reach of some parents. For example, publicly funded services will be required to meet higher standards for staffing and physical environment.

Individual publicly funded services will be required, as a condition of funding, to prepare 'a statement on quality', drawn up by their management committee after consultation with all stakeholders. The statement will incorporate the national 'core' standards together with additional objectives that reflect the values and principles of the particular service. These statements of quality will be subject to regular review by boards of management and will also form the basis for regular 'quality assessments', the results of which will determine future public funding for that service.

Quality assessments of all publicly funded services, and inspection of all privately funded services, will be undertaken by inspection staff who will form part of the early childhood service infrastructure.

9. Early childhood service plans

National government will provide a policy, legislative and funding framework and set targets for the development of early childhood services and training courses. Within this context, local authorities will be required to prepare area-based early childhood service plans, to guide their implementation of national policy and the achievement of targets. The plans will be closely related to the three-yearly review duty, which will provide the basis for assessing the effectiveness of existing plans and for drawing up new plans. The first round of plans might be for a four-year period, followed by two further three-year plans, covering altogether the ten-year transition period. A three-yearly review will then take place a year before the end of each plan, enabling the results of the review to inform the next round of planning.

Within the context of the area-based plans, services might be developed in each area through a process of bidding for funds, which will be allocated by the local authority. The bidding system will be open to the full range of providers (public, voluntary, private), and will encourage some diversity of provision in each area, including school-based and non-school-based centres and organised family day care. Tenders will be expected to show how providers expect to deliver a service that is flexible and multi-functional, and able to cover at least a three-year age range.

Services could lose their funding if their performance was consistently poor and, in particular, if their quality assessments prove unsatisfactory.

10. Early Childhood Service Development Fund

Central government will operate two separate funds. The National Development Funds for England, Scotland, Wales and Northern Ireland will be available to support innovative or experimental local and national projects, including services themselves, training, research and other aspects of infrastructure. They will be subject to bids in an annual competition held by the Department for Education, and the Scottish, Welsh and Northern Ireland Offices. Part of the Funds will be used for projects in priority areas identified by central government; but the rest will be open to any imaginative proposals.

There will also be a European Partnership Fund, with separate budgets for England, Scotland, Wales and Northern Ireland. These will be available to a wide range of individuals and institutions (services, training courses, infrastructure) to support exchanges and collaborative work with other European countries. Support will be given both to short-term projects and longer-term collaborations. These funds will be allocated through a bidding process.

RECONCILING EMPLOYMENT WITH THE CARE AND UPBRINGING OF CHILDREN

These measures specifically aimed at the development of a comprehensive, integrated and coherent early childhood service will be complemented by the development of a policy and implementation programme to support the reconciliation of employment and the care and upbringing of children. The development and implementation of this policy will need to bring together a number of government departments, local authorities, employers, trade unions and private organisations. There will need to be a 'lead' government department; a recognition of the wide range of needs and interests to be taken into account; and the development of structures, nationally and locally, where partnership between the wide range of interested groups can be promoted. It will also need a wide range of measures, with the development of the early childhood service playing an important role.

One measure is particularly important and relevant to the subject of this book. The ten-year transition period for introducing the early childhood service should also be used to develop leave entitlements for employed parents. As a minimum requirement, we propose that each parent will be given an entitlement to at least 6 months' leave per child (in addition to statutory maternity leave reduced to 16 weeks after birth and a new statutory 2-week paternity leave). Only part of this entitlement, up to 3 months, could be transferred between parents (except in the case of lone parents), so that each parent will have to use part of their allocation – or risk losing it. The leave will be available on a full-time or part-time basis and could be taken flexibly. For example, the 6 months allocation could be taken as 6 months full-time leave or as 3 months full-time leave and 6 months half-time leave or as 4 months full-time leave and 8 months quarter-time leave. It could be taken in up to 3 separate blocks of time, to be used at any time in a child's first 6 years. An earnings-related payment would be paid to parents on leave; not surprisingly, experience in other countries suggests that unpaid leave usually has a low take-up (EC Childcare Network, 1994b; OECD, 1995).

This proposal, as formulated, is a system of parental leave, that is leave equally available to mothers and fathers for the specific purpose of enabling them to give more time to the care of a young child; Britain, together with Luxembourg and Ireland, are the only countries in Europe which have no system of statutory parental leave – although the existing entitlements vary considerably between countries, for example, with respect to length, payment and flexibility (EC Childcare Network, 1994b). Alternatively, and more radically, a 'time account' scheme could be introduced, going further than parental leave by not restricting the taking of leave to caring for a young child. Instead, all men and women would start their working life with an allowance or credit of time that they could draw on as leave throughout their adult lives – at times of their choosing and for a wide range of reasons, including to spend time with children and not just when they are very young.

Parental leave, and even more so a 'time account' scheme, provides one way of trying to reverse a growing concentration of work, both paid and unpaid, within the relatively narrow age range of 25–49 – as employment grows among mothers, remains high for fathers, drops off among younger and older age groups and as the average age of first birth creeps ever higher, currently standing at around 28 for women. It will increase the choices open to parents in how they manage employment and family life. It will also provide a means for encouraging and supporting fathers to take a more equal share of the care and upbringing of young children.

Last, but not least, a well-developed system of parental leave or a 'time account' scheme will affect demand for early childhood services. Experience in the Nordic countries suggests that it will reduce the demand for full-time non-parental care for very young children (under 12–15 months). At the same time, there may be a corresponding increase in demand for an early childhood service to meet the support, socialisation and other needs of parents taking full-time or part-time leave and their children – emphasising again the importance of services that are flexible and multi-functional.

12

Transforming Nursery Education: What Would It Look Like?

We have argued throughout this book that the problems faced in early childhood services are structural and require political resolution. The lack of national policy has resulted in fragmented underfunded services, patchily distributed, to which children and parents have unequal access. Many early years workers – teachers and non-teachers alike – have made Herculean efforts to develop their own individual services and to influence practice in the areas where they work. It is a paradox that some of the most innovative and thoughtful provision is to be found in the UK, as well as some of the worst.

In the penultimate chapter we considered the content and implementation of a national policy on early childhood services. In this last chapter we speculate on what provision for young children might look like, if this national policy were put into place, offering three examples. In sketching some visionary services, we have drawn on our experiences in various European countries and further afield, as well as in Britain, selecting the features we think are exceptional. Our examples, therefore, are not so far fetched as they might appear, incorporating many features of existing provision both here and abroad.

We have stressed throughout the book that we value diversity – but diversity within a clear framework providing a coherent approach for critical areas such as funding, staffing and quality. We do not want services to be monolithic or monocultural, nor even necessarily provided by the public sector. We think that it is vital that local needs, conditions, resources and priorities are recognised. A comprehensive, integrated and coherent early childhood service does not mean identikit services. The three very different examples of how services might be organised, given below, are meant to be illustrative, not exhaustive.

We are imagining that, as in some other countries, childhood is regarded as an important and popular issue, well covered in the local and national press, radio and television and regularly debated in Parliament, local councils and other public forums. Many different aspects of living – such as transport, food and food advertising, public spaces – are considered in relation to children. Children are valued, and treated as citizens in their own right and with their own agenda. There is a consensus about the need for early childhood services, and there is lively debate about how demand can be met and how services can be developed imaginatively. There is real civic pride in local services. Just as the bus driver in the Italian town of Reggio Emilia – famous for its early childhood services – said to one of our colleagues 'Oh you've come to visit our nurseries then', so visitors to our three early childhood centres would have no trouble in finding them. Everyone would know where they were and would have something to say about them.

THE COMMUNITY CENTRE NURSERY

The first example is a small nursery based in a community centre in a prosperous semi-rural area in the south-west of England. The community centre-cum-library, which serves a large village and the surrounding area, made a successful bid to the local authority for a capital and revenue grant to open the nursery; the local authority funded the nursery as part of its early childhood plan for the area, which envisaged supporting three or four services for local children and parents. To prepare the bid, a steering group was set up including the playgroup leader, a community worker, a childminder, the librarian, the headteacher of the primary school, a health visitor from the local GP fundholders, practice, a representative from the OAP club based in the centre and a retired colonel who, after reading the RSA's 1994 *Start Right* report, became a campaigner for nursery education.

A local architect, herself a mother of a young child, offered to draw up the plans. She was part of the *Architects for Children* group, an informal group supported by the Royal Institute of British Architects, which has a considerable database about international practice. She based her plans on the generous brief developed by the *Architects for Children* group, in conjunction with the famous Frankfurt nursery programme. This programme, which ran from 1985 to 1995, provided Frankfurt with new centres combining early childhood services with care and recreation services for school-age children, designed by the world's leading architects who produced a series of beautiful and remarkable buildings. The brief for this programme allowed 4.7 square metres per child, with specifications that included: all buildings should have separate and exclusive areas for children's own use, cubbyholes where they can withdraw from adult surveillance; space, indoors and outdoors, for large-scale physical activities and games; and a child-proof kitchen in which children can safely enter (Burgard, 1994).

The enthusiasm of the local architect, and a trip to Frankfurt funded from the European Partnership Fund, inspired the steering group. Final plans included a landscape design for the field at the back of the community centre, which made imaginative use of a wonderful slope and dip and provided a sheltered sitting area that could be used by children from the nursery and other community centre users. It is now used, for example, by the chess club and the pensioners' Tai Chi classes.

The nursery was planned with 25 places for children from 0 to 6 years, with a further 25-place club providing care and recreation for school-age children. The centre is open from 8.00 a.m. to 6.00 p.m., covering the working year except for two weeks in August and a week each at Christmas and Easter. Parents can negotiate the hours their children attend, and usually about half the places for children under 6 are used on a part-time basis. The centre is open to all families, whether or not parents are employed, mainly on a first-come, first-served basis. However, some priority is given to children with special needs; normally three or four children attending the centre will have been referred by health or welfare agencies. As provision has increased, it has been possible to ensure priority for these children, while at the same time most places are filled by children off the general waiting list.

Originally the steering group anticipated a demand for children under one year. But the change in leave legislation, in particular the new parental leave entitlement, proved so popular that there was little demand for unaccompanied babies – although the nursery does provide a twice-weekly group for parents, babies and toddlers to which come several parents who are taking leave. There are other groups, too. A retired librarian runs an adult literacy scheme for young parents, realising that early parenthood is a time when parents with poor literacy skills are more likely to be keen and open to learning alongside their children. One of the two male members of staff has started a fathers' group, which has a committed membership of seven or eight men who welcome the opportunity to talk about parenthood and other issues. A training and employment counsellor holds regular sessions for women who would like to resume employment, change their jobs or get better qualifications.

The steering group recognised the needs not only of families in the village, but also of the more isolated families living outside the town and dependent on public transport. After discussion with local family day carers, a co-operative was established, offering a service to village and outlying families. The family day care co-operative was also a successful bidder for funds, so now forms a part of the range of early childhood services for the area. The centre provides support for the co-operative, offering sessions twice a week for family day carers and their children, and also other training and support facilities including attendance at training courses laid on by the centre. Among the services offered by the co-operative is a peripatetic family day carer, to provide temporary cover for other family day carers and parents at the nursery – for instance, in one week recently a parent taking leave to care for his sick child, who normally attended the nursery, needed to attend an important work meeting and a family day carer needed a day's cover to attend a funeral.

From the beginning, the steering group accepted that the nursery would have to share some space with other users of the community centre. This necessity has been turned to advantage. The OAP luncheon club shares the dining room with the nursery, which has led to some luncheon club members spending time with the children; the centre's hall is used by the nursery and adult classes, but this has led to some of the older children joining keep-fit and dance classes.

The original staff group included one nursery teacher, two nursery nurses and several untrained staff. After a year, they were joined by the leader of the village playgroup. The playgroup had originally operated twice a week in the centre, and the playgroup leader protested initially that the playgroup was being usurped by the new nursery. But over time she became convinced that the nursery offered not only better and more flexible facilities, but also a high level of parent participation, not least through membership of the centre's management committee which took over from the steering group. The playgroup closed and the leader took a job at the nursery.

Over time, the level of training among the staff group has increased. Some took advantage of the special training programme for existing staff, operating over the course of the ten-year transition period for the early childhood service. Vacancies have been filled with staff having the new 'early childhood teacher' qualification. After five years, half the staff at the centre have this qualification, and one of them is currently studying for a masters degree in early childhood on day release; the co-ordinator of the family day care co-operative (selected by the co-op's members) also has the new 'early childhood teacher' qualification, while two other centre staff and three family day carers are studying part-time to get the qualification. Other workers, both in the nursery and the family day care co-op, are working for their NVQ level 3, uncertain at this time whether they will go on to take the 'early childhood teacher' qualification.

The centre shares a programme of continuous staff training with staff from the early childhood service that has been developed on the local primary school site, as well as with the family day care co-operative. The two centres, at the school and the community centre, collaborate in other ways; for example, sharing a common pool cover system. Staff in both centres, as well as some family day carers in the co-operative, have also joined the early childhood section of the teachers' union and the union representative in the primary school is on the management committee of the community centre nursery. Originally doubtful about the new service and especially the new early childhood training and staffing arrangements, he has become a strong supporter over time, not least after becoming a father himself and taking 6 months parental leave. He is now about to have a 6-month secondment at the nursery centre, after which he may decide to take the conversion course to become an early childhood teacher.

The nursery centre, after a few teething problems, is now running smoothly. The co-ordinator of the nursery was a nursery teacher who took the conversion course to become an 'early childhood teacher' and is now studying for her masters degree in early childhood. Though some of the employment conditions, in particular the hours, are rather more onerous than in the old days when she worked in a nursery class, she finds the job much more fulfilling and enjoys the stimulation of working in a multi-functional setting. In particular, she likes the challenge of meeting the needs of the local community.

The colonel is the rather delighted chairman of the management committee of the nursery, visits and has lunch with the children most days, and knows all the children by name, although he has to be restrained from distributing sweets too liberally.

At present, 15 of the younger children attend full-time for a working day. A further 17 children share the remaining 10 places. Three of those children have disabilities, and one is profoundly disabled; each child with a disability counts for two places, and the cover budget can be used to provide more help if needed.

The pace of the day is carefully scheduled, because of the children who attend part-time. The children spend some time together before lunchtime, but for most of the time, the toddlers are in a separate group. The member of staff responsible for under-threes (who previously worked as a family day carer, before qualifying as an 'early childhood teacher' under the special programme) is familiar with heuristic play, and there is a stimulating range of natural and 'found' objects, with a range of textures and shapes and weights and subtle colours for the babies to explore, rather than crude brightly coloured plastic toys.

The activities for the 3–6 year olds link more closely with other community centre activities, including cooking (a speciality is jam-making and baking sessions with assistance from members of the WI), gardening (helped by members of the OAP gardening club) and dancing. The aerobics tutor who runs sessions for women and OAPs also agreed to do two sessions for children. The children have learned to move gracefully and with more suppleness, and have become more aware of the expressive potential of hands and feet. They can be seen playing games incorporating some of the exercises. All these activities involve the children in intense and continuous conceptual discussions with friendly and knowledgeable adults; for example, about the name and the rate of growth of the 'Morning Glory' climber as opposed to the non-climbing 'Evening Primrose'.

The club for school-age children makes a lot of use of the library, also housed in the community centre, with many literary games, crosswords and quizzes. Also popular are computer games and a chess club (there is a tournament between the OAPs and the club), outside camps and a tree-house. The local stables organise horse-riding in conjunction with the club, using the paddock end of the community centre field. The attention to detail in the nursery and the club is phenomenal; each aspect of every activity and the resources it needs has been carefully thought out and discussed and agreed with the staff group – an impossibility without the regular non-contact time in each staff member's week, which they can use for training, discussion and reflection.

The education inspectors, who amalgamated with the social services registration and inspection unit when responsibility for early childhood services passing to education, recently gave the nursery a good report. They praised its links with the local community, its curriculum, and the emphasis on homely activities such as gardening and cooking. They singled out the aerobics for special mention; they commented that young children are frequently under-exercised and that this programme was cleverly devised to stretch the children's physical capacities as well as being real fun. Everyone associated with the centre took great pride in this report. Since it started, there has been continuous and widespread discussion – among parents, staff, older children and members of the local community – about the objectives and values of the centre, leading to the 'statement on quality' which gave expression to the centre's distinctive identity and community role.

THE SCHOOL CAMPUS

Our second example could not be more different. The area is a vast council estate on the periphery of a city in the north-west. Male unemployment is high and many women work in various twilight jobs – cleaning, bar work, late supermarket shifts and so on. One of the main resources for the estate is a school campus, containing on one site an infant, junior and secondary school, as well as what had been a part-time nursery class sited next to the infant school and subject to its governance. It is bleak and windy and the 1950s buildings show many signs of decay and vandalism.

The headteacher of the secondary school realised that unless his school was 'owned' by its users, the youngsters and their parents, nothing was likely to improve. Together with the headteachers of the junior and infant schools he worked out a plan for the whole campus, borrowing the American idea of the 'school of the twenty-first century'. The vision statement they drew up outlined the following principles:

- the family at the centre: an approach to serving the needs of the whole family;
- co-ordination of a wide range of services to provide a more effective continuous service;
- communication of information regarding available services;
- co-operation within the community, community ownership and responsibility for development.

The headteachers' group worked with school governors and advisers from the local authority to implement their plan. They decided that to make this vision real they needed to be truly multi-functional and provide a range of services: a club offering care and recreation for children at the infant and junior schools; a centre for 0–6 year olds; an information service for parents which incorporated advice about training and career opportunities, benefits and housing issues; a personal counselling service which could be used by children or their parents, many of whom were under stress; a programme of youth and leisure activities for secondary children, and opportunities for parents to access lessons to gain GCSEs and GNVQs. Any surplus accommodation in the schools – and there was a great deal of space because of falling rolls – could be used for other activities run for and sometimes by parents.

Fortunately, the area had objective 1 status within the European Union, and it was possible to put together a bid to support the development of the whole scheme; a successful bid was also made to the local authority for money to fund the early childhood service part. It took a great deal of work to bring together the professional groups involved, the social services, housing and leisure departments, as well as the education department and the health authority (there was virtually no private enterprise in the area which could be tapped).

It was decided in line with the government's recommendations, that the 0–6 service and the care and recreation service for school-age children should be autonomous of the school. It is now independent with its own co-ordinator and management committee. Nevertheless, the early childhood service and the school work together closely; this close co-operation did not come easily. The headteacher of the secondary school, whose model of schooling was didactic and who valued obedience and orderliness from his pupils, comes from a very different tradition from the early childhood services co-ordinator, who trained as an 'early childhood teacher' and believes young children should have as much freedom as possible. There was some bitterness at first. But over time, mutual respect and understanding has developed, with the school probably the greater beneficiary – after seeing the autonomy of the 5 year olds, the secondary headteacher began to wonder about the lack of autonomy of the 15 year olds.

The sixth form students in the school doing their GNVQ (boys as well as girls) regularly do their placements in the early childhood centre, which their teachers regard as positive and practical training even if the students do not go on to work with young children. The early childhood service co-ordinator used this as an opportunity to widen discussions about the activities provided in the nursery. She was interested in the blend of autonomous and self-directed play, and in the idea of apprenticeship, of children learning alongside sympathetic adults as they engaged in long-term common tasks. The sixth formers made some useful suggestions about construction activities – which resulted in a dolls' house making competition in which the sixth formers teamed up with some of the 4 and 5 year olds to see who could make the most interesting homes and creatures to people them; one of the nursery workers went with a group of the sixth formers and nursery children on an outing to the Ideal Home exhibition as part of the project. The sixth formers also helped draw up and print – with the school's desktop publishing equipment – a curriculum plan for the nursery which was then discussed with parents and parent users from a range of groups inside the school.

The secondary school has a brass band, and puts on a termly performance for the nursery children and parents. These are prepared for with tapes, and offer opportunities for the young children to handle and try out the instruments. In two of the concert pieces, the nursery children joined in with timpani and drums – it took a great deal of practising!

The drop-in crèche, where mothers have an opportunity to be with their children and meet for a chat and can also leave their toddlers for a short break, or while they see the counsellor, or take classes, has also proved a success. Some of the year 6 pupils and sixth formers help out here too.

There has been a pay-off from the early childhood service and other school-based activities. Delinquency and vandalism in the area have dropped. The school's performance as measured by GCSE passes has improved. Very little can alter the massive unemployment in the area, but people have gained some degree of hope and self-respect, while the nursery has encouraged some parents to seek jobs outside the immediate area.

THE NURSERY SCHOOL AND OUT-OF-SCHOOL CLUB IN THE PARK

Our third example is a depressed town in the industrial north-east. It has a large Victorian park, within which were the ruins of a large castellated house, Saltwell Towers, once long ago the summer residence of a local manufacturing family. The house had been closed for twenty years because of dry rot.

The Saltwell Towers project was set up by the local FE college as an independent project. Its objective was to establish a working group and trustees, commission design briefs for the refurbishment of the castellated house, carry out an ecological survey of the surrounding grounds and put forward suggestions for their communal use, and to publicise and secure support for the project locally.

The group, led by Robin, an early years teacher on sabbatical from his school, applied for Millenium Commission money to renovate the house. They argued that the building was originally constructed with pride and care, and had a quirky magicality to which young people relate (an older generation remembers playing in and around the house when they were children). The site itself in the park is child-friendly and has great potential as a wildlife area, as well as having plenty of attractive safe and cared for green space. The park is uniquely placed in the town, providing a common meeting ground for all sections of society.

The design brief specified four group rooms, each a base for 12–15 children and 2–3 adults, plus a well-resourced soft play area within the building; a library with multi-media facilities; a room for music-making, listening, dance and drama; and an arts and crafts room. A well-equipped child-accessible kitchen was to be a centrepiece of the project, since the working group believed strongly that children should contribute towards the choice and preparation of the food they eat. Outside, in the grounds, were designated wild spaces, a sunken garden with nooks, crannies and sitting areas, and imaginative climbing structures in the park itself. In the park there are enclosures with goats, hens, rabbits, guinea pigs, etc., and a boating pond with swans, ducks and geese.

The Millenium Commission were impressed with the plans, and keen to support the interests of children which they felt have been too long neglected. But they insisted that there was a guarantee of revenue funding for the project.

This came from the National Early Years Development Fund, with the local authority guaranteeing to assume responsibility for funding when this money ends after three years. On this basis, Saltwell Towers was lovingly restored (almost as lavishly as a National Trust mansion!) and has been open a year now.

It provides places for children aged 0–6, and a club offering care and recreation for school children; during school holidays many older children also attend for play activities and workshops. The curriculum emphasis is on positive social interaction, developing communication skills and symbolic and imaginative play, with lots of creative activities. The curriculum also includes developing a familiarity with healthy nutritional eating habits and a proper delight in food (the ice-cream vans in the park provide organic ice cream and Mexican snacks but they do not stock sweets or burgers). The groups have timetabled access to the specialist areas within the centre – like the arts and crafts workshop (with a potter in residence sponsored by Northern Arts) and the surrounding park. For instance, the animal keeper explained about the annual geese cull, and explored with the children the dividing line between animals as pests and animals as pets. The secret garden is a great success, and is used in summer and winter alike. In summer in particular there are stories, painting, parties, group games, parachute games, etc.

The multi-media library is also a success, and the council's Libraries and Leisure department provide workshops for adults as well as children. Several video histories have been made, of old age pensioners reminiscing about their memories of the house and the social attitudes of the 1930s, which have been used in local schools.

The project has lived up to its expectations in terms of staff. It has attracted both men and women to work, half of whom have the new early childhood teachers degree. Their main role is as enablers and facilitators of children's activities. They are concerned to find ways of listening to children and enabling children to articulate their point of view. There is a continuous training programme for them, in order to develop their practice, to enable the children to meet new challenges with excitement, and to support children in recovering from the minor knocks, fears and setbacks that are part of growing up in a challenging environment.

Parents are on the management committee of the project, and are encouraged to take part in as many of the activities as they like. For example, some class activities are timetabled for evenings or weekends, so they can be family events. Mealtimes are open to parents. A member of staff, who also has counselling skills, is supernumerary, in order to service the management group, and provide information, support and advice for parents.

CONCLUSION

Is this fanciful or could it happen here? The three projects whose proposals we have borrowed and elaborated on hope that it can. The projects are innovatory in many ways. While they all hold children at the centre, they blur the traditional distinctions between education and community, between adult and child, between professional and non-professional, between formal and informal settings, and for that matter between rich and poor. They see education as a life-long process; learning is exciting and zestful for the youngest children but it can go on being pleasurable into old age. They are characterised by a flexibility of approach and a responsiveness to the needs and situation of the local community. Above all they are based on the inclusion of a range of stakeholders in discussions and decisions – none take their point of view for granted, and realise that in order to develop and progress they must seek out and earn consensus and commitment. They have all earned public acceptance and legitimacy through their inclusive approach.

It may take a shift in attitudes to view services in this way, but perhaps not as much as we think. There are already projects like this in existence. If funding were made available for such grass roots initiatives, then more ideas like these – child-focused, creative, community-based, diverse – would be forthcoming. We have great confidence in the energy, resourcefulness and talent in British society.

We think that nursery education transformed into a comprehensive, integrated and coherent early childhood service, flexible and multi-functional, could be a rich and enhancing experience for everyone involved in it – children first and foremost, but also parents, staff, members of the local community. But to make the transformation, nursery education must break the current rigid mould of curriculum and child development, of part-time nursery classes and reception classes full of 4 year olds being schooled before their time. It must engage with the daily complex reality of children's lives.

References

Alexander, G. (1995) Instigating change in the early years: financial management implications, *International Journal of Educational Management*, Vol. 9, no. 3, 10–12.

Audit Commission (1995) *Local Authority Performance Indicators: Appendix to Volumes 1 and 2*, HMSO, London.

Audit Commission (1995) *Where Did You Learn That: Education of Children Under Five*, Audit Commission, London.

Balaguer, I. (1994) The paradox of services for children 0–3 years, in EC Childcare Network *Annual Report 1992*, European Commission Equal Opportunities Unit, Brussels.

Ball, C. (1994) *Start Right: the Importance of Early Learning*, Royal Society of Arts, London.

Belle, D. (ed.) (1989) *Children's Social Networks and Social Supports*, Wiley, New York.

Blenkin, G. M., and Kelly, A. V. (eds.) (1987) *Early Childhood Education: A Developmental Curriculum*, Paul Chapman, London.

Blenkin, G. M., and Kelly, A. V. (1994) *The National Curriculum and Early Learning*, Paul Chapman, London.

Blenkin, G., Hurst, V., Whitehead, M. and Yue, N. (1995) *Principles into Practice: Improving the Quality of Children's Early Learning – Phase One Report*, mimeographed report from Early Childhood Education Research Project, Goldsmiths' College.

Bloom, L. (1993) *The Transition from Infancy to Language*, Cambridge University Press, Cambridge.

Bornstein, M. (ed.) (1991) *Cultural Approaches to Parenting*, Lawrence Erlbaum: London.

Bowlby, J. (1952) *Maternal Care and Mental Health*, World Health Organisation, Geneva.

Bradburn, E. (1976) *Margaret McMillan*, Denholm House Press – National Christian Education Council, Surrey.

Brannen, J., Meszaros, G., Moss, P. and Poland, G. (1994) *Employment and Family Life: A Review of Research in the UK*, Employment Department, London.

Brice-Heath, S. (1983) *Ways with Words: Language, Life and Work in Communities and Classrooms*, Cambridge University Press, Cambridge Mass.

Bronfenbrenner, U. and Crouter, A. (1983) An evolution of environmental models in developmental research, in W. Kessen (ed.) *History, Theory and Methods; Handbook of Child Psychology*, Vol. 1, Wiley, New York.

Bruner, J. (1980) *Under Fives in Britain*, Grant McIntyre, London.

Burgard, R. (1994) *Archigrad 1: The Frankfurt Kindergarten Programme*, Corporate Identities Production, Frankfurt.

Central Advisory Council on Education (1967) *Children and Their Primary Schools* (the Plowden Report), HMSO, London.

Central Statistical Office (1995a) *Social Trends 25 (1995 Edition)*, HMSO, London.

Central Statistical Office (1995b) *Economic Trends*, HMSO, London.

Clark, M. (1988): *Children under Five: Educational Research and Evidence. Final Report to the Department of Education and Science*, Gordon and Breach, London.

Cochran, M. (ed.) (1993) *International Handbook of Childcare Policies and Programmes*, Greenwood Press, Connecticut.

Cohen, B. and Fraser, N. (1991) *Childcare in a Modern Welfare State*, Institute of Public Policy Research, London.

Commission on Social Justice (1994) *Social Justice: Strategies for National Renewal*, Vintage, London.

Consultative Committee on the Primary School (1931) *Report of the Committee*, HMSO, London.

Corsaro, W. (1985) *Friendship and Peer Culture in the Early Years*, Ablex Publishing Co., Norwood NJ.

Dahlberg, G. and Åsén, G. (1994) Evaluation and regulation: a question of empowerment, in P. Moss, and A. Pence (eds.) *Valuing Quality in Early Childhood Services*, Paul Chapman, London.

Davies Jones, H. (1993) The social pedagogues in Western Europe – some implications for European inter-professional care, *Journal of Interprofessional Care*, Vol. 8, no. 1.

Davies Jones, H. (1994) *Social Workers or Social Educators? The International Context for Developing Social Care*. National Institute of Social Work Paper No.2, National Institute of Social Work, London.

Dearing, R. (1995) Interview in *Guardian Education*, 16 May.

Deasey, D. (1978) *Education Under Six*, Croom Helm, London.

Department for Education (1995) *Pupils under Five Years of Age in Schools in England – January 1995 (Statistical Bulletin 2/95)*, Department for Education, London.

Department of Education and Science (1973) *Circular 2/73*, HMSO, London.

Department of Education and Science (1989) *Aspects of Primary Education: The Education of Children Under Five*, HMSO, London.

Department of Education and Science (1990) *Starting with Quality: The Rumbold Report of the Committee of Inquiry into the Quality of the Educational Experience offered to 3- and 4-year-olds*, HMSO, London.

Department of Health (1995) *Children's Day Care Facilities at 31 March 1994 England*, Department of Health, London.

Department of Health and Social Security/Department of Education and Science (1976) *Low Cost Day Provision for the Under-Fives*. Papers from a Conference held on 9–10 January 1976.

Department of Social Security (1993) *Households below Average Income: a Statistical Analysis*, HMSO, London.

Doise, W. and Palmonari, A. (eds.) (1984) *Social Interaction and Individual Development*, Cambridge University Press, Cambridge.

Duncan, A., Giles, C. and Webb, S. (1995) *The Impact of Subsidising Childcare*, Equal Opportunities Commission, Manchester.

Dunn, J. (1993) *Young Children's Close Relationships: Beyond Attachment*, Sage, London.

Early Years Curriculum Group (1992) *The Early Years Curriculum*, Trentham Books, Stoke on Trent.

Education Enquiry Committee (1929) *The Case For Nursery Schools*, George Phillip & Son, London.

Education, Science and Arts (House of Commons) (1988) *Educational Provision for the Under Fives, Vol 1*, HMSO, London.

Edwards, A. and Knight P. (1994) *Effective Early Years Education*, Open University Press, Buckingham.

Elfer, P. (1995) *Parental Views on the Development of Day Care and Education Services for Children under Eight in England*, National Children's Bureau, London.

EC Childcare Network (European Commission Network on Childcare and Other Measures to Reconcile Employment and Family Responsibilities) (1994a) *Men as Carers: Towards a Culture of Responsibility, Sharing and Reciprocity between Women and Men in the Care and Upbringing of Children*, European Commission Equal Opportunities Unit, Brussels.

EC Childcare Network (European Commission Network on Childcare and Other Measures to Reconcile Employment and Family Responsibilities) (1994b) *Leave Arrangements for Workers with Children*, European Commission Equal Opportunities Unit, Brussels.

EC Childcare Network (European Commission Network on Childcare and Other Measures to Reconcile Employment and Family Responsibilities) (1995) *The Costs and Funding of Services for Young Children*, European Commission Equal Opportunities Unit, Brussels.

EC Childcare Network (European Commission Network on Childcare and Other Measures to Reconcile Employment and Family Responsibilities) (forthcoming) *Services for Young Children in the European Union 1990–1995*, European Commission Equal Opportunities Unit, Brussels.

Faulkner, D. (1990) *Working with Under Fives: In Service Training Pack PE 635*, Open University School of Education/Centre for Human Development and Learning, Milton Keynes

Ferri, E., Birchall, D., Gingell, V. and Gipps, C. (1981) *Combined Nursery Centres*, MacMillan, London.

Froebel, F. (1897) *Pedagogics of the Kindergarten*, Edward Arnold, London.

Gardner, D. (1969) *Susan Isaacs*, Methuen Educational, London.

Ghedini, P., Chandler, T., Whalley, M. and Moss, P. (1995) *Dad, How Did You Learn to Care for Me? The Role of Services for Young Children in Supporting More Equal Sharing of Family Responsibilities*, European Commission Equal Opportunities Unit, Brussels.

Goodman, A. and Webb, W. (1994) *For Richer, For Poorer: the Changing Distribution of Income in the United Kingdom 1961–1991*, Institute for Fiscal Studies, London.

Goodnow, J. and Collins, A. (1990) *Development According to Parents: The Nature, Sources and Consequences of Parents' Ideas*, Lawrence Erlbaum Associates, London

Harrop, A. and Moss, P. (1995) Trends in parental employment, *Work, Employment and Society*, Vol. 9, no. 3, pp. 421–44.

Holtermann, S. (1995) *Investing In Young Children* (revised edn) National Children's Bureau, London.

Holtermann, S. (1992) *Investing In Young Children: Costing and Funding an*

Educational and Day Care Service for Young Children, National Children's Bureau, London.

Howes, C., Hamilton, C. and Matheson C. (1994) Children's relationships with peers: different associations with aspects of teacher-child relationships, *Child Development*, Vol. 65, no. 1, pp. 253–63.

Huang Cen (1989) *Comparison of nursery education in Scotland and Guandong Province, China*. Unpublished MEd thesis, Glasgow University.

Hughes, M., Wikeley, F. and Nash, T. (1994) *Parents and Their Children's Schools*, Blackwell, Oxford.

Hurst, V., Lally, M. and Whitehead, M. (1993) *Early Education in Jeopardy*, Early Years Curriculum Group/BAECE, London.

Hutton, W. (1995a) *The State We're In*, Jonathon Cape, London.

Hutton, W. (1995b) Forget Austerity era – Britain's rich, *Guardian,* 16 October.

Isaacs, S. (1929) *The Nursery Years: The Mind of the Child from Birth to Six Years*, Routledge, London.

Isaacs, S. (1930) *Intellectual Growth in Young Children*, Lund Humphries, London.

Isaacs, S. (1954) *The Educational Value of the Nursery School*, Nursery School Association of Great Britain and Northern Ireland, London.

Jenkins, S. (1994) *Winners and Losers: a Portrait of the UK Income Distribution during the 1980s (Swansea Economic Discussion Paper 94–07)*, Department of Economics, Swansea.

Jensen, C. (1994) Fragments for a discussion about quality, in P. Moss, and A. Pence (eds.) *Valuing Quality in Early Childhood Services*, Paul Chapman, London.

Jensen, J. (1993) Age integrated centres in Denmark, in EC Childcare Network *Annual Report 1992*, European Commission Equal Opportunities Unit, Brussels.

Jensen, J. (forthcoming) *Men as Workers in Services for Young Children*, European Commission Equal Opportunities Unit, Brussels.

Kagan, J. (1984) *The Nature of the Child*, Basic Books, New York.

Konner, M. (1991) *Childhood: A Multicultural View*, Little, Brown and Company, London.

Kumar, V. (1993) *Poverty and Inequality in the UK: the Effects on Children*, National Children's Bureau, London.

Lamb, M., Sternberg, K., Hwang, C. P., and Broberg, A. (eds.) (1992) *Childcare in Context*, Lawrence Erlbaum Associates, London.

Light, P., Sheldon, S. and Woodhead, M. (1991) *Learning to Think*, Routledge, London.

Mallory, B. and New, R. (eds.) (1994) *Diversity and Developmentally Appropriate Practice*, Teachers College Press, New York.

McGurk, H., Caplan, M., Hennessy, E. and Moss, P. (1993) Controversy, Theory and Social Context in Contemporary Day Care Research, *Journal of Child Psychiatry and Psychology,* Vol. 34, no. 1, pp. 3–23.

McGurk, H., Mooney, A., Moss, P., and Poland, G. (1995): *Staff-Child Ratios in Care and Education Services for Young Children*, HMSO, London.

McMillan, M. (1930) *The Nursery School*, 1930 Edition, Dent, London.

McRae, S. (1991) *Maternity Rights in Britain: the PSI Report on the Experience of Women and Employers*, Policy Studies Institute, London.

Meltzer, H. (1994) *Day Care Services for Children*, HMSO, London.

Ministerio de Educación y Ciencia (1989) *Ejemplificaciones del Diseño Curricular Base: Infantil y Primaria*, Ministerio de Educación y Ciencia, Madrid.

Ministerio de Educación y Ciencia (1991) *General Law of Spanish Educational System*, Ministerio de Educación y Ciencia, Madrid.

Ministry of Education (1944) *Education Act 1944*, HMSO, London.

Ministry of Health (1945) *Circular 221/45*, HMSO, London.

Moss, P. (1992) 'Employee Child Care' – or services for children, carers and employers, *Employee Relations*, Vol. 14, no. 6, pp. 20–32.

Moss, P. and Pence, A. (eds.) (1994) *Valuing Quality*, Paul Chapman, London.

Moss, P. (ed.) (1995) *Father Figures: Fathers in the Families of the '90s*, HMSO, Edinburgh.

Munn, P. and Schaffer, H. R. (1993) Literacy and numeracy events in social interactive contexts, *International Journal of Early Years Education*, Vol. 1, no. 3.

National Commission on Education (1993) *Learning to Succeed. Report of the Paul Hamlyn Foundation*, Heinemann, London.

National Union of Teachers (1977) *The Needs of the Under Fives*, National Union of Teachers, London.

Nelson, N. and Wright, S (1995) *Power and Participatory Development*, Intermediate Technology Publications, London.

Nursery World (1995) *The Professional Nanny, September 1995*, Nursery World, London.

OECD (Organisation for Economic Co-operation and Development) (1994) *Education at a Glance, OECD Indicators,* OECD, Paris.

OECD (Organisation for Economic Co-operation and Development) (1995) Long-term leave for parents in OECD countries, in *Employment Outlook, July 1995,* OECD, Paris.

Olmsted, P. and Weikart, D. (1989) *How Nations Serve Young Children*, High Scope Press, Ypsilanti, Michigan.

Owen, C. and Moss, P. (1989) Patterns of pre-school provision in English local authorities, *Journal of Education Policy*, Vol. 4, pp. 309–28.

Owen, G. (1928) *Nursery School Education*, Dutton, London.

Owen, R. (1836): *A New View of Society and other Writings*, 1927 edition, Everyman's Library, London.

Piaget, J. (1964) Development and learning, *Journal of Research in Science Teaching*, Vol. 2, pp. 176–86.

Pence, A. (1995) *Cross-Cultural Partnerships in Training*. Paper given at the Institute of Education Early Years Seminar Series, July.

Penn, H. (1990) *The Rise of Private Nurseries*. Paper given at a Local Government Management Board/EOC Conference. INLOGOV. BirminghamUniversity.

Penn, H. (1992) *The View from Strathclyde*. Scottish Academic Press, Edinburgh.

Penn, H. (1995a) Nursery education: What is it for?, *International Journal of Educational Management*, Vol. 9, no. 3, pp. 4–9.

Penn, H. (1995b) Development of integrated provision for pre-fives in the UK, *Early Child Development and Care*, Vol. 108, pp. 5–18.

Penn, H. (forthcoming) The Relationship of Private Daycare and Nursery Education in the UK, *European Early Childhood Education Research Journal*.

Potts, P., Petrie, P. and Statham, J. (1992) *Learning for All: Right from the Start (Unit 5, Course E242)*, Open University, Milton Keynes.

Powney, J., Glissov, P., Hall, S. and Harlen, W. (1995) *We Are Getting Them Ready for Life*, SCRE, Edinburgh.

Pugh, G. (1994) *The Sooner the Better: Early Education*. Paper given at a Conference 'Our Children, Our Future', Birmingham, 18–19 November.

Riley, D. (1983) *War in the Nursery*, Virago, London.

Rogoff, B. (1990) *Apprenticeship in Thinking: Cognitive Development in Social Context*, Oxford University Press.

School Curriculum and Assessment Authority (1995) *Pre-school Education Consultation: Desirable Outcomes for Children's Learning and Guidance for Providers*, SCAA, London.

Schweinhardt, L. J., Weikart, D. P. and Larner, M. B. (1986) Child-initiated activities in early childhood programs may help prevent delinquency, *Early Childhood Research Quarterly*, Vol. 1, pp. 303–11.

Schweinhardt, L. J., and Weikart, D. P. (1993) *A Summary of Significant Benefits: The High Scope Perry Pre-School Study Through Age 27*, High Scope UK, Ypsilanti, Michigan.

Silver, H. (1969) *Robert Owen on Education*, Cambridge University Press.

Solity, J. (1995) Psychology, teachers and the early years, *International Journal of Early Years Education*, Vol. 3, no. 1, pp. 5–23.

Steedman, C. (1990) *Childhood, Culture and Class in Britain: Margaret McMillan 1860–1931*, Virago, London.

Super, C. M. and Harkness, S. (1986) The developmental niche: a conceptualization of the interface of child and culture, *International Journal of Behavioural Development*, Vol. 9, pp. 546–69.

Taylor, B. (1983) *Eve and the New Jerusalem: Socialism and Feminism in the Nineteenth Century*, London, Virago.

Thompson, C. (1995) Business Basics, *Who Minds* Summer, 22–3.

Tizard, B. (1985) 'Social relationships between adults and young children and their impact on intellectual functioning' in R. Hinde, A.-N. Perret-Clermont and J. Stevenson-Hinde, (eds.) *Social Relationships and Cognitive Development (Fyssen Foundation Symposium)*, Clarendon Press, Oxford.

Tizard, B. and Hughes, M. (1984) *Young Children Learning: Talking and Thinking at Home and at School*, Fontana, London.

Tizard, J., Moss, P. and Perry, J. (1976) *All Our Children*, Temple-Smith, London.

Van der Eyken, W. (ed.) (1973) *Education, The Child and Society: A Documentary History*, Penguin Books, Harmondsworth.

Vygotsky, L. S. (1978) *Mind in Society*, Harvard University Press, Cambridge Mass.

Vygotsky, L. S. (1986) *Thought and Language (revised and edited by A. Kozulin)*, MIT Press, Cambridge Mass.

Wachs, T. (1992) *The Nature of Nurture*, Sage, London.

Weikart, D. (1989) High/Scope curriculum in practice, in F. Macleod (ed.) *The High/Scope Project (Perspectives 40)*, School of Education, University of Exeter.

Weisner, T. (1989) Cultural and universal aspects of social support for children: evidence from the Abuluyia of Kenya, in D. Belle (ed.) *Childrens' Social Networks and Social Support*, Wiley, New York.

Wells, G. (1987) *The Meaning Makers: Children Learning Language and Using Language to Learn*, Hodder & Stoughton, London.

Whiting, B. and Whiting, J. (1975) *Children of Six Cultures – A Psycho-Cultural Analysis*, Harvard University Press, Cambridge Mass.

Wilkinson, J. E. (1994) *Flagships: An Evaluation/Research Study of Community Nurseries in Strathclyde Region 1989–92*, Department of Education, University of Glasgow.

Williamson, H. and Butler, I. (1995) Children Speak: Perspectives on their Social

Worlds, in Brannen, J. and O'Brien, M. (eds) *Childhood and Parenthood* (1995) London. Proceedings of the International Sociological Association Committee for Family Research Conference, Institute of Education, pp. 294–308.

Winnicott, D. W. (1964) *The Child, the Family and the Outside World*, Penguin Books, Harmondsworth.

Wood, D. (1988) *How Children Think and Learn*, Blackwell, Oxford.

Woodhead, M. (1988) The case of early childhood intervention, *American Psychologist*, Vol. 43, no. 6, pp. 443–54.

Working Party on Early Childhood Care and Education (1988) *Education to be More*, Government Printer, Wellington.

Index